The Environmental Imagination

The Environmental Imagination explores the relationship between technics and poetics in environmental design in architecture. Working thematically and chronologically from the eighteenth century to the present day, this book aims to redefine the historiography of environmental design. The author looks beyond conventional histories to recognise that environmental matters are not purely a technical matter: they are a collaboration between poetic intentions and technical means.

The essays in this book assess the work of several leading nineteenth- and twentieth-century figures to demonstrate the growth of environmental awareness. A consideration of the qualitative dimension of the environment is added to the existing, primarily technological, narratives. Essays on earlier buildings highlight the response of pioneering architects to the 'new' technologies of mechanical services and their influence on the form of buildings, while the late twentieth-century design is explored in particular depth to illustrate individual strands of the environmental diversity of modern practice. The architects discussed range from John Soane to Peter Zumthor.

The Environmental Imagination will appeal to those interested in both architectural technology and history and theory.

Dean Hawkes is Emeritus Fellow at Darwin College, University of Cambridge and Emeritus Professor of Architectural Design at Cardiff University. He is also visiting professor at the Departments of Architecture in the University of Huddersfield and the Chinese University of Hong Kong and honorary visiting professor at the Mackintosh School of Architecture, Glasgow School of Art.

For Christine

Dean Hawkes

The
Enviro
Imagir

Technics and poet

Routledge
Taylor & Francis Group

London and New York

First published 2008 by Taylor and Francis

2 Park Square, Milton Park, Abingdon, Oxon, OX14 4RN

Simultaneously published in the USA and Canada by Taylor and Francis
270 Madison Avenue, New York, NY10016

Taylor and Francis is an imprint of the Taylor & Francis Group,
an informa business

© 2008 Dean Hawkes

Designed by Gavin Ambrose

Printed and bound in Great Britain by The Cromwell Press,
Trowbridge, Wiltshire

British Library Cataloguing in Publication Data
A catalogue record for this book is available from the British Library

Library of Congress Cataloging- in-Publication Data
A catalog record for this book has been requested

ISBN10 0-415-36086-2 (hbk)
ISBN10 0-415-36087-0 (pbk)
ISBN10 0-203-79941-0 (ebk)

ISBN13 978-0-415-36086-9 (hbk)
ISBN13 978-0-415-36087-6 (pbk)
ISBN13 978-0-203-79941-3 (ebk)

Contents

Preface   vi

Acknowledgements   viii

Introduction   x

Part I   **From Enlightenment to Modernity**   1

Essay 1   Soane, Labrouste, Mackintosh: 3
                   pioneers of environment

Part II   **The Twentieth-Century Environment:**   31
                   themes and variations

Essay 2   Le Corbusier and Mies van der Rohe: 33
                   continuity and invention

Essay 3   The 'other' environmental tradition: 61
                   Erik Gunnar Asplund and Alvar Aalto

Essay 4   The poetics of 'served' and 'servant': Louis I. Kahn   87

Essay 5   'I wish I could frame the blue of the sky':   111
                   Carlo Scarpa

Essay 6   Architecture of adaptive light: Sigurd Lewerentz   129

Part III   **Image and Environment**   143

Essay 7   The sheltering environment: Fehn and Zumthor   145

Essay 8   The art museum: art, environment, imagination   157
                   – Moneo, Siza, Caruso St John, Zumthor

Essay 9   Sacred places: Zumthor, Siza, Holl   185

Essay 10   Airs, waters, places: Therme Vals   203

Selected bibliography   220

Index   226

Illustration credits   233

Preface

A decade ago, I assembled a collection of essays, *The Environmental Tradition.*[1] In these I attempted to make connections between the theory and the practice of environmental design in architecture. I also sought to bring a historical perspective to the field. A further aim, and with hindsight perhaps the most important, was to show that the nature of the environment within a building lies at the very heart of the architectural project.

The present book tries to penetrate more deeply into the thinking of architects as they imagine the *environment*, the *atmosphere*, the *ambience* of their buildings. In most circumstances this involves establishing some kind of relationship between the elements of architecture, *space, form, material,* and mechanical systems for *heating, ventilating, lighting*. Together, these constitute the *technics* of the architectural environment, but *technics* or *techniques* or *technologies* alone, however important their role, fail to touch the central point. As I hope these essays go some way to show, the significant environmental propositions in architecture rest upon acts of *imagination* in which *technics* are brought to bear in the service of *poetic* ends.

Although the book follows a broad chronological structure, spanning the nineteenth and twentieth centuries, it does not attempt to present a continuous historical account of environmental design in this period. The method is to examine the work of specifically selected architects, identifying and exploring a variety of themes. The description, analysis and interpretation of the major buildings that are discussed are based on extensive visits and observations, supplemented by documentary and archival research. The essence of the environment that I am trying to capture must be directly experienced; it cannot be completely discerned from images and verbal descriptions alone. For the purposes of this kind of research the only reliable instruments of observation are the human senses. As a consequence, I have spent many hours in some remarkable buildings. These include: churches by Steven Holl, Sigurd Lewerentz, Alvaro Siza and Peter Zumthor; art museums by Caruso St John, Carlo Scarpa, Sverre Fehn, Louis Kahn, Rafael Moneo, Alvaro Siza, Peter Zumthor; Asplund's Gothenburg Law Courts and Aalto's Säynätsalo Town Hall; and the waters at Zumthor's Therme Vals. This is the most indulgent research imaginable, but at all times it has, I hope, been purposeful.

The works of many other architects could, maybe should, have served to demonstrate my thesis. For example, I am conscious of the absence of Semper, Schinkel and Horta from my account of the nineteenth century. In the twentieth century, Scharoun and Terragni could be represented as major poets of the architectural environment, to say nothing of Barragan and Utzon, and I am acutely aware of the absence of Wright; then there is Ando. I also recognise that very few British architects are represented here. Maybe in the future these and others will be given their due attention.

1   Hawkes, Dean, *The Environmental Tradition: Studies in the Architecture of Environment*, E. & F.N. Spon, London, 1996.

Acknowledgements

I wish to acknowledge the help of many in supporting this project. First of all, I thank the Leverhulme Trust for the award of an Emeritus Research Fellowship, 2002–2003. This funded my series of research visits to buildings in Europe and the USA and made a substantial contribution towards the cost of making new drawings of many of the buildings. I am grateful to Peter Carolin and Malcolm Higgs for their support of my application to Leverhulme. The drawings were prepared with care and excellent judgement by Simon Blunden.

Many individuals went to great lengths to allow me access to buildings and archives. I am particularly grateful to Katariina Pakkomaa and colleagues at the Alvar Aalto Archive in Jyväskylä and to Patricia Cummings Loud, who welcomed me to the Kimbell Art Museum in Fort Worth and, later, read and helped me to improve my essay on Louis I. Kahn. I also thank Margaret Richardson at the Sir John Soane Museum in London, for a long and insightful conversation on Soane. My long-standing friendship with Sergio Los has for many years inspired and informed my thinking on the architectural environment. On numerous occasions we have together visited and discussed Carlo Scarpa's buildings in the Veneto. In specific connection with this book I enjoyed the hospitality of Sergio and Natasha Pulitzer in Vicenza and benefited from Sergio's critique of my Scarpa essay. I wish also to thank Mary Ann Steane in Cambridge for conversations and for her helpful comments on some of the essays. I am also grateful for the help, over many years, of the Librarians at the Welsh School of Architecture in Cardiff and the Faculty of Architecture and History of Art at Cambridge, Silvia Harris and Maddy Brown respectively.

Over the years I have been privileged to work with many outstanding students whose work has, either directly or indirectly, contributed to these essays. Among these Todd Willmert occupies a special place. His distinguished research on Sir John Soane, which he began when he was a post-graduate student in Cambridge, laid the foundation for my discussion of Soane and his recent work on Le Corbusier's fireplaces inspired me to undertake my comparison of Corbusier and Mies. Other students whose work has been of direct help are Nigel Craddock, again on Soane, and Edward Ng for his insights into both Soane and Mackintosh. I should like to express my thanks to Emma Toogood, whose graphic analysis of the insolation of the Villa Mairea provided precise verification of my empirical observations. I wish also to thank numerous other colleagues and students in Cardiff, Cambridge and elsewhere who have helped to shape my thoughts.

The raw material of these essays formed the basis of a series of lectures that I gave in 2003–2004 as Visiting Professor at the Department of Architecture, University of Huddersfield. I am grateful to the Head of Department, Richard Fellows, for inviting me to join the school in that capacity and for his willingness to expose his staff and students to my ideas as they took shape. I must also, as always, thank Caroline Mallinder at Taylor & Francis for her patience and tact in bringing the book to print.

For over forty years, I have enjoyed the tolerance, care and love of my wife, Christine. I dedicate this book to her.

Dean Hawkes, Cambridge, February 2007

Introduction

I only wish that the first really worthwhile discovery of science would be that it recognised that the unmeasurable is what they're really fighting to understand, and that the measurable is only the servant of the unmeasurable; that everything that man makes must be fundamentally unmeasurable.[1]

I begin with this quotation from Louis Kahn because it seems to me that it poses a fundamental question about the nature and utility of science and its cousin, technology, and their relationship to the concerns of architecture. The aim of this book is to explore the relationship between the scientific method and the devices of technology as they have been applied to the determination of the environmental properties of buildings. To establish a wide context for the discussion, I begin with a brief historical review of the emergence of what may be termed 'architectural science'.

0.1
Andrea Palladio,
Villa Capra, Vicenza (1565–1566)

My starting point is the Renaissance and, specifically, with the works of Andrea Palladio (1508–1580) and his English contemporary, Robert Smythson (1537(?)–1614). The Villa Capra (1550–1551), also known as La Rotonda, near Vicenza (Figure 0.1) is arguably Palladio's most celebrated villa.[2] It may be represented as the summation of the ideals of Renaissance architecture in its synthesis of form, proportion and symbolism. But it was also conceived as a practical dwelling in which these same principles of form and proportion serve as precisely calculated mediators between the variables of the climate of the Veneto and the more moderate conditions required for domestic life. In the *Four Books*,[3] Palladio explained the principles by which the size of windows should be related to the dimensions of the rooms which they serve:

> It is to be observed in making the windows, that they should not take in more or less light, or be fewer or more in number, than what necessity requires: therefore great regard ought to be had to the largeness of the rooms which are to receive the light from them; because it is manifest, that a great room requires more light to make it lucid and clear, than a small one: and if the windows are made either less or fewer that that which is convenient, they will make the places obscure, and if too large, they will scarce be habitable,

because they will let in so much hot and cold air, that the places, according to the season of the year, will either be exceeding hot or very cold, in case the part of the heavens which they face, does not in some manner prevent it.

0.2
Robert Smythson,
Hardwick Hall (1590–1597)

A similar complex unity of the symbolic and the practical may be seen in Smythson's Hardwick Hall (1590–1597). Here (Figure 0.2), in the very different conditions of Elizabethan England, a complex order of symmetry and proportion is fused with the organisation of solid and void, of perimeter and core, to achieve a balance of light and heat, in both winter and summer, that served both the domestic practicalities and grand ritual that the house was intended to accommodate.[4]

The point to be emphasised here is that this acute perception of the relationship between the cultural and symbolic qualities of these buildings and what we now refer to as their 'environmental' function, was an indissoluble part of their conception and realisation. But, as practical science and its related technologies developed and found application in architecture from the end of the eighteenth century, this unity was eroded as reductive codification and specialisation took its place. This process coincided with and accelerated as technology advanced during the nineteenth century to meet the demands of industrial production and urbanisation.

To give some indication of the nature of this transformation I refer to *Gwilt's Encyclopaedia of Architecture*, first published in 1825.[5] This tome, which underwent many revisions and remained in print until the twentieth century, is, on the model of the Renaissance treatises, divided into Four Books:

Book I, History of Architecture
Book II, Theory of Architecture
Book III, Practice of Architecture
Book IV, Valuation of Property.

Alongside the catalogue of the styles that constitutes Book I, Book II's 'Theory of Architecture' is, in effect, a technical manual containing chapters on:

> Mathematics and Mechanics of Construction
> Materials Used in Building
> Use of Materials or Practical Building – this includes sections
> on ventilation and warming
> Medium of Expression – a manual on draughtsmanship.

The section on 'Warming of Buildings' contains practical guidance on how to calculate the relationship between a room and its heating system:

> One foot of superficies of heating surface is required for every 6
> feet of glass; the same for every 120 feet of wall, roof and ceiling;
> and an equivalent quantity for every 6 cubic feet of air withdrawn
> from the apartment by ventilation per minute.

This prescription provides an indication of the extent to which central heating design was placed on a precise quantitative basis early in its development. It was from these beginnings that the enterprise of architectural science rapidly developed.

Moving on to the twentieth century, the early decades saw the key work in establishing the foundations of the theory of environmental comfort. Here the objective was to establish connections between physical descriptors of environmental conditions, of heat, light and sound, within buildings and human needs.[6] In many cases, this work continues to provide the basis of present-day environmental design practice.

All this was taking place at the same time as the emergence of the Modern Movement in architecture, with its fundamental transformation of the relationship of technique to form and language. As represented by the analysis of Le Corbusier's *Cinq points d'une architecture nouvelle*,[7] this proposed the expression of distinct functions through specific and separate elements of the composition. *Structure* and *enclosure* are no longer achieved through the single, portmanteau, element of a wall punctured by carefully dimensioned openings – the method of Palladio and, in a different way, of Smythson – but by the separate elements of frame and envelope respectively. In this new conception, the potential of mechanical systems for heating, cooling, ventilation and lighting was quickly appreciated and both the language of architecture and the nature of the architectural environment were, thereby, transformed.

For architects like Palladio and Smythson, the environmental function of architecture was embraced by the philosophical and intellectual synthesis of the Renaissance. By the twentieth century, it had become a matter of specialisation and quantification. The enterprise of building – or architectural – science has received relatively little attention from the historians. But, it may be claimed, it has played a key role in extending the potential of architecture to address the increasingly precise and complex demands made of buildings during, first, the industrial, then the post-industrial and, now, the digital eras. Pragmatically this may be judged a success. It is now possible to design buildings in which quantitatively and precisely specified environments can be delivered by calculated configurations of building fabric and mechanical plant. But this success has, it seems, often been bought at a high price.

My concern hinges around the emphasis of the *quantitative* as the principal object of environmental design, around precisely the conflict of the *measurable* and the *unmeasurable* expressed by Louis Kahn. In the present book I aim to develop an account of the environmental strategies adopted by important architects over the past two centuries. I hope this will demonstrate that quantification and mechanisation may co-exist with a poetic interpretation of the nature of the architectural environment.

Architecture is frequently, and with good reason, considered to be about providing shelter from the naturally occurring climate. From the earliest times, humankind has sought to construct enclosures to offer protection against the extremes of heat, cold, wind and rain. Studies in the ethnography of architecture[8] have shown how effectively the material resources of diverse places have been used to this end; they equally clearly show that such structures are quickly transformed to acquire meaning beyond mere practicality. Modern buildings continue to protect their occupants and their activities from the elements, but this is achieved for diverse and demanding ends by a vast and ever expanding array of technical means.

Writing in 1969, Reyner Banham pointed out that:

> mechanical servicing ... has been almost entirely excluded from
> historical discussion ... Yet however obvious it may appear ... that
> the history of architecture should cover the whole of the
> technological art of creating habitable environments, the fact
> remains that the history of architecture found in the books ... deals
> almost exclusively with the external forms of habitable volumes as
> revealed by the structures that enclose them.[9]

In his ground-breaking book, Banham established the significance, in the
historiography of nineteenth- and twentieth-century architecture, of mechanical
systems for heating, ventilating, cooling and lighting buildings. The argument added
an environmental dimension to the established narrative, represented by authors such
as Collins, Giedion, Pevsner and Richards.[10] In this, nineteenth-century innovation in
the technologies of building was shown to prepare the ground for the new architecture
of the twentieth century. To this, Banham added a provisional history of
developments in heating, ventilation and lighting in elucidating the process by which
the industrial revolution led to the emergence of new technical and stylistic
possibilities in architecture. This constituted a major contribution to scholarship and
has influenced a significant body of work in the past thirty years.

Banham described his work as 'a tentative beginning'. He sensed that there
was almost certain to be a vast undiscovered body of material concerning the theory
and practice of environmental techniques in building. The subsequent research that
his book inspired has proved the accuracy of this intuition. Bruegmann, Olley and
Willmert,[11] among others, have uncovered the extent to which mechanical services
were applied in buildings of many kinds and styles throughout the nineteenth century.
Their work has also revealed something of the theoretical basis for the design of these
systems, as it was represented in numerous treatises on the specifics and generalities of
the sizing of pipes and the layout of distribution systems.[12] Significantly, these authors
have shown that mechanical systems were developed and put into widespread use as
early as the last decades of the eighteenth century and that they were adopted by
architects of such eminence as Robert Adam and Sir John Soane.

Terminological reflections

Banham's felicitous title, *The Architecture of the Well-tempered Environment*, has, over the years, come to articulate and define an entire field of scholarship and practice. 'Environmental Design' is now universally the basis of courses, texts and professional practice. There is general consensus on its meaning and content.

The generic definition of 'environment' is 'the surroundings or conditions in which a person, animal or plant lives or operates'.[13] According to *Chambers Dictionary*, the use of the noun 'environment' in this generic sense first occurred in Carlyle's writings early in the nineteenth century[14] The adjective 'environmental' appeared in 1887 and the idea of 'environmentalism' first came into use in 1923. More specific meanings, such as the ecological sense of environmental concern, came early in the 1970s, with the emergence of the so-called 'environmental movement'.

Banham's use of the term 'environment' in 1969 was almost certainly its first occurrence in architectural writing. Its now widespread present use is an indication of its appropriateness and of the relevance of his insight. But environmental design, whether it is regarded from the viewpoint of history, theory or practice, is seen, by Banham and most of those that have followed him, primarily as a matter of technology.

One of Banham's principal ideas was to propose a taxonomy of three 'modes' of environmental management: the 'Conservative', the 'Selective' and the 'Regenerative'. These categories derive from historical analysis and empirical observation. For example, the 'Conservative' mode, which is 'the ingrained norm of European culture', is named in honour of Sir Joseph Paxton's 'Conservative Wall' at Chatsworth, whereas the 'Selective' acknowledges the practice, 'common to humid or tropical climates... which employs structure not just to retain desirable environmental conditions, but to admit desirable conditions from outside'. The 'Regenerative' mode is that of 'applied power', of mechanical, energy-consuming systems for heating, ventilating, cooling and lighting buildings.

While these definitions effectively characterise the scope of environmental management in architecture, they are principally concerned with the instrumental. They define the function of building almost entirely in technical terms as an environmental or climate modifier. The aim is to establish a defined and constrained set of conditions of heat, light and sound within a building that, together, constitutes the idea of comfort. The development of strategies for environmental management is paralleled by a process of codification of degrees of temperature, ventilation, illuminance, noise levels and so on, that have, in contemporary practice, rendered the environment within buildings as almost entirely a matter of calculation realised through the mechanisms of engineering.

There is, however, a critical dimension of the experience of architecture that this approach fails to represent. The interaction of light and air and sound with the form and materiality of architectural space is of the very essence of the architectural imagination. The complex sensory experience that we enjoy in buildings implies a wholly different dimension to the idea of the architectural environment from the pragmatic and mechanical processes of climate modification and comfort engineering.

The distinction is, perhaps, expressed by the terms *technics* and *poetics*, insofar as these differentiate between, on the one hand, the objective or quantitative and, on the other, the subjective or qualitative. This is not to propose that these are mutually exclusive categories, but to make the point that the architectural environment is much more than a matter of pragmatic prescription and technical realisation, however useful that might be. To explore this further, it is, perhaps, useful to consider other terminological possibilities.

In Italian, the equivalent of the English *environment* is *ambiente*. This shares its roots with the French *ambiance*, translated as *atmosphere* in English, and the English use of *ambiance* (or *ambience*) that is defined as 'the character and atmosphere of a place' (*OED*), and *atmosphere*, in its non-scientific sense, is 'the pervading tone or mood of a place' (*OED*). In French, *environment* is *milieu* or *environnement*.

Character, atmosphere, tone, mood and milieu are terms that seem more readily to capture the poetic qualities of architecture. Indeed, Sir John Soane, in his lectures to the Royal Academy in London, used the presence or absence of 'character' to differentiate between the work of a 'useful builder' and that of an architect, 'without which architecture becomes little more than a mere routine, a mere mechanical art.'[15] As we shall see, Soane occupies a significant place in the history of the architectural environment.

The question arises of whether these questions are important. The idea of Soane as 'environmentalist' usefully relates him and his works to the modern discourse upon environmental design in architecture. But his engagement with 'character' rather than 'environment' proposes intentions that are quite distinct from the pragmatic and technological basis of much present-day environmentalism. The same distinction may also be discovered in the work of many other architects during the nineteenth and twentieth centuries. For example, Henri Labrouste and Charles Rennie Mackintosh both merged poetic sensibility with the environmental technologies of the nineteenth century in the invention of distinctive and expressive character within their buildings. It is also possible to bring this perspective to bear on the works of many major twentieth-century figures. Le Corbusier, Mies van der Rohe, Alvar Aalto, Erik Gunnar Asplund, Sigurd Lewerentz, Louis Kahn and Carlo Scarpa all can be shown to have sought quite specific qualities in the conception and realisation of the environmental character of their designs. The same may be said of contemporary architects. Sverre Fehn, Peter Zumthor, Rafael Moneo, Alvaro Siza, Caruso St John and Steven Holl have all, in recent years, made important contributions to the continuing vitality of environmental inquiry.

The environmental imagination

Just to hint at the essence of the argument, consider Sir John Soane's house at Lincoln's Inn Fields or his Dulwich Picture Gallery. These demonstrate a profound poetry of space, material and light, and these were realised through a pioneering engagement with the potential of the new techniques of illumination and heating and ventilating that were developing at the end of the eighteenth century. In France, Henri Labrouste brought together advanced structural and servicing techniques and a poetic environmental vision in creating the reading rooms of the Bibliothèque Ste-Geneviève and the Bibliothèque Nationale. Then, in the closing years of the nineteenth century, Charles Rennie Mackintosh achieved a different, but equally rich synthesis in his Glasgow buildings. In these he readily applied the engineering idioms of late Victorian building technology and of the shipyards of the River Clyde in the realisation of his complex and original visions.

The Modern Movement led to new conceptions and configurations of architecture, not least in respect of its environmental nature and potential. Le Corbusier's call for 'only one house for all countries' and Mies van der Rohe's design for a glass skyscraper in Berlin are both symbols of the adventurous spirit of the modernist environment. But beyond the symbols, the work of these two architects can be shown to take quite distinct approaches to the intention and realisation of new kinds of environment.

Elsewhere it is possible to identify the presence of an 'alternative environmental tradition'. The bright volume of the reading room in Erik Gunnar Asplund's Stockholm Library and the central hall of the Gothenburg Law Courts are examples of a sensibility that is deeply rooted in a response to the Nordic climate and the cultures that have long inhabited it. This sensibility may also be found in Alvar Aalto's work. A sequence of buildings, spanning from the Viipuri Library to Säynätsalo Town Hall, illustrate his deep understanding of the northern condition.

In contrast, Carlo Scarpa's works consistently offer insights into the nature and history of the *ambiente* and *materiale* of the Veneto. The luminosity of the Gipsoteca Canoviana at Possagno vividly demonstrates this as do his interventions at Castelvecchio and Querini Stampalia. In a very different context, the Banca Popolare in Verona shows that the office building can rise above the mechanistic assumptions of most conventional designs.

Returning north, Sigurd Lewerentz brought a unique sensibility to bear in his response to the northern latitudes. His realisation of the potency of darkness and the human ability visually to adapt to it, as it was ultimately realised at the churches of St Mark's at Björkhagen and St Peter's at Klippan, is among the most remarkable acts of the environmental imagination.

Finally, in this litany of twentieth-century exponents of the architectural environment, we must mention Louis Kahn, whose buildings, with their distinction of 'served' and 'servant', over and over again bring environmental qualities to the service of human institutions.

An equal, if different, environmental sensibility can be observed in the work of many leading contemporary architects. Sverre Fehn's Archbishopric Museum at Hamar and Peter Zumthor's shelter for Roman remains at Chur reach back to the origins of architecture as shelter and open up new possibilities for the modern environment. Throughout its history the art museum has been the object of environmental priorities through, first, questions of lighting works of art and, latterly, through the growing concerns for their protection and preservation. Buildings by Caruso St John, Moneo, Siza and Zumthor show how these concerns have stimulated invention in creating new and diverse environments for art. Equal diversity exists in recent explorations of the sacred environment. Zumthor's St Benedict's chapel, Siza's Santa Maria church and Holl's St Ignatius chapel are quite different from each other, in context and concept. They, nonetheless, fashion the media of form, space and material to establish original and appropriate settings – environments, ambiences and atmospheres – for Christian worship.

In *Experiencing Architecture*,[16] Steen Eiler Rasmussen wrote with deep insight about the environmental qualities of architecture. His chapters on daylight, colour and sound remain among the most compelling texts to capture the ambience of buildings. More recently, Juhani Pallasmaa's *The Eyes of the Skin*[17] is, perhaps, the most persuasive attempt to explore the relationship between the human senses and architecture. In the Conclusion to his book Pallasmaa writes:

> In memorable experiences of architecture, space, matter and time
> fuse into one single dimension, into the basic substance of being
> that penetrates consciousness. We identify ourselves with this space,
> this place, this moment and these dimensions become ingredients
> of our very existence. Architecture is the art of reconciliation
> between ourselves and the world, and this mediation takes place
> through the senses.

In *Studies in Tectonic Culture*,[18] Kenneth Frampton clarifies the distinction between spatiality and tectonics in architecture and develops a powerful argument for the re-establishment of the significance of the tectonic in relation to the dominant position of space in much of twentieth-century theory. In this, the tectonic is represented as more than a mere instrument of construction, resisting the notion that it is an end in itself. The concern is with the *poetics* of construction: 'The full tectonic potential of any building stems from its capacity to articulate both the poetic and the cognitive aspects of its substance.' Frampton's argument presents an implicit challenge to the historians and theoreticians of the architectural environment to develop a parallel account of its evolution. This book is, to some degree, a response.

Notes

1   Louis I. Kahn, 'Silence and Light', lecture given at ETH, Zurich, 1969, in Heinz Ronner and Sharad Jhaveri, *Louis I. Kahn: Complete Works*, Birkhäuser, Basel, 1987.

2   A comprehensive description of the Villa Capra is given in *La Rotunda*, in the series *Novum Corpus Palladianum*, Centro Internazionale di Studi di Architettura 'Andrea Palladio' di Vicenza, Electa, Milan, 1988.

3   Andrea Palladio, *I Quattro libri dell'architettura*, Venice, 1570; English translation, Isaac Ware, *The Four Books of Andrea Palladio's Architecture*, London, 1738; reprinted as *Andrea Palladio: The Four Books of Architecture*, Introduction by A. K. Placzek, Dover, New York, 1965.

4   See Chapter 4 of Mark Girouard, *Robert Smythson and the Elizabethan Country House*, Yale University Press, New Haven, CT, 1983, for an extended description of Hardwick Hall.

5   Joseph Gwilt, *An Encyclopaedia of Architecture: Historical, Theoretical and Practical*, Longman, Brown, Green and Longmans, London, 1825. This was based on William Chamber's *Treatise on Civil Architecture*, 1759, succeeded in 1867 by a revised edition 'with alterations and considerable additions, by Wyatt Papworth'. Further revisions were made in 1836, 1876 and 1888 and the book remained in print into the twentieth century.

6   Building scientists, such as Bedford, Dufton, Gagge, Houghten, Missenard, Vernon and Yaglou in the thermal field; Hartridge, Hecht, Luckeish and Walsh in lighting; and Sabine, Watson, Knudsen, Hope Bagenal and Wood in acoustics, all carried out fundamental work in the period between the world wars.

7   Le Corbusier, *Les Cinq points d'une architecture nouvelle*, in *Œuvre complète*, Volume 1, 1910–1929, Editions Girsberger, Zurich, 1929.

8   See Bernard Rudofsky, *Architecture without Architects: A Short Introduction to Non-pedigreed Architecture*, Doubleday, New York, 1964, and Amos Rapoport, *House Form and Culture*, Prentice-Hall, Englewood Cliffs, NJ, 1969.

9   Reyner Banham, *The Architecture of the Well-tempered Environment*, The Architectural Press, London, 1969.

10 The following offer accounts of the implications of developments in structural and constructional technology during the nineteenth century for the new architecture of the twentieth century. Peter Collins, *Changing Ideals in Modern Architecture*, Faber & Faber, London, 1965; Sigfried Giedion, *Space, Time and Architecture*, Harvard University Press, Cambridge, MA, 1st edn, 1941, 4th edn, 1962; Nikolaus Pevsner, *Pioneers of Modern Design*, Penguin Press, Harmondsworth, 1960, first published as *Pioneers of the Modern Movement*, Faber & Faber, London, 1936; J. M. Richards, *An Introduction to Modern Architecture*, Penguin Press, Harmondsworth, rev. edn, 1961.

11 Important studies of pioneering applications of mechanical services include, Robert Bruegmann, 'Central Heating and Forced Ventilation: Origins and Effects on Architectural Design', *Journal of the Society of Architectural Historians*, XXXVII, 1978, pp. 143–160; John Olley, 'The Reform Club', in Dan Cruickshank (ed.), *Timeless Architecture*, The Architectural Press, London, 1985; John Olley, 'St George's Hall, Liverpool', Parts 1 and 2, *The Architects' Journal*, 18 and 25 June 1986; Todd Willmert, 'Heating Methods and their Impact on Soane's Work: Lincoln's Inn Field and Dulwich Picture Gallery', *Journal of the Society of Architectural Historians*, LII, 1993, pp. 26–58.

12 Examples of such texts include, Thomas Tredgold, *Principles of Warming and Ventilating*, London, 1824; Marquis J. B. M. F. Chabannes, *On Conducting Air by Forced Ventilation, and Regulating Temperature in Dwellings*, London, 1818; D. B. Reid, *Illustrations of the Theory and Practice of Ventilation*, London, 1844; W. Bernan, *On the History and Art of Warming and Ventilating, Rooms and Buildings, etc.*, London 1845.

13 *New Oxford Dictionary of English*, Oxford University Press, Oxford, 1998.

14 *Chambers Dictionary of Etymology*, Chambers Harrap Publishers, Edinburgh, 1998.

15 David Watkin (ed.), *Sir John Soane: The Royal Academy Lectures*, Cambridge University Press, Cambridge, 2000. A more extensive presentation and discussion of the lectures may be found in David Watkin, *Sir John Soane: Enlightenment Thought and the Royal Academy Lectures*, Cambridge University Press, Cambridge, 1996.

16 Steen Eiler Rasmussen, *Experiencing Architecture*, MIT Press, Cambridge, MA, 1959.

17 Juhani Pallasmaa, *The Eyes of the Skin: Architecture and the Senses*, Academy Editions, London, 1996. Revised edition, Wiley Academy, Chichester, 2005.

18 Kenneth Frampton (ed.), *Studies in Tectonic Culture: The Poetics of Construction in Nineteenth and Twentieth Century Architecture*, MIT Press, Cambridge, MA, 1995.

Part I

From Enlightenment to Modernity

Essay 1
Soane, Labrouste, Mackintosh
Pioneers of environment

> A new movement appeared in industrial society which had been gathering headway almost unnoticed from the fifteenth century on: after 1750 industry passed into a new phase, with a different source of power, different materials, different social objectives. This second revolution multiplied, vulgarized, and spread the methods and goods produced by the first: above all, it was directed toward the quantification of life, and its success could be gauged only in terms of the multiplication table.

This statement, from Lewis Mumford's *Technics and Civilization*,[1] expresses a commonly held interpretation of the period from the middle of the eighteenth century to the end of the nineteenth. In those years, applied science and technology reshaped the way in which artefacts were conceived and manufactured and this was often thought to be a triumph of quantity over quality. My aim in this essay is to examine the nature of the architectural environment as it was influenced by the new technologies that came into use during the nineteenth century. I have chosen to look at the works of three architects, Sir John Soane, Henri Labrouste and Charles Rennie Mackintosh, which span the beginning, middle and end of the period.

Throughout the nineteenth century, in the field of building construction, new materials and techniques, allied with tools for calculation and analysis, allowed the dimensions of clear span, enclosed spaces to increase and for new configurations of space to be proposed. These themes have been the focus of extensive study in works such as Reyner Banham's *Theory and Design in the First Machine Age*[2] and Peter Collins' *Changing Ideals in Modern Architecture*[3] and, more recently, Kenneth Frampton's *Studies in Tectonic Culture*.[4] In parallel with the tectonic there was a corresponding line of development in environmental technology, although this has received relatively little historical or critical attention. Banham's *The Architecture of the Well-tempered Environment*[5] was the first to break into this ground and remains an important text. But the there treatment of events in the nineteenth century tells only a part of the story. The book hardly touches upon the works of significant architects until it reaches Banham's important studies of the environmental achievements of Frank Lloyd Wright at the Larkin Building and the Robie House.

In the intervening years other studies have begun to fill in many gaps. For example, Robert Bruegmann has made an important study of the general effect of developments in central heating and ventilation on architectural design in the nineteenth century[6] and the series of 'Masters of Building' studies, first published in *The Architects Journal*,[7] explored a group of significant British buildings. One of the most detailed studies of the relationship between environmental technology and the work of a major architect is Todd Willmert's research into Sir John Soane's application of new methods of space heating in his designs for his own house at Lincoln's Inn Fields and at the Dulwich Picture Gallery.[8] This provides the point of departure for this sketch of the architectural environment as it evolved from the Enlightenment to the threshold of Modernity.

Sir John Soane

> The due and equally warming of rooms in cold climates, it must be admitted, is of great importance to the health and comfort of the inhabitants of every dwelling, from the cottage of the servant to the palace of the sovereign. So necessary is warmth to existence that we cannot be surprised at the various inventions that have been produced for the better and more economical warming of our houses.

> The architect will do well to examine and reflect on the different modes adopted by painters of introducing light into their studios. The 'lumière mystérieuse' so successfully practised by the French artists, is a most powerful agent in the hands of a man of genius, and its power cannot be too fully understood, not too highly appreciated. It is, however, little attended to in our architecture, and for this obvious reason, that we do not sufficiently feel the importance of character in our buildings, to which the mode of admitting light contributes in no small degree.

Sir John Soane (1753–1837) made these statements in Lecture VIII of the series that he delivered, between 1810 and 1820, in his capacity as Professor of Architecture at the Royal Academy of Arts.[9] This is the lecture in which he most directly addressed aspects of the environment in buildings. 'Warming', a more felicitous term than our modern reference to 'heating', is identified quite pragmatically as an element of 'health' and 'comfort', whereas light, although of practical value, is considered to be an 'agent' of 'character' in architecture. While the statements maintain separation between the thermal and the luminous environments and seem to distinguish between the quantitative – warming – and the qualitative – lighting – it may be argued that in the realisation of his buildings Soane brought together all of the dimensions of environment into a complex synthesis.

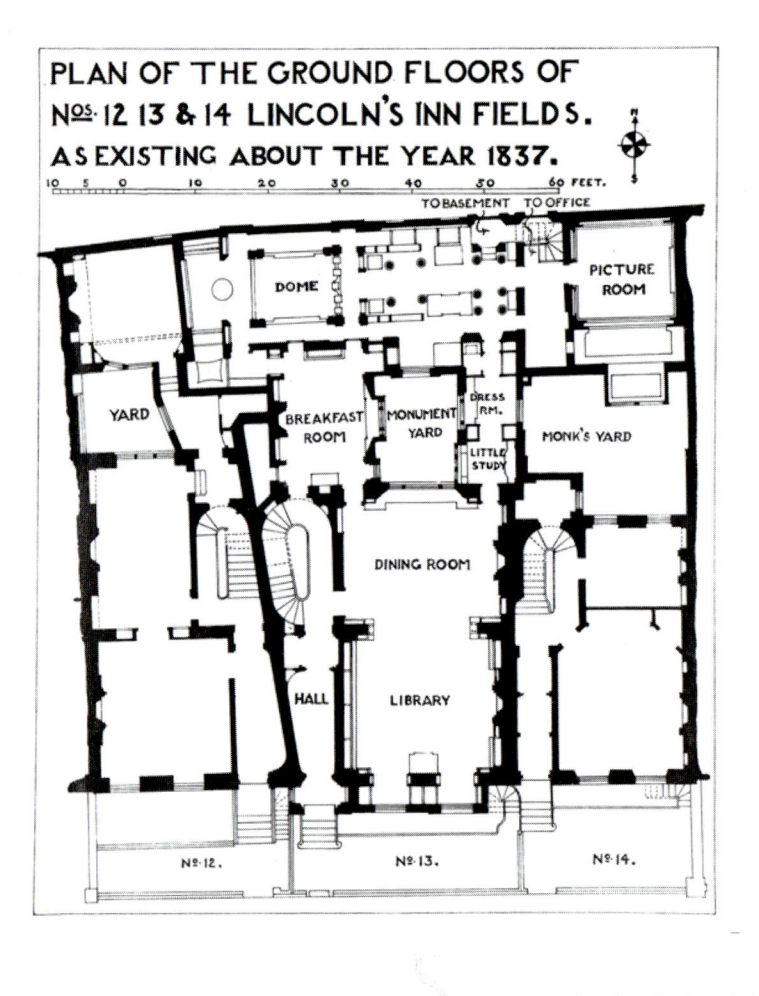

PLAN OF THE GROUND FLOORS OF
Nᵒˢ· 12 13 & 14 LINCOLN'S INN FIELDS.
AS EXISTING ABOUT THE YEAR 1837.

1.1
Soane house and museum,
ground floor plan in 1837

Soane first occupied a part of the premises on the north side of Lincoln's Inn Fields in 1792 and lived there up to his death in 1837. The process of reconstruction of the houses numbers 12, 13 and 14 continued for much of this period and is well documented.[10] As the years passed and Soane took over yet more of the buildings it is possible to see how the arrangement in plan, particularly in the museum and office, became less cellular, more interconnected (Figure 1.1). This process also occurred in cross-section as the rear yards were progressively covered over and vertical links established as the accommodation for the office and the museum took shape.

Willmert has shown the extent of Soane's interest in innovations in methods of warming, as they are revealed by both the texts of the Royal Academy lectures and the contents of his library, in which there are no less than seventeen books and pamphlets on the subject.[11] But even more authoritative than these documents is the evidence of his practical application of new systems of warming into designs for buildings from as early as the steam heating installation at Tyringham House that was completed in 1797. Experiments in heating were made in the works at the Bank of England and in many other projects. This direct experience of the design, installation and use of these devices, as Willmert attests, equipped Soane to apply them in the reconstruction of his own house.

In the forty-five years that Soane lived at Lincoln's Inn Fields, he seems to have almost continuously experimented with all conceivable methods of heating, encompassing stoves, fireplaces and three kinds of central heating installation using, in turn, steam, warmed air and hot water as the heating medium.[12] These were applied to the apartments at the northern edge of the house, behind the windowless façade facing the mews at Whetstone Park that contained Soane's professional office and the museum that housed his ever-expanding collection of works of art. In contrast the heating arrangements of the main body of the house were relatively conventional, retaining the tradition of the open hearth as the principal, usually the sole, source of heat. In explanation, Willmert cites Soane declaring that in their houses the English must, 'see the fire, or no degree of heat will satisfy'.[13]

The realisation of effective heating in the museum took Soane many years and numerous false starts were made, but finally, in 1832, the installation of a hot water system by the engineer A. M. Perkins seems to have solved the problem. This is extensively described in Charles James Richardson's, *A Popular Treatise on the Warming and Ventilation of Buildings*, first published in 1837[14] (Figure 1.2). Richardson was an architect who worked in Soane's office from 1824 and his book is devoted exclusively to the illustration of Perkins's system. With reference to Lincoln's Inn Fields, Richardson wrote of, 'The perfect success of Mr. Perkins's system … especially as I

1.2
Perkins' hot water heating system at 12–14 Lincoln's Inn Fields, from the frontispiece to Charles James Richardson's *Popular Treatise*

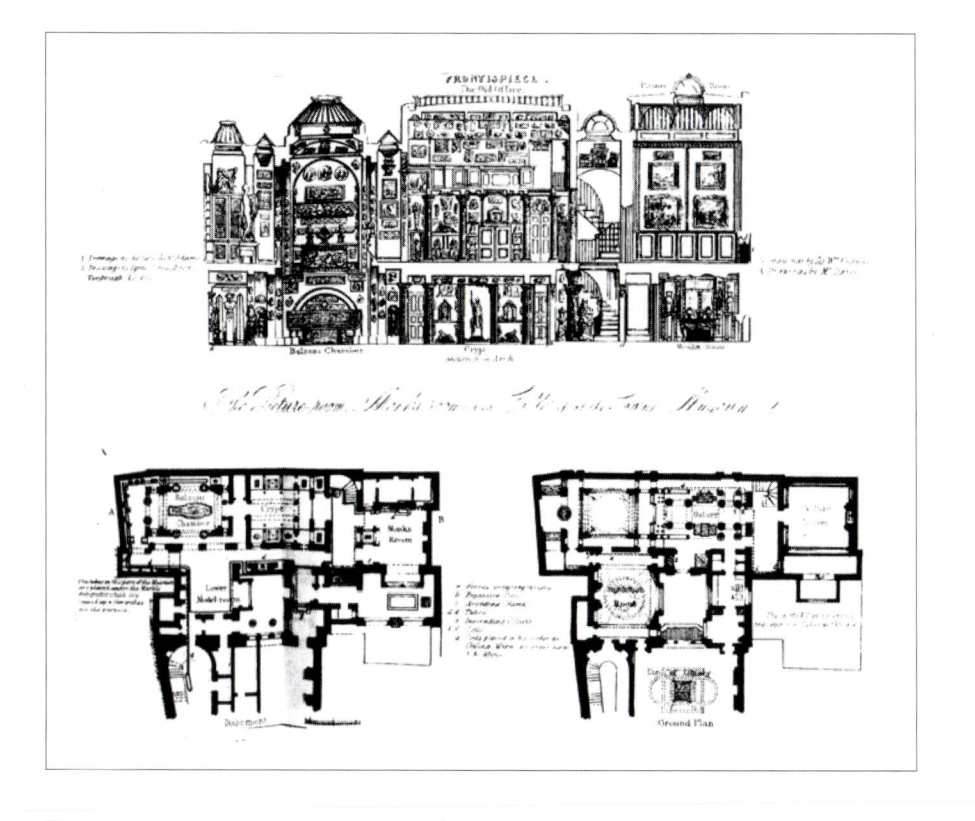

well remembered the miserable cold experienced in the office during former periods'.[15] The extent of the installation was described in full technical detail.

> There are 1,200 feet of pipe in the Soane Museum. It is divided into two circulations; one of which warms the picture-room, and the two rooms beneath. The other, which has the largest circulation annexed to it, first warms the office in which the expansion and filling pipes are placed; the pipe then traverses the whole length of the Museum, then passes through the breakfast-room under the long skylight, intended to counteract the cooling effect of the glass; it then passes through the floor into the lower room, forms a coil of pipe of 100 feet in the staircase, and returns to the furnace, passing in its course twice round the lower part of the Museum; a coil from this circulation is likewise placed under the floor of the dressing-room, which, by an opening in the floor and the side of the box, admits a current of warm air into the room above.[16]

This was almost certainly one of the first instances in the history of architecture in which a complex and specialised spatial organisation was rendered thermally comfortable by an advance in technology. It anticipates by nearly a century Frank Lloyd Wright's synthesis of heating with the open plans of the Prairie houses, as described by Reyner Banham.

> Here, almost for the first time, was an architecture in which environmental technology was not called in as a desperate remedy, nor had it dictated the forms of the structure, but was finally and naturally subsumed into the normal working methods of the architect, and contributed to his freedom of design.[17]

By common assent, Soane's over-riding environmental concern was with the quality of the luminous environment of his buildings. As David Watkin shows,[18] the ideas of Le Camus de Mézières, most particularly in relation to the effects of light, *la lumière mystérieuse*, lay at the centre of Soane's architecture.[19] The essential instruments in the realisation of these effects were the use of top-light, false or mysterious light and reflected light. John Summerson proposed that top-lighting, which Soane adopted as a matter of necessity in his work at the Bank of England, 'becomes an essential of the style' in the works of the so-called 'Picturesque Period' from 1806 to 1821.[20] In addition, Soane consistently used colour to modify the effect of light. This was achieved in two ways. First, he used coloured glass directly to modify the tonality of the light that entered a building, false or mysterious light. Second, he made precise judgements about the colours that he painted internal surfaces and, thereby, controlled the nature of reflected light. In developing these techniques Soane referred to sources such as the contemporary philosophy of Edmund Burke, the aesthetic theories of Goethe, Kant and Price and the scientific work of Thomas Young, Sir David Brewster and Moses Harris. He was also much influenced by J. M. W. Turner's experiments in painting.[21]

The nature of the artefacts in Soane's collection, their dimension, material and form, inspired the development of a complex sequence of inter-connected spaces in the Museum. These were almost exclusively top lit by an array of different forms of rooflight, no less than nine different types of top-light and one clerestorey, that allowed precise calibration of the quantity, quality and effect of the illumination of the spaces below and their contents.[22] The sky, even when overcast, is brightest at the zenith. This means that rooflights such as those in Soane's museum cast a strongly directional light vertically through tall narrow volumes. This dramatises the space and gives the strongest possible modelling of three-dimensional objects that it illuminates. The well-known cross-section through the Dome, rendered by George Bailey, effectively represents Soane's deep understanding of the physical distribution of light in architectural space (Figure 1.3). From autumn to spring these rooflights receive no direct sunlight because of the overshadowing of the main body of the houses to the south. In summer, however, the roof is sunlit throughout most of the day, creating even more dramatic effects. With or without direct sunlight, the illumination of the museum is enhanced by the use of coloured glass in the rooflights, yellow to suggest the effect of midday sun and red in the west facing rooflight in conformity with Turner's colour symbolism, where crimson is associated with the evening.[23]

The breakfast room is one of Soane's most remarkable inventions and, as we have seen from Richardson's description of the Perkins heating system, was one of the few domestic apartments in the house that enjoyed the benefits of central heating (Figure 1.4). But, as always, the preoccupation is with light. This compressed, land-locked space is lit by the ingenious combination of a small lantern placed, in the canopy of the vaulted ceiling, directly above the breakfast table and two linear lights, glazed with yellow tinted glass, that wash the yellow painted north and south walls. The effect of these is softened by sidelight that enters through the window that overlooks the Monument Yard, the east light of morning appropriately illuminating breakfast. Convex mirrors occupy the four corners of the ceiling vault and bring further complexity to the light by inter-reflection. Further mirrors are laid into the decoration and furniture and add yet more visual detail. Soane described the room in the following terms:

> The views from this room into the Monument Court and into
> the Museum, the mirrors in the ceiling, and the looking-glasses,
> combined with the variety of outline and general arrangement
> of the design and decoration of this limited space, present
> a succession of those fanciful effects which constitute the poetry
> of architecture.[24]

1.3
The Dome in 1810, cross-section looking east, drawn by Soane's chief clerk, George Bailey

1.4
Cross-section and plan of the breakfast room

The main body of the house at 13 Lincoln's Inn Fields is less elaborate than the museum, but, even in the absence of top-lighting, its illumination is as deeply considered. The front façade faces almost exactly due south and the principal rooms, at ground floor the library and dining room are, in effect, a single space divided only by a hanging arched screen. The drawing rooms are connected by wide double doors, but these function more obviously as separate rooms. The window openings at both floors are framed by the stone loggia that Soane added to the house in 1812 and these bring floods of sunlight into the house. The walls of the library and dining room are painted a deep Pompeian red that absorbs much of the light. Set against these, large and small panels of mirror again provide supplementation and transformation of the quality and quantity of the light. The loggia was originally open, but was glazed in 1829. The piers between the openings are faced with mirrors as are the inner faces of the sliding shutters. When the shutters are closed, almost the entire south wall of the library is a continuous plane of mirrors. The drawing rooms are bright yellow and, in the south drawing room in particular, this enhances the direct sunlight from the south. As elsewhere, mirrors bring yet more sparkle to these rooms.

The Dulwich Picture Gallery is quite different in purpose from Soane's house and museum.[25] Soane began the design in 1811 and construction was completed in 1813, so the two projects are exactly contemporary, but his approach in designing the first independent purpose-built picture gallery to be built in the British Isles[26] was, certainly at first sight, almost scientific in comparison with the complexity and symbolism that are so powerfully in evidence at Lincoln's Inn Fields. The building had a complex genesis and was required to accommodate the 360 paintings bequeathed to

Dulwich College by the painter Sir Peter Francis Bourgeois and a mausoleum to contain the remains of Bourgeois himself and those of his friend Noel Desenfans and, eventually, of Desenfans's wife, Margaret. In addition to these, the college required the building to re-house six almswomen, whose existing quarters were to be demolished to make space for the gallery.

Although the design went through many stages, this idiosyncratic brief was eventually resolved in a plan of the greatest simplicity, with the almshouses and mausoleum symmetrically disposed alongside the body of the gallery block. By placing the galleries with their long axis perpendicular to the existing buildings of the college, in particular, to the chapel, Soane contrived a perfect orientation for the exhibition spaces. His lantern rooflights thereby cast their principal east and west light directly onto the upper parts of the long walls of the *enfillade* picture rooms and limit the penetration of high-angled south light (Figure 1.5). This again reveals Soane's deep understanding of the physical behaviour of natural light in architectural space that was noted at Lincoln's Inn Fields, but here the intention would seem to be to provide consistent and controlled illumination of the paintings arrayed on the walls. It is interesting and surprising that the lighting of the gallery was much criticised by contemporary critics[27] when it has subsequently been seen as a prototype for many gallery designs.[28] In later alterations, carried out early in the twentieth century, more glazing was added to the lanterns, the condition in which the building is found today.

Against the objective lucidity of the galleries, however, Soane juxtaposed the solemn and mysterious light of the mausoleum (Figure 1.6). In the earlier designs this was placed to the east of the picture galleries, but, quite late in the day, in November 1811, the college decided that it should be to the west and even after this date the final design was not fixed.[29] The design, as built, presents the mausoleum on the axis through the entrance. It is approached through a narrow arched opening that leads to the circular, columned, vaulted 'chapel'. The floor of which is set one step below the level of the picture galleries. Beyond this the black sarcophagi stand in arched recesses. A tall lantern rises above the central space; glazed with Soane's much-loved yellow tinted glass. This glowing light floods the white plaster of the walls and the light stone paving, in contrast to the clear illumination of the galleries. These apparently simple means, the combinations of material, tone and illumination, emphatically establish the distinction between the realms of living and the dead.

Dulwich also has a place in Soane's experiments with the technologies of space heating.[30] From the outset, the picture galleries were conceived to be centrally heated using a steam system installed by Matthew Boulton and James Watt. The dark cylindrical objects that are visible in Gandy's perspective are part of the original heating system, presumably cast-iron registers warmed by the steam pipes in the duct below.[31] This duct is clearly visible in an on-site watercolour made in 1812 (Figure 1.7). This image also indicates a fireplace opening set into the gallery wall. It is not clear whether the fireplaces were part of the original heating scheme, intended to operate in combination with the steam system, or whether their purpose was to ventilate the

1.5
Dulwich Picture Gallery interior, watercolour by J. M. Gandy. The dark-coloured cylinders in the centre of the image were part of the original heating system.

1.6
Dulwich Picture Gallery, mausoleum

1.7
Dulwich Picture Gallery,
view under construction
showing the heating duct

building. In the event, the central heating installation caused problems almost from the completion of the building, when leaks from the expansion joints in the pipe work soon led to dry rot in the timber floor.

The almshouses were heated by open fireplaces, as one would expect from Soane's views on the heating of domestic apartments. Whether the mausoleum was connected to the central heating is not known. Plans of the building clearly show the gallery fireplaces or flues located in the west wall, as is confirmed by the watercolour perspective, but other images of the mausoleum fail to confirm this. Willmert[32] speculates that this space was unheated, using the chill of its atmosphere further to signify its distinction from the galleries. This reinforcement of the visual by the thermal might reasonably be said to be characteristic of Soane's imagination.

Just as Soane is now firmly established as a pioneer in the use of new systems of heating, we should, briefly, consider his interest in artificial lighting. Nigel Craddock has noted the exact parallel between Soane's career as a practising architect, from 1781 to 1833, and developments in lighting technology that allowed much higher and to some degree more controllable sources of illumination than simple candles or oil lamps.[33] First among these was the Argand lamp, developed in 1783. This used the discovery by Lavoisier that flames will burn more brightly if they are fed by a good supply of oxygen. Argand's lamps consisted of two concentric glass tubes that drew a double current of air over the wick over a hollow cotton wick placed between them. Craddock argues that Soane used such lamps at Lincoln's Inn Fields, on the evidence of the light decorations that he employed that would be quickly discoloured by the soot from traditional lamps.

Soane also experimented with gaslight, but at Lincoln's Inn Fields this was limited to the servants quarters in the basement and a single wall bracket in the Monument Court. At the Bank of England gas lighting was used extensively on the exterior of the building, in the circulation areas and other utilitarian areas. At Wimpole Hall in Cambridgeshire, where he carried out a variety of projects.[34] Soane installed practical gas lighting, similar to that at the Bank. Two major interventions here, made in the 1790s, were the formation of the Yellow Drawing Room and the construction of a rooflight over the Great Staircase. The Drawing Room has a tall vaulted ceiling surmounted by a circular lantern that rises through the whole height of the house and the Great Staircase is lit by a similar, but square lantern that replaced an earlier east-facing window that was obstructed by the construction of the Drawing Room. Both of these lanterns incorporated gasoliers. It is uncertain whether these were Soane's work,[35] but their integration into the structure of the rooflights was both a practical solution to the problem of ventilating such devices and coincides with Soane's constant interest in applying technology in the service of the quality of the environment.

All accounts of Soane's fascination with the power of light in architecture refer to the event that he organised at Lincoln's Inn Fields in March 1825. The previous year he had purchased the Sarcophagus of Seti that had been discovered in 1817 by the Egyptologist, Giovanni Belzoni (Figure 1.8). At three evening parties, attended by some 890 guests, the sarcophagus, that he had placed in the crypt, and the ground floor and basement of the house were illuminated by candles and oil lamps specially hired for the occasion and the exterior of the house was lit by 256 lamps, all in special glass containers.[36] It has been recorded that Soane 'lit the ground floor and basement at night to exploit to the full the contrasts of light and shadow around the house and to create the maximum romantic atmosphere in which to appreciate the sarcophagus'.[37] The lamps in the museum were concealed, placed close to mirrors or shaded with coloured glass and it has been suggested that some were placed inside the sarcophagus, which would then have become itself a source of mystical light. The spectacle is further evidence of Soane's acute awareness of the relation of light to space.

1.8
Sarcophagus of Seti in the crypt at Lincoln's Inn Fields

Henri Labrouste

John Soane's working life bridged the transition from the eighteenth to the nineteenth centuries. As we have seen, he was one of the true pioneers in exploring the use of new methods of warming and illuminating buildings. While he was daring and inventive in his spatial schemes, he was quite conservative in his approach to structure and construction. For example, the domed spaces at the Bank of England were of traditional brick construction. On the other hand, by the time Henri Labrouste (1801–1875) began his remarkable practice with the design of the Bibliothèque Ste. Geneviève in Paris (1838–1850), the use of iron structures was relatively commonplace and it is primarily for this reason that his work has attracted the attention of historians of the Modern Movement and of architectural technology.[38]

At first sight, the Bibliothèque Ste-Geneviève inhabits a totally different world from the Dulwich Picture Gallery. The great reading room on the first floor is dominated by its double-vaulted iron roof structure supported on the central row of slender iron columns (Figure 1.9). The relationship of the iron structure to the enclosing masonry walls has been widely discussed and admired. Kenneth Frampton describes it as

> the insertion of a prefabricated, fireproof iron armature into a masonry shell tectonically prepared for its reception ... It is of the utmost importance ... that the arcuated iron ribs go around the corner at the end of the long volume, thereby unifying the space and forestalling a reading of the library structure as two parallel lines of vaults.[39]

Compare this with the simple load-bearing brick wall structure and primitive carpentry of Soane's lantern roof system at Dulwich, where all is concealed behind the applied plaster surface.

When we turn to environmental matters, however, we discover some affinity between the two architects and their buildings. Approaching the mid-point of the century, Labrouste had available tried and tested heating systems that could be applied to meet the needs of the new urban population as they sought to make the fullest use of new public institutions and the buildings that they inhabited. At both the Bibliothèque Ste-Geneviève and later at the Bibliothèque Nationale (1860–1868), Labrouste was able to respond to these needs.

The site of the Bibliothèque Ste-Geneviève stands at the northern edge of the Place du Panthéon, with the long axis of the building aligned almost exactly east–west. This situation was to be of great importance in its environmental conception. A further significant factor was that the library was intended to be open in the evenings.[40] It would be expected to be light and warm late into the winter's evenings and this need was addressed by the installation of gas lighting and a central heating system. While these were less visible than the expressed iron structure, they

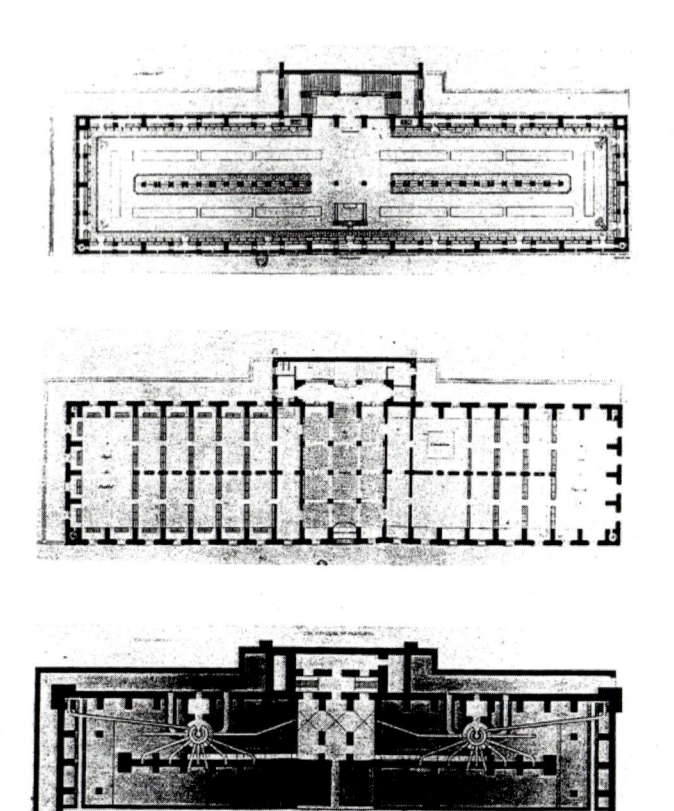

1.9
Bibliothèque Ste-Geneviève, first
floor, ground floor and basement
plans. The basement plan shows
the layout of the heating and
ventilating ducts that serve the
upper floors.

were equally essential to the conception of the building. They were elements of a
complete vision of the building's environment that embraced all times of day and
seasons of the year (Figure 1.10).

The route from the Place du Panthéon passes from the unlimited light of the
city, and moves north through the dimly lit vestibule, where fictive nature in the form
of the blue painted ceiling that continues onto the side walls as part of two painted
vistas of tree tops replaces reality. At the half landing, the route turns to the south and
arrives in the full light of the reading room. The location of the reading room on the
first floor is reminiscent of Sir Christopher Wren's library at Trinity College,
Cambridge. In both buildings the windows are placed high in the walls above the book
stacks and flood the interior with daylight. But at Trinity the windows face to the east
and west and thus only admit relatively low angle sunlight, whereas at Ste-Geneviève
the long sides of the room face north and south so that there is a distinct asymmetry
of light as the sun tracks diurnally from east to west. The continuation of the windows
at the east and west ends of the room gives further emphasis to this. David Van Zanten
has analysed this situation:

the building is a library, a place illuminated properly for reading, and … proper lighting is difficult here since the site is flattened and oriented along its whole vast length directly toward the southern sun. The only means Labrouste had to provide a diffused, comfortable light was to protect the interior by a light, deep arcade whose thin piers would act as sunscreens, breaking the direct rays and diffusing the sunlight by reflection off their flat, unornamented sides.[41]

This interpretation is supported and further developed by Neil Levine who wrote:

> The most obvious quality of the reading room is its openness and lightness. The deep, girding arcade, letting in daylight on all four sides, and acting as a brise-soleil for most of the day. One is constantly made aware of the passage of time by the movement of the sun and of the fact that it is the skeletal iron construction that allows for this perception of the cycle of the day.[42]

Levine shows that the room's orientation and inhabitation are further marked by a subtle inflection of its ornamentation. The decoration of the eight exposed surfaces of the stone piers that support the central iron columns, four of which face east and four west, are carved with female terms representing day and night. Those in the centre of the room facing west are described as having 'knitted brows, open eyes and an intense look of concentration'. The eyes of those that face east 'are heavy lidded and give the figures a dreamy look'. When seen from within the room, the open eyes of Day are

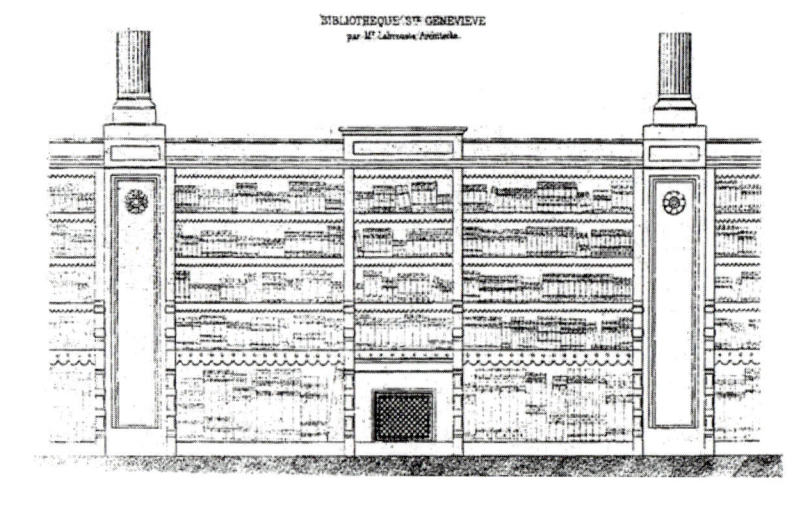

1.10
Bibliothèque Ste-Geneviève.
Detail showing the incorporation of the heating outlet into the bookcases that originally stood between the central columns of the reading room.

thus seen against the bright morning light, and sleepy Night is set against the backdrop of the setting sun.

The commission for the building required it to be gas-lit and fireproof, a necessary connection at the time, and the original lighting of the reading room was straightforward and functional. But Labrouste's use of artificial illumination was also turned to poetic ends. The entrance sequence has been widely analysed and Levine has proposed that the requirement that the building should be open in the evening mean that 'The lamps (gas lights) at the entrance condense into one "sign" the reason for the library's being where it is, its hours of opening and the possibility of enlightenment that its use offers.'[43]

Labrouste's last building, the Bibliothèque Nationale (1859–1868), occupies the western edge of the site that lies between the rue Vivienne to the east and the rue de Richelieu to the west and north of the rue des Petits-Champs (Figure 1.11). It essentially consists of a sequence of three great spaces, in sequence from north to south comprising the open Cour d'Honneur, the Grande Salle des Imprimés and the Magasin Central des Imprimés that lie behind narrow ranges to the west and south. As at the Bibliothèque Ste-Geneviève, the sequence of movement from outside to the interior takes the visitor on a journey from bright light, through relative darkness to arrive in a luminous interior, but here this is all arranged at ground floor level.

The Girande Salle des Imprimés is a square space, roofed by nine domes that are supported on a slender iron structure (Figure 1.12). The principal light of the salle comes from the oculi at the zenith of each dome, supplemented by a rooflight over the apse to the south and three great north-facing lunettes above the entrance.[44] As at Ste-Geneviève, the structure defines and organises the primary environmental qualities of the room and translates the evident tectonics into a simultaneously practical and poetic setting for study. Labrouste recorded his idea of the reading room in the following terms:

> When I was in lycée, before or after classes I would go and study in the Luxembourg Garden and especially in the Pépinière. There, where nothing disturbed me, my eyes as well as my mind would repose happily on the beautiful and luxuriant foliage that surrounded me. I thought that in a place of study the representation of what had had so much charm for me would be in a library a decoration without pretension, first of all, and also an occasion for rest for the minds of the readers occupying the room.[45]

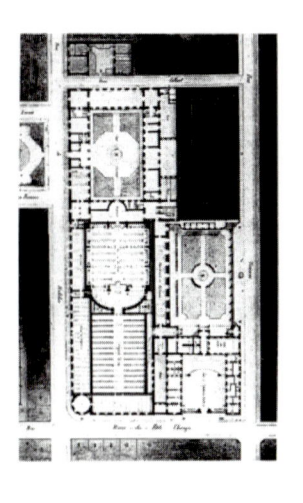

1.11
Bibliothèque Nationale, ground plan with north to the top

It is probably erroneous too literally to interpret the Salle as a representation of the Pépinière, even though the blind lunettes to east and west are painted as with vistas of sky and treetops to mimic the view through the north windows when, in the nineteenth century, the Cour d'Honneur was planted with trees. To over-emphasise this would distract attention from the precision with which Labrouste's design provides practical illumination for the task of study. The relationship of solid to void, of direct light to reflection in the design of the roof, supplemented by the shadowless north light of the lunettes, achieves excellent distribution of light throughout this large space, which was designed to accommodate four hundred readers. The reflectance of the white porcelain structures of the domes receives light directly from the oculi and these become powerful secondary sources of illumination. Van Zanten describes these 'as if they were cloth awnings in a gusting breeze'.[46] When the building opened in 1868, night-time light was provided by gas lamps placed in the pendentives. These, in anticipation of the 'uplighting' techniques of the twentieth century, directly illuminated the domes, making them the principal light source.

The Salle was, of course, centrally heated. This is unsurprising in view of Labrouste's earlier installation at Ste-Geneviève. At this point in the nineteenth century such installations were commonplace in buildings throughout Europe, including Sydney Smirke's contemporary reading room at the British Museum in London. Just like the installation in London, Labrouste's system delivered warmth by two means. Cast-iron *émetteurs de chaleur* stand in composed relationship to the

1.12
Bibliothèque Nationale,
Salle des Imprimés

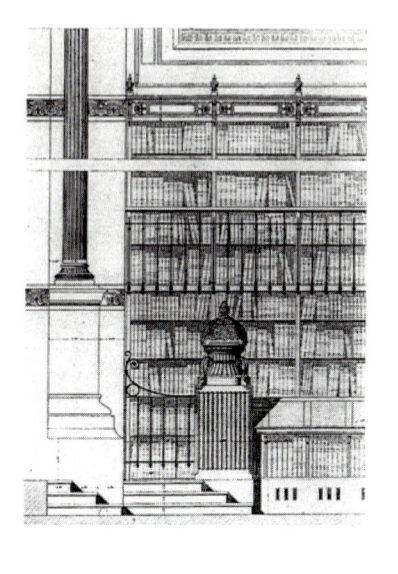

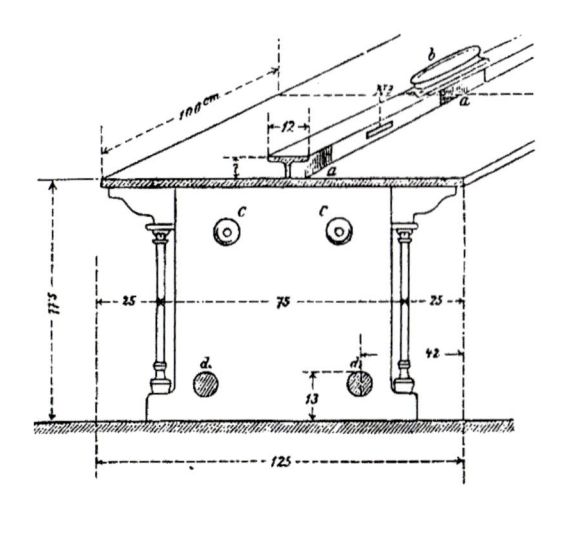

perimeter columns that support the roof canopy and supply the general background warmth to the Salle and this was supplemented by further hot water pipes that ran within the readers' tables (Figures 1.13 and 1.14).

Behind the Grande Salle des Imprimés stands the private, but equally spectacular Magasin Central des Imprimés – the closed book stack (Figure 1.15). This seized the attention of historians of the Modern Movement, most particularly Sigfried Giedion, who saw it, in its unornamented simplicity, as a clear anticipation of the architecture of the twentieth century. He wrote in 1940 that:

> Labrouste's masterpiece is the Grand Magasin or stack room … The
> whole area was covered with a glass ceiling. Cast-iron floor plates in
> a grid-iron pattern permit the daylight to penetrate the stacks
> from top to bottom … This hovering play of light and shadow
> appears as an artistic means in certain works of modern sculpture as
> well as in contemporary architecture … In this room – one never
> meant for public display – a great artist infolded new possibilities
> for architecture.[47]

More recent critics have rejected Giedion's interpretation and have properly relocated Labrouste in his own time and place.[48] It is there that the true nature of these buildings may be perceived. Then the significance of the public rooms of these two buildings becomes clear. Their mastery resides in the synthesis of means and ends; in bringing then quite new technologies of structure and environment into such assured relationships one with the other. This synthesis was, however, not contained within the realm of technics alone, but opened up powerful new possibilities for the poetics of architecture.

1.13
Bibliothèque Nationale, detail of *émetteurs de chaleur* in the Salles des Imprimés

1.14
Bibliothèque Nationale, detail showing heating elements integrated into the reading tables

Charles Rennie Mackintosh

It is precisely this synthesis that informs the work of Charles Rennie Mackintosh (1868–1928). In his lecture/essay 'Seemliness', dated 1902,[49] Mackintosh wrote that an architect

> must possess technical invention in order to create for himself suitable processes of expression – and above all he requires the aid of invention in order to transform the elements with which nature supplies him – and compose new images from them.

1.15
Bibliothèque Nationale, Magasin Central des Imprimés

In his recorded observations on architecture Mackintosh consistently stressed the primacy of 'expression' in his work, but this was always related to the need to understand the nature and potential of materials.[50] At no point in his spoken/written statements did Mackintosh refer directly to environmental questions, but the evidence of his buildings reveals both a deep sensibility to the very particular climatic conditions of Glasgow and the west of Scotland, where the buildings are situated and also to the potential of the engineering culture that was the basis of the local economy at the end of the nineteenth century. To illustrate both of these elements of Mackintosh's work I will examine his greatest building, the Glasgow School of Art (1896–1909).

In 1896, the Governors of the Glasgow School of Art held a competition for the design of a new building on a site on Renfrew Street in the centre of the city. The winning design was announced in January 1897 and was by the Glasgow practice of Honeyman and Keppie in which Charles Rennie Mackintosh worked as an assistant. Construction began later that year and the first stage was completed in 1899. In 1904, Mackintosh became a partner in Honeyman and Keppie and work on the Art School recommenced in 1907 and was completed in 1909.[51]

The plan of the building is very straightforward (Figure 1.16). A simple four-storey block of studios occupies the northern edge of the site facing Renfrew Street. Behind this, three smaller wings project southwards over the steeply sloping interior of the site and house more specialised spaces, such as the central, first floor museum and, to the west, the celebrated library. It is in the cross-sections that the building's complexity is found (Figure 1.17). The studios are lit by the unchanging light from enormous north-facing windows, in absolute conformity with the conventions of the painting studio. But circulation through the building takes one through diverse and ever changing lights and the important public rooms are invested with individual qualities through their lighting.

From the street the entry is into a dark vestibule, beyond which one is led towards the light that floods in from the wholly glazed roof of the museum above (Figure 1.18). The south-facing slope of glass allows direct sunlight to penetrate deep into the building. To left and right at the entrance level there are corridors lit by south-facing windows and above these there are corresponding corridors, that to the east lit

1.16
Glasgow School of Art, ground
floor and basement plans. The
plant rooms are shown in the
centre of the basement plan.

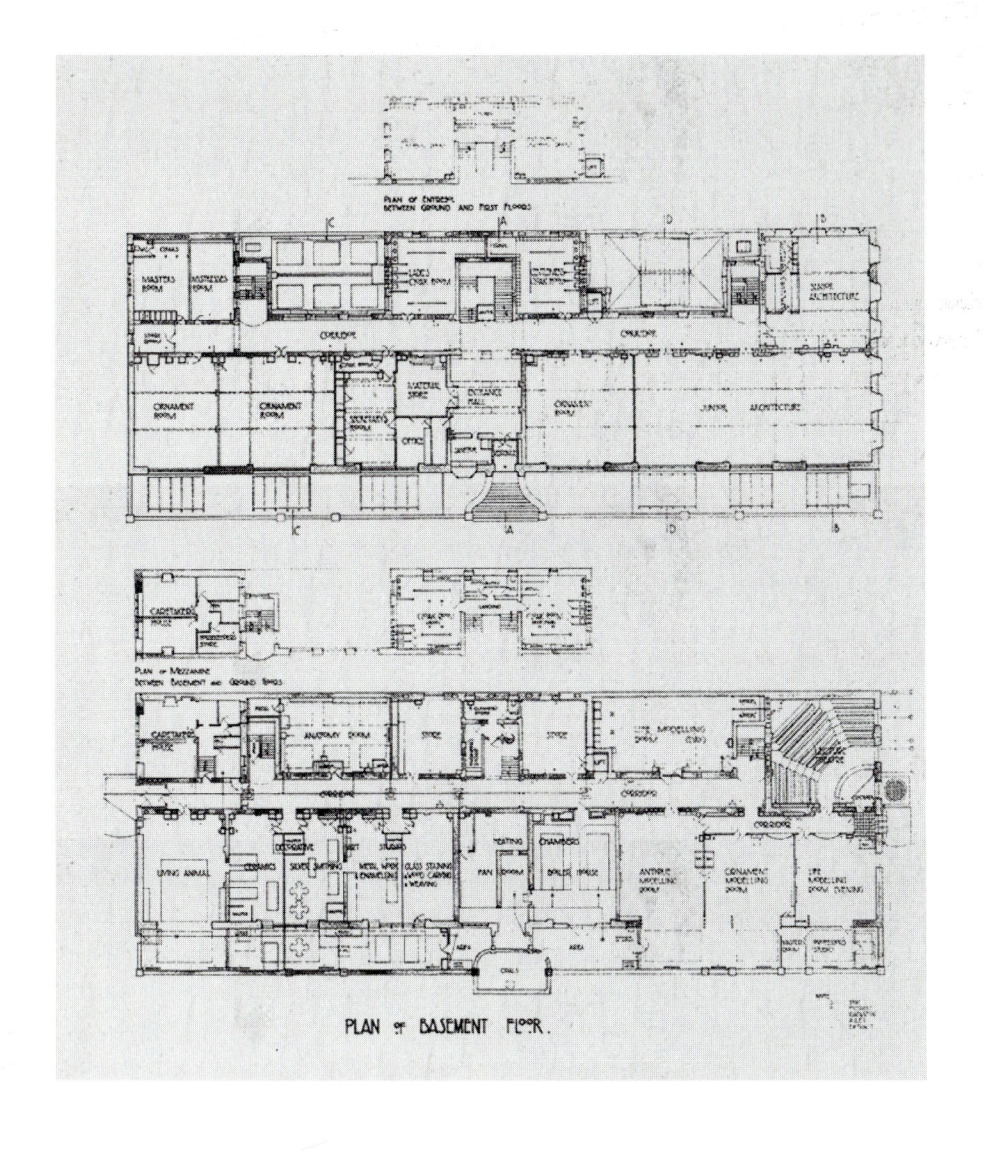

PLAN of BASEMENT FLOOR.

by wonderfully shaped rooflights, the other by south-facing windows that here are framed by window seats. On the second floor, circulation is by the loggia and the 'hen run' that seemingly hang out above the city and capture the ever-changing light and weather of this north-western city (Figure 1.19). The library (Figure 1.20), at the south-west corner of the building, is lit by three deeply incised windows in the south wall, one of which rises high to the gallery level, and to the west are three tall oriel windows that project beyond the face of the wall with widely splayed reveals. Together, these illuminate the library with the most dynamic light.

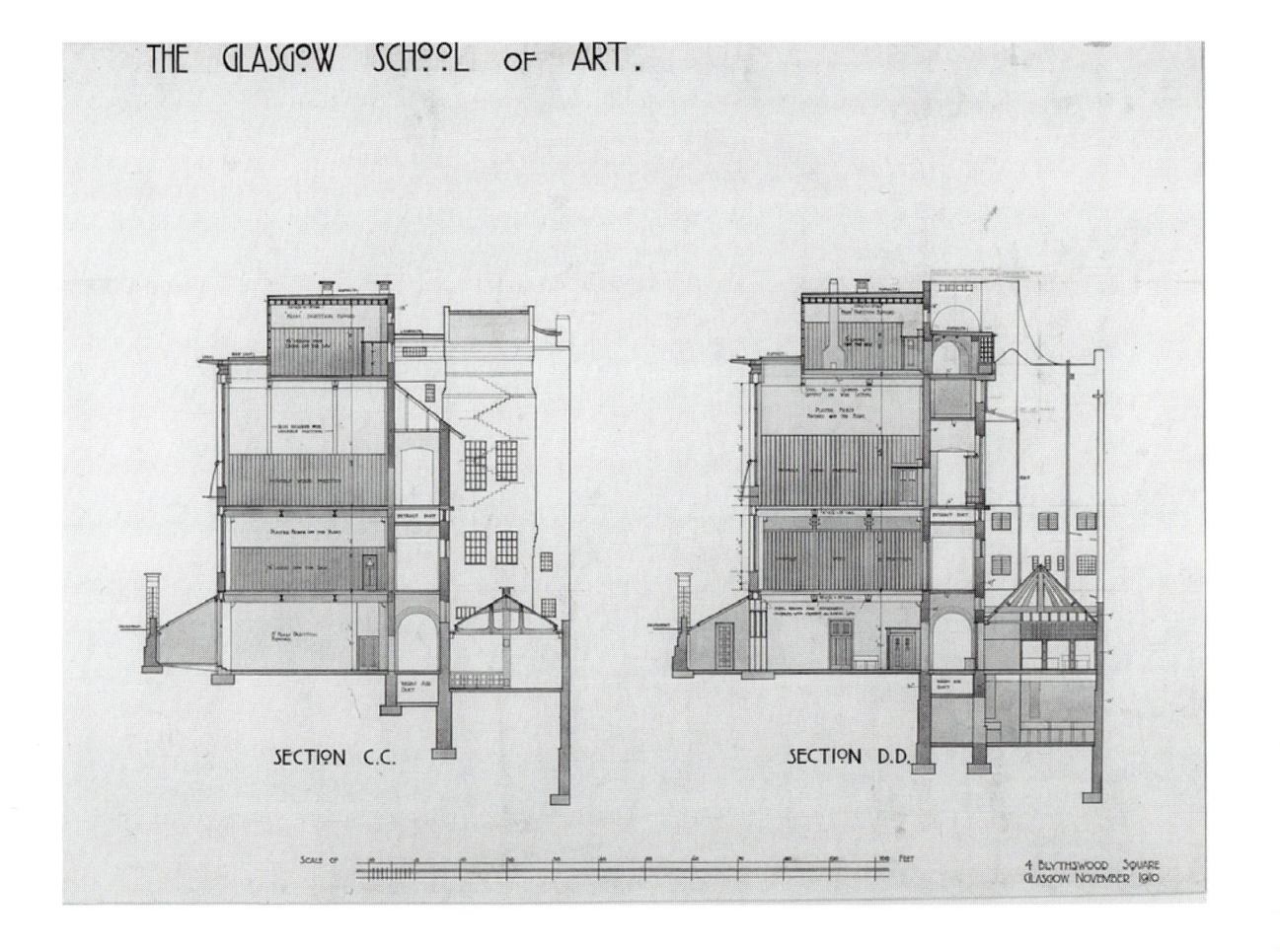

1.18
Glasgow School of Art, museum

1.19
Glasgow School of Art,
the 'hen run'

It is, at first sight, surprising that the structure of the Art School is of load-bearing masonry, with iron beams supporting the intermediate floors, and many of the roofs are supported on timber trusses. This is very conservative in comparison with Labrouste's iron structures half a century earlier. But Mackintosh stated his position on the question of structural technology and material as early as 1892:

> These two comparatively modern materials iron & glass though eminently suitable for many purposes will never worthily take the place of stone because of this defect the want of mass. With the advent of the Crystal Palace and the many rosetinted hallucinations of that period arose the belief in the invention of a new style. At last common sence (sic) it was shouted prevails – no more connection with the works of the past … But time has passed, and practical experience has shown that … the want of appearance of stability is fatal.[52]

The principal environmental systems of the building were, in contrast, absolutely of their day. This was noted by Banham in 1969 when he wrote:

> the Glasgow School of Art … used a Plenum ventilation system – which is not surprising in William Key's home town – whose upcast ducts appear, uncommented in practically all the standard photographs of the studios and workspaces of the school. The provision of such a system of hot air ventilation and heating was a necessary concomitant of Mackintosh's use of huge north-facing windows in these rooms and a humane provision where the life-class is concerned, for Glasgow is a chill city for nude models.[53]

Inspection of the plans of the building show the vertical ducts of the system built into or attached to the spine wall that runs the full length of the building. Many of the rooms were also served by cast-iron radiators placed beneath the windows to counteract the down draughts that inevitably fall over such large cold surfaces. The original plant has now been replaced, but the outlet grilles are still visibly present throughout the building.

But the evidence of Mackintosh's technological conservatism, that is seen in the structure and material of the Art School, is also expressed in the building's environmental arrangements. Even though the heating and ventilating system is carried throughout the building, there are numerous points where it is supplemented by traditional fireplaces. These could be more symbolic than functional, but, even if this is the case, they reveal how Mackintosh was at pains to hold onto the symbolism of these traditional elements. For Mackintosh, there was no inconsistency in incorporating domestic elements in an institutional building, if the nature and use of a room made this appropriate, and this almost certainly played an important role in the symbolic content of the building. As you move through the Art School, it is striking how the environment of its spaces is finely tuned to their purpose. This is realised and expressed by the use of different levels of material and finish. The studios are robust with expressed construction and durable materials. On the other hand, the Board Room and the library are exquisitely finished, the one lined with timber panelling, the other with glass-fronted bookcases.

By the date of the Art School, electric lighting was commonplace and Mackintosh used it as both a practical component of the building's technical equipment and as a means of further expressing the distinction between its functions. In the studios and other practical spaces the lighting was provided by simple groups of incandescent lamps, in some cases unshaded, in others provided with simple glass or metal shades. These were often suspended on pulley systems, to allow light to be brought exactly to where it was most needed, and the supply wires became web-like as they festooned the upper reaches of the rooms (Figure 1.21). This pragmatism contrasts with the attention given to the artificial lighting of the Board Room and the library. In the former, three identical light fittings bring, by the standards of the time, copious light to this dark-panelled room. The fittings are of wrought iron and each has nine lamps, each with a polished copper reflector. The lighting of the library is dominated by the group of silver and black lamps that hang low over the central magazine table. These have coloured glass inserts that refer to the luminescent colours of the chamfered spindles of the upper gallery balustrade.

1.20
Glasgow School of Art, Library

The new environment

At the beginning of the nineteenth century the first technological fruits of the industrial revolution were already being applied in transforming the environment within buildings. At the century's end, mechanical means for heating, and ventilating were commonplace and the development of electric light and power brought new flexibility of use and precision of control. With the exception of effective mechanical means of cooling,[54] all the elements of the modern environmental system were in place. This marked the possibility of redefining the relationship between climate and architecture and thereby to propose a fundamental change in the nature of architecture itself, characterised by Lewis Mumford as 'the quantification of life'.

Soane, Labrouste and Mackintosh have all been represented as forerunners of this change. Their experiments in and implementation of mechanical heating and ventilating, of gas and electric light could easily support this interpretation, but in all of their work we see these technological means consistently applied in the service of qualitative ends, *technics* subservient to *poetics*. This is their most important contribution to the history of the architectural environment and is a legacy that can be traced throughout the work of the most significant architects who followed them.

1.21
Glasgow School of Art. Second Floor Studio showing electric lighting, cast iron radiators beneath the windows and the timber cased air ducts on the inner wall.

Notes

1   Lewis Mumford, *Technics and Civilization*, Routledge & Sons, London, 1934.

2   Reyner Banham, *Theory and Design in the First Machine Age*, The Architectural Press, London, 1960.

3   Peter Collins, *Changing Ideals in Modern Architecture*, Faber & Faber, London, 1965.

4   Kenneth Frampton, *Studies in Tectonic Culture: The Poetics of Construction in Nineteenth and Twentieth Century Architecture*, MIT Press, Cambridge, MA, 1995.

5   Reyner Banham, *The Architecture of the Well-tempered Environment*, The Architectural Press, London, 1969.

6   Robert Bruegmann, 'Central Heating and Forced Ventilation: Origins and Effects on Architectural Design', *Journal of the Society of Architectural Historians*, Vol. XXXVII, 1978, pp. 143–160.

7   Dan Cruickshank (ed.), *AJ Masters of Building: Timeless Architecture*, The Architectural Press, London, 1985. This volume contains studies of the following buildings: Edward Prior's St Andrew's Church, Roker, by Dean Hawkes; Charles Barry's Reform Club, by John Olley; Waterhouses' Natural History Museum, by John Olley and Caroline Wilson; a study of Soane's Dulwich Picture Gallery by Colin Davies and concludes with Horta's Hôtel Tassel, by Eric Parry and David Dernie.

8   Todd Willmert, 'Heating Methods and Their Impact on Soane's Work: Lincoln's Inn Fields and Dulwich Picture Gallery', *Journal of the Society of Architectural Historians*, Vol. LII, 1993, pp. 26–58.

9   Sir John Soane, Lecture VIII, The Royal Academy Lectures. The lectures are reproduced in full with an extensive commentary in David Watkin, *Sir John Soane: Enlightenment Thought and the Royal Academy Lectures*, Cambridge University Press, Cambridge, 1996. The same texts with a shorter Introduction may be found in David Watkin (ed.), *Sir John Soane: The Royal Academy Lectures*, Cambridge University Press, Cambridge, 2000.

10 The standard source for this is the 'Description' of the residence that has been published in various editions from 1830 to the present. The latest of these is *A New Description of Sir John Soane's Museum*, 10th revised and fully illustrated edition, 2001. This is based on the edition first published in 1955 during Sir John Summerson's curatorship. That succeeded the 1930 edition that, itself, followed Soane's original text. The evolution of the House-Museum is recounted in detail in Susan G. Feinberg, *Sir John Soane's 'Museum': An Analysis of the Architect's House-Museum in Lincoln's Inn Fields, London*, PhD dissertation, The University of Michigan, 1979. University Microfilms International, Ann Arbor, MI. Elements of this may be found in Susan G. Feinberg, 'The Genesis of Sir John Soane's Museum Idea: 1801–1810', *Journal of the Society of Architectural Historians*, Vol. XLIII, 1984, pp. 225–237.

11 Todd Willmert, op. cit.

12 Ibid.

13 Ibid.

14 Charles James Richardson, *A Popular Treatise on the Warming and Ventilation of Buildings: Showing the Advantage of the Improved System of Heated Water Circulation*, John Weale, Architectural Library, London, 1837. The book is entirely devoted to the presentation of Perkins' system in both principle and application. The installation at Lincoln's Inn Fields is illustrated as the frontispiece. Other examples include one installed in 1837 at Robert Adam's Edinburgh Register Office (1774).

15 Ibid.

16 Willmert, op. cit., records that the archives at the Soane Museum contain an even more extensive description of the installation in Perkins' hand.

17 Reyner Banham, op. cit.

18 David Watkin, ops. cit.

19 Robin Middleton, in his introduction to Le Camus' *The Genius of Architecture; Or the Analogy of That Art with Our Sensations*, trans. David Brett, The Getty Center, Santa Monica, CA, 1992, also comments that, 'These themes had long been at the center of Soane's quest, and there can be little doubt that Le Camus inspired them.'

20 John Summerson, 'Soane: the Man and the Style', in *John Soane*, Architectural Monographs, Academy Editions, London, 1983. Here Summerson proposes five periods of Soane's career: Student Period, 1776–1780, Early Practice Period, 1780–1791, Middle Period, 1791–18056 Picturesque Period, 1806–1821 and Last Period, 1821–1833.

21 Important sources here include John Gage, *Colour in Turner: Poetry and Truth*, Studio Vista, London, 1969 and Martin Kemp, *The Science of Art: Optical Themes in Western Art from Brunelleschi to Seurat*, Yale University Press, New Haven, CT. The specific relationship of philosophy, aesthetic theories and science to the lighting of Soane's architecture is examined in Nigel Craddock, 'Sir John Soane and the Luminous Environment', MPhil dissertation, Department of Architecture, University of Cambridge, 1995, unpublished.

22 A comprehensive taxonomy of the rooflights at Lincoln's Inn Fields may be found in Nigel Craddock, op. cit.

23 Craddock's research includes detailed studies of the insolation of the museum roof made using a scale model mounted on a Heliodon. He also explores the relation of Soane's use of coloured glass to Turner's colour symbolism.

24 From Soane's original 'Description', written in 1835, cited in Arthur T. Bolton's 11th edition of *The Official Handbook of Sir John Soane's Museum*, Oxford University Press, Oxford, 1930.

25 The most accessible sources on the building are: G.-Tilman Mellinghof, 'Soane's Dulwich Picture Gallery revisited', in *John Soane*, Architectural Monographs, Academy Editions, London, 1983; Colin Davies, 'Dulwich Picture Gallery: Soane', in Dan Cruickshank (ed.), *Timeless Architecture*, op. cit.; Giles Waterfield, *Collection for a King: Old Master Paintings from the Dulwich Picture Gallery*; Giles Waterfield, *Soane and After: The Architecture of Dulwich Picture*

Gallery, Dulwich Picture Gallery, London, 1987; Giles Waterfield (ed.), *Palaces of Art: Art Galleries in Britain 1790–1990*, National Gallery of Art Washington/Los Angeles County Museum of Art, 1985, Dulwich Picture Gallery, London, 1991; Francesco Nevola, *Soane's Favourite Subject: The Story of Dulwich Picture Gallery*, Dulwich Picture Gallery, London, 2000.

26 G.-Tilman Mellinghof, op. cit., offers a good review of contemporary developments in the design of picture galleries and their relationship to Soane's design at Dulwich.

27 Again G-Tilman Mellinghof, op. cit., is a good source, citing, among others, William Hazlitt, who considered the pictures to have been better displayed at Desenfans's house. Artificial lighting was not introduced into the gallery until 1977 and is now in almost permanent use. On a visit on an overcast afternoon early in 2004, the author was able to experience the building in almost its original state, as a result of a power failure. The pictures were gently, but clearly lit.

28 Robert Venturi explicitly adopted and adapted the Dulwich cross-section in his design for the Sainsbury Wing at the National Gallery in London, completed in 1991. See Dean Hawkes, 'The Sainsbury Wing, National Gallery, London', in *The Environmental Tradition*, E & FN Spon, London, 1996.

29 Details of these events are given in Francesco Nevola, op. cit.

30 As before, Todd Willmert's researches are the authoritative source, op. cit.

31 This is suggested by Giles Waterfield in Margaret Richardson and MaryAnn Stevens (eds), *John Soane, Architect: Master of Space and Light*, London Royal Academy of Arts/Yale University Press, New Haven, CT/London, 1999.

32 Todd Willmert, op. cit.

33 Nigel Craddock, op. cit.

34 See *Wimpole Hall*, The National Trust, 1979.

35 Nigel Craddock, op. cit., suggests that the gasolier over the Great Staircase probably dates from 1840, three years after Soane's death. The author recalls seeing the remains of a small 'gas house' in the grounds, to the east of the house, in the mid-1970s, shortly after the house was bequeathed to the National Trust. This apparently produced combustible carbide gas that was piped to the house.

36 Helen Dorey, 'Sir John Soane's acquisition of the Sarcophagus of Seti I', in *The Georgian Group Journal*, 1991, cited in Nigel Craddock, op. cit.

37 Ibid.

38 Sigfried Giedion in *Space, Time and Architecture: The growth of a New Tradition*, Harvard University Press, Cambridge MA/Oxford University Press, Oxford, 1st edn, 1941, 4th, enlarged edition, 1963, was one of the first to represent Labrouste as a proto-modernist. A similar view was expressed by Henry-Russell Hitchcock in *Architecture: Nineteenth and Twentieth Centuries*, Penguin Books, Harmondsworth, 1958, 3rd edn, 1969. It is Labrouste's 'typological rigour with tectonic

invention and symbolisation' that Kenneth Frampton commends in *Studies in Tectonic Culture*.

39 Kenneth Frampton, op. cit.

40 Neil Levine's essay, 'The Book and the Building: Hugo's Theory of Architecture and Labrouste's Bibliothèque Ste-Geneviève', in Robin Middleton (ed.), *The Beaux-Arts, and Nineteenth-Century French Architecture*, Thames and Hudson, London, 1982, is a key source of information and interpretation of the building.

41 David Van Zanten, *Designing Paris: The Architecture of Duban, Labrouste, Duc, and Vaudoyer*, MIT Press, Cambridge, MA, 1987.

42 Neil Levine, op. cit.

43 Ibid.

44 David Van Zanten, op. cit., provides a detailed description and analysis of the Salle.

45 E. Bailly, *Notice sur M. Henri Labrouste*, Paris, 1976, cited in David Van Zanten, op. cit.

46 Van Zanten, op. cit.

47 Sigfried Giedion, op. cit.

48 In his Introduction to *The Beaux-Arts and Nineteenth Century French Architecture*, op. cit., Robin Middleton wrote that, 'with the publication, in 1977, of *The Architecture of the Ecole des Beaux Arts*, edited by Arthur Drexler … the sheer silliness of Giedion's account was laid bare'.

49 Charles Rennie Mackintosh, 'Seemliness', in Pamela Robertson (ed.), *Charles Rennie Mackintosh: The Architectural Papers*, White Cockade Publishing, Wendlebury, in association with the Hunterian Museum,

Glasgow, 1990. It is suggested that the lecture might have been given to the Northern Art Workers' Guild in Manchester in January 1902.

50 For recent interpretations of Mackintosh's work see, Timothy Neat, *Part Seen, Part Imagined: Meaning and Symbolism in the Work of Charles Rennie Mackintosh and Margaret Macdonald*, Canongate Press, Edinburgh, 1994, and Anna-Maija Ylimaula, *Origins of Style: Phenomenological Approach to the Essence of Style in the Architecture of Antoni Gaudí, C. R. Mackintosh and Otto Wagner*, Acta Universitatis Ouluensis, University of Oulu, 1992.

51 The standard works on Mackintosh's life and work are Thomas Howarth, *Charles Rennie Mackintosh and the Modern Movement*, 1st edn 1952, 2nd edn 1977, Routledge & Kegan Paul, London, and Robert Macleod, *Charles Rennie Mackintosh*, Country life, London, 1968. Howarth casts Mackintosh in the Pevsnerian paradigm as a 'Pioneer of Modern Design'. Macleod, on the other hand, explores Mackintosh's relationship with the social and cultural situation in *fin-de-siècle* Glasgow. A useful outline of Mackintosh's principal projects is given by Jackie Cooper (ed.), *Mackintosh Architecture: The Complete Buildings and Selected Projects*, Academy Editions, London, 1978. Important sources in connection with the Glasgow School of Art are *Charles Rennie Mackintosh and Glasgow School of Art*, Glasgow School of Art, 1st edn 1961, 2nd edn 1979. This has an essay by Douglas Percy Bliss and contains important photographs of

the building taken about 1909 by Bedford Lemere & Company. James Macaulay, *Glasgow School of Art: Charles Rennie Mackintosh*, Architecture in Detail, Phaidon, London, 1993 is a first-rate modern source.

52 Charles Rennie Mackintosh, untitled paper on architecture, *c.* 1892, in Pamela Robertson, op. cit.

53 Reyner Banham, op. cit. William Key was a Glasgow engineer whose Plenum system of warm air heating and ventilation was widely used in late nineteenth century buildings in Britain.

54 Rayner Banham, op. cit., is again an invaluable source for the early history of air-conditioning. The term was first used by Stuart W. Cramer in lectures and patent documents as early as 1904/1906, but Banham identifies Willis Havilland Carrier as the 'father of his art'. He proposes the Milam Building in San Antonio, Texas (1927) as the first fully air-conditioned office building.

Part II

The Twentieth-
Century
Environment

Themes and variations

Essay 2
Le Corbusier and Mies van der Rohe
Continuity and invention

> Every country builds its houses in response to its climate.
> At this moment of general diffusion, of international scientific techniques, I propose: only one house for all countries, the house of *exact breathing*.
>
> The Russian house, the Parisian, at Suez or in Buenos Aires, the luxury liner crossing the Equator will be hermetically sealed. In winter it is warm inside, in summer cool, which means that at all times there is *clean air* inside at *exactly* 18°.
>
> The house is sealed fast! No dust can enter it. Neither flies nor mosquitos. No noise![1]

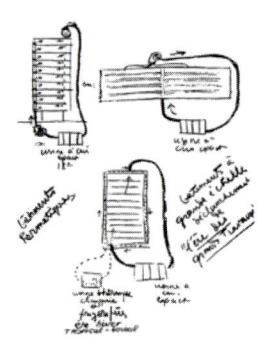

In these statements, made in 1929 during one of his Buenos Aires lectures, Le Corbusier aligns himself unambiguously with the internationalist vision of the future of architecture. The existence of 'international scientific techniques', by which we should assume the apparatus of mechanical environmental control – central heating, mechanical ventilation, air-conditioning, electric light – offers the prospect of releasing architecture from its historical relationship with the specific, geographical conditions of climate. This is an environmental counterpart to the structural, constructional and spatial propositions represented by the *Cinq points d'une architecture nouvelle*.[2] As such, it portends a revolution in way in which architecture fulfils one of its deepest functions.

2.1
Usine à air exact, from
Le Corbusier, *Précisions*, 1930

2.2
Mies van der Rohe,
Friedrichstrasse Glass
Skyscraper Project, Berlin, 1922

The lecture was illustrated by diagrams that indicate the relationship of plant to building envelope. These show rectilinear forms – 'bâtiments hermétiques' (airtight buildings) – that are umbilically connected to the 'usine à air exact' (air conditioning plant) (Figure 2.1).

In 1921, eight years before Le Corbusier gave this lecture, Mies van der Rohe submitted a design in a competition for a glass skyscraper on a site in Berlin's Friedrichstrasse. The perspective drawing, viewed from the north, of this became one of the most potent images of the early modern age (Figure 2.2).

Writing of this project, Mies declared:

> Skyscrapers reveal their bold structural pattern during construction. Only then does the gigantic steel web seem impressive. When the outer walls are put in place, the structural system which is the basis of all artistic design, is hidden in a chaos of meaningless and trivial forms ... Instead of trying to solve new problems with old forms, we should develop the new forms from the very nature of the new problems.
>
> We can see the new structural principles most clearly when we use glass in place of the outer walls, which is feasible today since in a skeleton building these outer walls do not actually carry weight. The use of glass imposes new solutions ...
>
> I discovered by working with actual glass models that the important thing is the play of reflections, and not the effect of light and shadow as in ordinary buildings.[3]

It is, perhaps, significant that Mies' discussion of the design was in terms of structure and its expression, of 'new forms' developing from 'new problems', rather than from any argument for the environmental benefits that might be bestowed by the glass envelope. He was interested in the reflection of light off the envelope, not its passage into the interior of the building as an environmental service. Unlike Le Corbusier's practical proposals concerning the mechanisms of environmental management, Mies offered the poetic paradox of the glass box that is not about the transmission of light. It is almost certain that this building, if built, would have been uninhabitable, given the then state of development of mechanical environmental systems.

In spite of their differences, these pronouncements, nonetheless, confirm the status of Le Corbusier and Mies van der Rohe as innovators, as promoters of a radically new vision of architecture. There is a huge body of evidence to support this reading of their work, but there is much also to suggest that the picture is more complex, and an important element of this concerns their positions in the field of the architectural environment. The aim of this essay is to explore this evidence.

Le Corbusier's Villa Savoye at Poissy was designed and built in 1929–1931. Mies van der Rohe's Tugendhat House near Brno is dated 1928–1930 (Figures 2.3 and 2.4). Each building marks an important point in the work of its architect at which the ideas and explorations of earlier projects reach a refined synthesis. William Curtis[4] has shown how the Villa Savoye was the fullest and most expressive presentation of the *Cinq points*, with *Les pilotis, Les toits-jardins, Le plan libre, La fenêtre en longueur* and *La façade libre* fully displayed. At the Tugendhat House, Mies translated the abstract perfection of his design for the contemporary Barcelona Pavilion, 1929, into one of the most eloquent statements of the potential of new materials and techniques to redefine and transform the nature of the house. In many respects, these houses can be shown to share much common ground. This is particularly the case when we examine their environmental credentials, but this analysis also reveals quite crucial differences that, it will be argued, assume significance in the later works of their architects.

If we begin by examining the common ground shared by the two houses, we can note that they both pay careful attention to the question of orientation. The Tugendhat House, on its south-facing slope, exhibits most of the planning and environmental features of an Arts and Crafts house, entered from the north with all of the principal rooms to the south (Figure 2.5). The inversion of the conventional cross-section, with the main entrance at the upper level, allows the living room to enjoy an easy connection to the open space of the garden.

In the fifth of his Buenos Aires lectures Le Corbusier went to some lengths to explain the orientation of the Villa Savoye, then under construction, in relation both to the sun and the view (Figure 2.6):

> The site: a big lawn, slightly convex. The main view is to the north, therefore opposite to the sun; the front of the house would usually be inverted … Receiving views and light from around the periphery of the box, the different rooms center on a hanging garden that is there like a distributor of adequate light and sunshine. It is on the hanging garden that the sliding plate glass walls of the salon and other rooms of the house open freely: thus the sun is everywhere, in the very heart of the house.[5]

2.3
Le Corbusier, Villa Savoye, Poissy, 1929–1931

2.4
Mies van der Rohe, Tugendhat House, Brno, 1928–1930

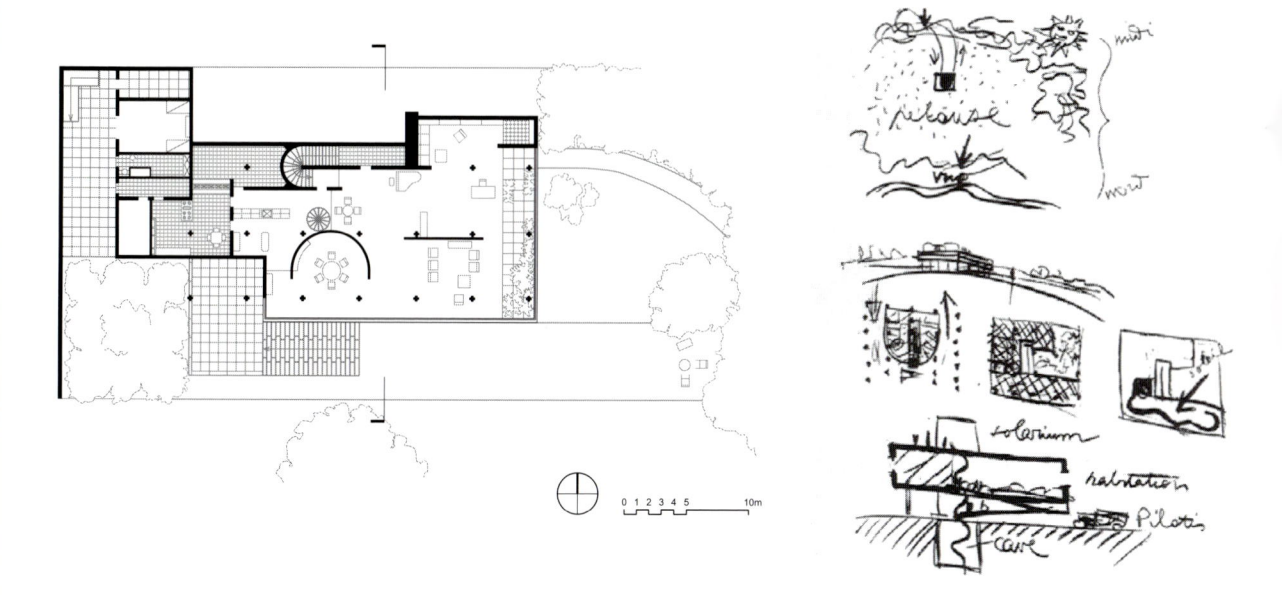

In most publications, from Volume 2 of the *Œuvre complète* onwards, the plan is presented without a north point, but with south to the top. The most reproduced exterior image is almost certainly that from the north, where the piloti are most clearly visible in front of the curved glass screen of the ground floor, and the free forms of the solarium dramatise the silhouette. As soon as the plan is oriented conventionally the environmental logic becomes clear (Figure 2.7). The salon slides out to face south over the open terrace and also enjoys evening sunlight, the principal bedroom, boudoir and covered terrace look south. The kitchen is at the cool northeast corner. The solarium, as it should be, is sheltered from the wind, private and sun-filled.

Curtis has noted that 'The building has continued to occupy the imagination as the image *par excellence* of the "machine à habiter".'[6] The familiar images sustain that judgement. The view of the salon from the *Œuvre complète*, Volume 2, shows the connection with the terrace and, of its environmental systems, the large radiator beneath the west-facing window and the continuous electric light fitting. Whether by accident or design, and one suspects that nothing was accidental in these images, the fireplace, that is such a crucial element in the spatial organisation and iconography of the room, is omitted. The house would be adequately heated by the central heating system and this would allow a kind of 'free' occupation of space, without the constraints that follow from traditional localised heat sources. One can imagine a thermal comparison of these alternative means of heating alongside the relation of *fenêtre en longueur* and traditional windows in the *Cinq points*. But the fact of the fireplace fundamentally transforms the interpretation and mode of occupation

2.5
Tugendhat House, principal floor plan

2.6
Le Corbusier, sketch from lecture 5, Buenos Aires, 1929

of the salon (Figure 2.8). Even if the fireplace had only a marginal function as a heat source, it would establish a particular territory, a focus, within the free, relatively undifferentiated space. Its physical integration in the overall composition of the building and in the arrangement of the room is precisely considered in every respect. In plan, it is precisely in line with the paving grid of the terrace and with the jamb of the boudoir window seen across the terrace. In the vertical plane the mantelpiece lines through with and is a continuation of the sill of the north-facing window and the square flue is aligned with the load-bearing columns. The sides of the fireplace and the firebox itself are of brick – the only occurrence of this traditional material in the house. All of this implies that, consciously or otherwise, the force of tradition survives alongside the argument for innovation in this seminal work of the Modern Movement.

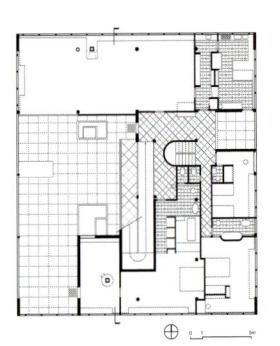

2.7
Villa Savoye, principal floor plan

2.8
Villa Savoye, salon showing fireplace and flue

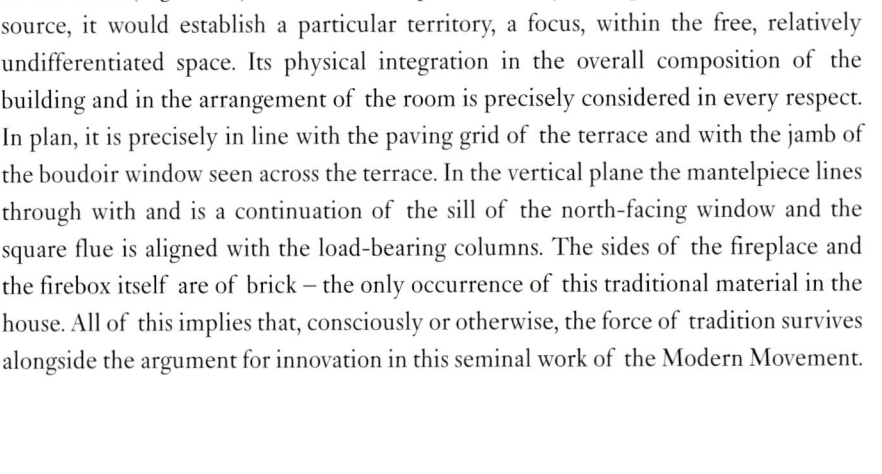

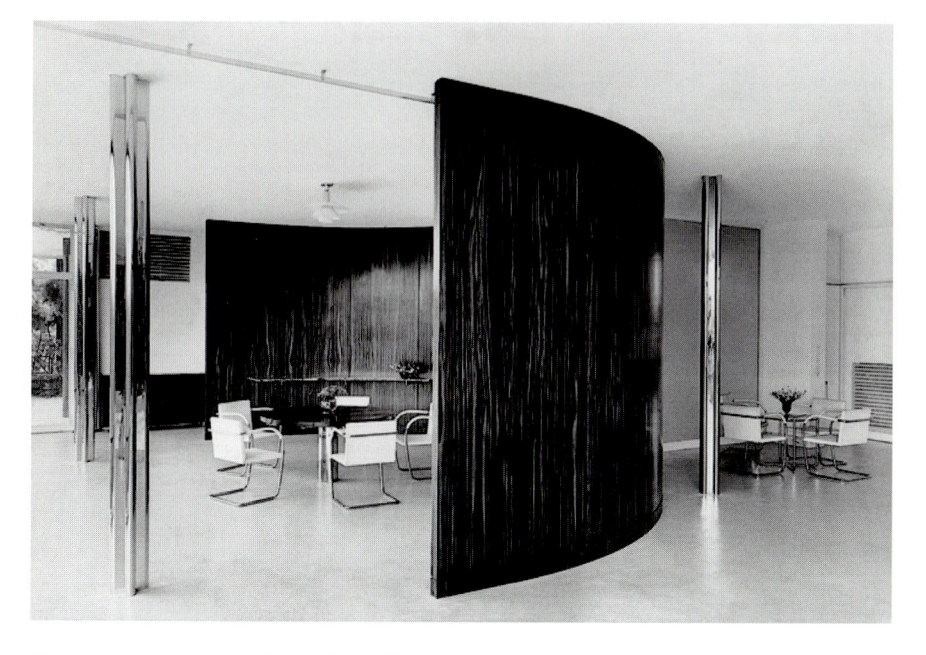

Turning now to the Tugendhat House, we can begin a comparison between Le Corbusier's and Mies van der Rohe's approaches to the environment of the Modern Movement. A striking difference between Savoye and Tugendhat lies in the nature and expression of their respective heating systems. In contrast to the strong presence of the cast-iron radiators and the fireplace at Savoye, Mies sought to suppress the visible evidence of the complex installation at Tugendhat, that has been said to be, 'absolutely state of the art and surpassed in many respects even today's standards'[7] (Figures 2.9 and 2.10). This installation is described in the following terms by Tegethoff:

> Whilst most of the rooms were outfitted with radiators or heat flues, the large living area had an additional warm air heating system that could also be used for cooling on warm summer days. The intake shaft is found below the front court, where to the east the surface is sunk about an additional one and a half meters. A complicated filtering system cleaned and humidified the air before it was forwarded to the two vents in the living area.[8]

In addition to these mechanical installations, the south-facing wall of the living space is a sophisticated mechanism of environmental control. Two entire sections of the glazing can be mechanically lowered below the sill line to open the entire space to the elements on summer days. The window head houses retractable roller blinds to shade the glass and interior from unwanted solar heat gains. The whole of the glazed wall could be covered at night by full-height silk curtains.

From statements made by the Tugendhat family, these systems worked perfectly. In response to the question, 'Is the Tugendhat House habitable?' Fritz Tugendhat replied:

> After almost a year of living in the house I can assure you without hesitation that technically it possess everything a modern person might wish for. In winter it is easier to heat than a house with thick walls and small double windows. Because of the floor-to-ceiling glass wall and the elevated site of the house the sunlight reaches deep into the interior. On clear and frosty days one can lower its windows, sit in the sun and enjoy the view of a snow-covered landscape, like in Davos. In summer, sunscreens and electrical air-conditioning ensure comfortable temperatures … In the evenings the glazed walls are hidden behind silk curtains to avoid reflexions of light.[9]

His daughter, Daniela Hammer-Tugendhat has written:

> The basement contained a sophisticated air conditioning system next to the laundry and the darkroom, a combination of heating system, ventilator, and humidifier. Despite the fact that such systems had only rarely been used in private houses, it worked perfectly … Not only was Mies an aesthete, he also was a good engineer, who paid much attention to the technical installations of the house.[10]

2.10
Tugendhat House, cross-section showing heating vent connection between basement and living room and machine room beneath the retractable south-facing windows

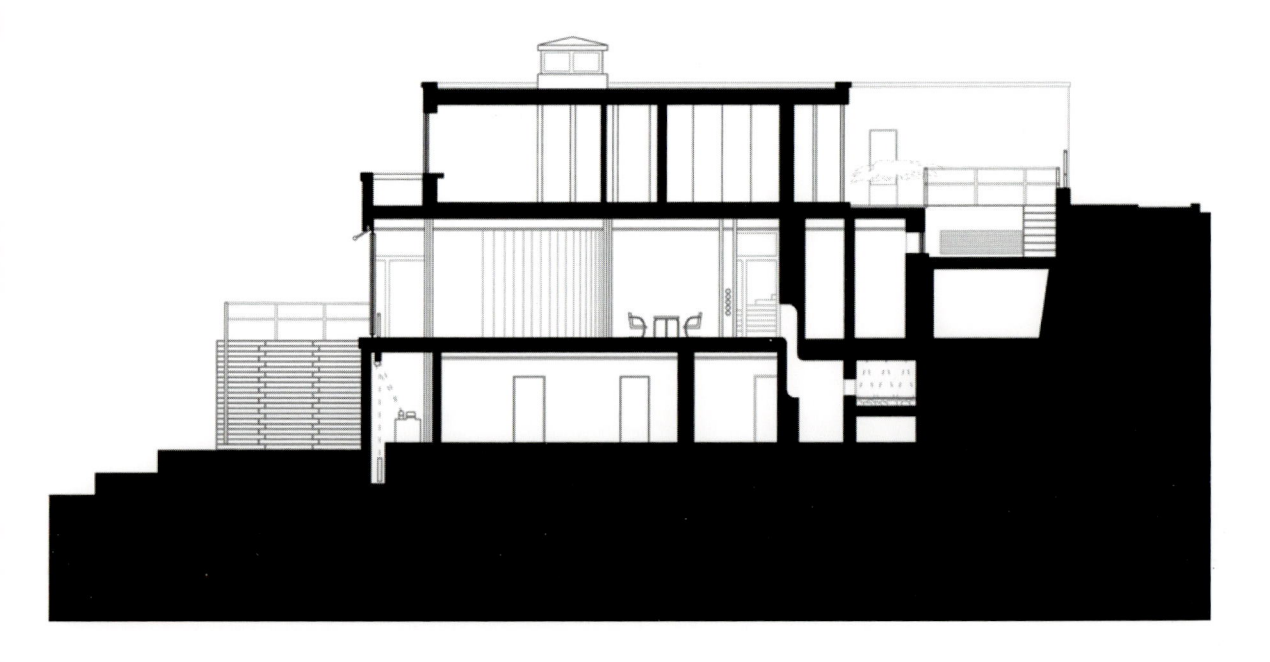

The relationship between the Barcelona Pavilion and the Tugendhat House has often been noted. Among others, Curtis has commented:

> the luxury of the Barcelona Pavilion was reproduced in a domestic setting, with clear, semi-reflective or tinted planes of glass, chrome-faced cruciform columns, white and gold polished onyx planes, and a curved ebony partition defining the dining alcove.[11]

An exhibition pavilion is relieved of many of the apparent necessities of a dwelling. The Barcelona Exposition was open from May 1929 to January 1930. The pavilion would thus endure the climates of summer and winter, but it had no heating system.[12] Environmentally it was purely a roof canopy and a glazed enclosure. The building had an extremely original, if technically inadequate lighting system, in which an etched glass, roof-lit box brought diffuse daylight into the heart of the plan, at night, electric light bulbs aimed to reproduce the effect of daylight (Figure 2.11).[13] This idea was repeated at the Tugendhat House in the back-illuminated, etched glass screen that stands behind the curved Macassar ebony screen of the dining space.

Nonetheless, the pavilion can be interpreted as a statement on the nature of the ideal dwelling and, specifically in the present discussion, as an image of the ideal

2.11
Barcelona Pavilion, interior showing the etched glass light box

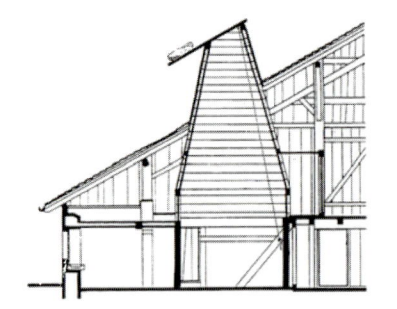

2.12
Jura farmhouse, Mont Cornu,
cross-section showing fireplace
and chimney

2.13
Le Corbusier, *La Cheminée*, 1918

environment. The essence of this lies in the absence of traditional elements of the domestic interior. In place of the specific conditions of hearth, the separation of functions of sitting from dining, even of winter from summer spaces, we find at the Barcelona Pavilion and at its adaptation in the living room of the Tugendhat House an environment for all seasons. The fabric and envelope of the dwelling are brought into a new relationship with mechanical plant that enables the limits of diurnal and seasonal climate to be transcended. This is a far cry from the Villa Savoye where, in spite of its status as the ultimate icon of Corbusian modernity, the power and significance of domestic tradition live on.

H. Allen Brooks has written at length about the 'Swiss interlude' in 1910, when the young Jeanneret lived in a Jura farmhouse on the slopes of Mont Cornu.[14] The most prominent feature of this house type is its aedicular fireplace and chimney that occupies the heart of the plan and plays a vital role in its environmental function (Figure 2.12). Brooks sees this tapering flue as a formal antecedent of the great shaft of the parliament chamber in the Assembly Building at Chandigarh, but there is much evidence that the fireplace as such occupied a deeper and more symbolic place in Le Corbusier's thinking throughout his life's work. In a wide-ranging study, Todd Willmert[15] has explored the occurrences, and occasional absences, of fireplaces in buildings ranging in time from the La Chaux-de-Fonds days through to the late works. This establishes grounds for a re-reading of the nature of Le Corbusier's modernism and places it in a new relationship to Mies' contemporary work.

Willmert points out that the early designs for houses in La Chaux-de-Fonds, Villas Fallet (1905), Jaquemet (1908) and Stotzer (1908), and the later Villa Favre-Jacot (1912), did not have fireplaces, but they did appear in the house Le Corbusier designed for his parents, Villa Jeanneret-Perret (1912), and the Villa Schwob (1916). The last of these houses had an extensive and unusual central heating system in which heating pipes were integrated into the masonry of the walls, which rendered the fireplaces of little value in supplying heat to the spaces. On the other hand, the specific location of the stack of three fireplaces, in relation to the south-facing glazing of the double height living room, hints at the establishment of particular zones of comfort within the otherwise generalised environment of the house.

2.14
Le Corbusier, Ozenfant Studio,
Paris, 1922, image from *Œuvre
Complète*, vol. 1

2.15
Maison La Roche, studio fireplace

In 1918, Le Corbusier joined with Amédée Ozenfant in exhibiting paintings at the Galerie Thomas. One of the two works shown by Le Corbusier was *La Cheminée* (Figure 2.13). He later claimed this to be his first oil painting, ignoring his earlier works executed in La Chaux-de-Fonds. The piece is usually discussed dismissively in relation to Ozenfant's work at that time and Le Corbusier's own strikingly more sophisticated, genuinely Purist paintings of 1920 onwards.[16] But Willmert suggests that the subject matter might have a close relationship to the recurring image of the briar pipe, from its appearance in the Conclusion of *Vers une Architecture* into numerous paintings, and hence connect with the significance of the fireplace in Le Corbusier's architecture. Whether such an explicit connection can be proved or not, when we come to the architectural explorations of the Purist period in the 1920s, the fireplace is found to be almost always present, most significantly in the Ozenfant Studio house (1922).

The familiar image of Ozenfant's painting studio, from Volume 1 of the *Œuvre complète* (Figure 2.14), looking towards the great steel-framed windows, with the gridded lay light hovering above and the curved enclosure of the library accessed by its steep ladder, is usually interpreted as probably the first built essay in architectural Purism:

> The Ozenfant Studio was a small fragment of Le Corbusier's machine-age dream: a limpid shrine dedicated to L'Esprit Nouveau. The glazing had to be made specially by hand to look mass-produced; tubular railings and metal companion ladders evoked the era of steam power. Thonet chairs, guitars, a Purist still life stated the morality of sober 'objets-types'. Through an intense abstraction, naked industrial facts were transformed into icons of a new way of life. The studio was evidence that Le Corbusier was at last able to translate his vision of a new architecture into a haunting and tangible reality.[17]

In these commentaries attention is never drawn to the presence of the fireplace located, almost in Arts and Crafts manner, in the 'nook' beneath the overhanging library. The prominent finned tube radiators, located beneath the windows, and the ducts that run up the internal wall, venting the lower floors, are absolutely consistent with the modernist reading, but the fireplace, with its projecting mantlepiece, almost exactly like that depicted in La Cheminée, proposes a more ambiguous circumstance.

Willmert has detected a further environmental curiosity of this space. This concerns the artificial lighting. The 'approved' image shows no light sources, save the four electric light bulbs on the sill of the north window. Other images, however, show that lamps were located at the edge of the lay light, but had been masked out of the *Œuvre complète* image.

A brief survey can illustrate the presence, and hence, significance of fireplaces in other buildings by Le Corbusier in the period between the Ozenfant Studio and Villa Savoye. In the sequence in which they appear in the *Œuvre complète*, we find them beneath the balcony in the gallery of the Maison La Roche (Figure 2.15) and in the living room of the Jeanneret house next door (1923).

Fireplaces are also found in the houses at Pessac (1925), but there was none in either the unbuilt Villa Meyer or the Pavillon l'Esprit Nouveau of the same year. The Maison 'Minimum' was also without an open hearth, probably a necessity in such a small building. But, in 1926, the almost free-standing fireplace occupies a crucial position at the junction of the *Salle* and the *Salle à manger* of the Maison Cook (Figure 2.16). The Villa Stein-de-Monzie at Garches was built without a fireplace, although it had its full complement of strongly displayed cast-iron radiators, and the heating plant was awarded an almost sculptural significance in an image of the garage. Later, however, when the house changed hands in 1935, designs were made for a fireplace to be placed on the wall between the salon and the terrace.

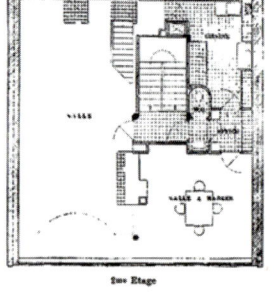

2.16
Maison Cook, first floor plan

2.17
Villa Church, library

Le Corbusier's work at the Villa Church at Ville d'Avray (1928–1929) was an addition of a music room, salon and guest wing to an existing building. Within the restoration of the existing pavilion, the free-standing fireplace of the *bibliothèque*, is seen, in juxtaposition with furniture by Le Corbusier and Charlotte Perriand, and a hovering circular rooflight, to constitute one of the most complete representations of the conjunction of modernity and tradition in a domestic interior (Figure 2.17). The relationship of the curved back surface of the fireplace and the cast-iron radiator incorporated into the balustrade of the stairwell is particularly telling.

Much attention has been paid to the Bestegui Apartment on its rooftop high above the Champs Elysées in Paris (1929–1930). It is here that the fireplace achieves its least functional and most symbolic manifestation in the whole of Le Corbusier's *œuvre*. Tim Benton has described this as, 'one of the most exotic and puzzling of Le Corbusier's works'[18] and Curtis as 'the last luxurious gasp of the Purist style'.[19] The image of the Rococo fireplace of the outdoor room of the highest of a series of roof terraces, with the Arc de Triomphe composed as the mantlepiece clock, moves here across the boundary of practical iconography into the realm of the Surreal. But it is still, perhaps, revealing of the architect's continuing fascination with the essence of the dwelling (Figure 2.18).

In the 1930s Le Corbusier's work took a new direction. Curtis has described this period as a turn to 'Regionalism and Reassessment',[20] in which a sequence of projects, particularly for houses, made use of traditional materials, stone and timber, in some instances in load-bearing structures and, of particular relevance in the present discussion, of specific response to climate.

The second volume of the *Œuvre complète* opens with the full presentation of the Villa Savoye that had appeared in Volume 1 as a work in progress. The next 'residential' project is the installation at the Salon d'Automne, 1929, in which the full range of furniture designed in collaboration with Charlotte Perriand was displayed in a setting that was truly a *machine à habiter*, but over the page we find the project of 1930 for the Errazuris House in Chile.

2.18
Bestegui Apartment, roof terrace

2.19
Antonin Raymond, Summer House, Asama Mountain, Japan, 1933, from Raymond McGrath, *Twentieth Century Houses*, 1935

In its forms and materiality this image is an almost shocking departure from the Purism of the Villa Savoye. But Le Corbusier was at pains to insist that this was consistent with his principles:

> La rusticité des matériaux n'est aucunement une entrave à la manifestation d'une plan clair et d'une esthétique moderne.[21]
> (The rusticity of the materials is in no way a hindrance to the expression of a clear plan and a modern aesthetic.)

The plan of the house is perfectly clear with the single, double-height living room differentiated from the compact two-storey sleeping and service zone. It also observes good principles of orientation with, in the southern hemisphere, the tall north-facing window admitting copious warming sunlight to the space and smaller west-facing openings bringing in the evening sun and views out of the Pacific Ocean.

The drawing of 'La grande salle et la Cheminée' is vitally important in the account of the significance of the fireplace in Le Corbusier's domestic architecture. It shows a very precise relationship between the natural warmth of the sunlight flowing through the tall window to the right-hand – north – end of the room and the almost primitive environment of the sunken cavern, beneath the ramp, containing the hearth. The relationship of the hearth and the ramp is explicitly represented in a drawing in the *Œuvre complète*. Although the house was not built, the *Œuvre complète* contains photographic images (Figure 2.19). These are of a house of almost identical form built in Japan by Antonin Raymond in 1933.[22] Le Corbusier commented that:

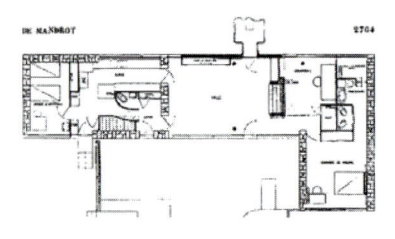

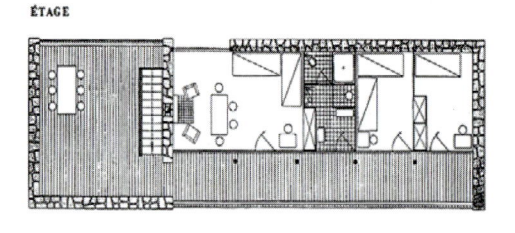

2.20
Villa Mandrot, plan of main house

2.21
Villa at Mathes

The reader ought not to be deceived, it was not photographs of our house but rather a creation by Mr. Raymond! The least one can say is that great minds think alike! Be that as it may, we have had a true satisfaction in seeing ideas that are dear to us realized with such taste.[23]

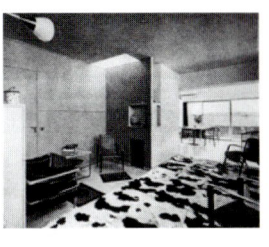

Raymond's house is much larger, with greatly extended quarters, including rooms based on tatami mat configurations. The orientation is rotated so that the long axis of the main room is east–west not north–south. The other major departure is that it is a timber-framed structure, not the masonry of Le Corbusier's design.

Fireplaces are also found in two of the other 'Regionalist' houses of the 1930s, the Villa Mandrot in Le Pradet in the south of France (1930–1931) and the house at Mathes on the Atlantic coast north of Bordeaux (1935) (Figures 2.20 and 2.21). At Mandrot, the fireplace, identified in plan by its brick hearth, divides the living room from the library in the central part of the composition where three structural columns take over from the load-bearing masonry of the wings. In the holiday house at Mathes, the fireplace is accommodated in the thickness of the stone cross wall at the first floor. In each case, this is appropriate and well judged in the wider context of the design, but two other projects of this period are of even greater significance in the account of the fireplace in Le Corbusier's work.

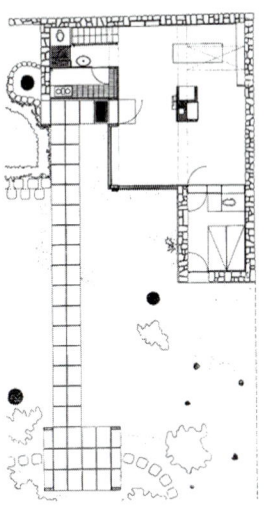

The apartment building at rue Nungesser et Coli in Paris (1933) is of particular importance because this is where Le Corbusier made his own home and studio on the top floor. The plan disposes the dwelling and the studio on either side of the internal light wells that rise through the building. Above this, is the *toit-jardin* and guest room. At the heart of the principal floor, a top-lit recess opens from the living room and there we find a fireplace (Figure 2.22).

The contrast between the brick and stone rubble party walls of the Le Corbusier penthouse and the precise, machine-made steel, glass and glass-block construction of the lower floors and façades of the building has been taken to suggest the special significance of the apartment.[24] This supposition is reinforced by the presence and nature of the fireplace. Its simple opening in the plastered wall, with no attempt at defining a proper hearth, suggests that it was not intended to make a practical contribution to heating the apartment, but its presence in so many of the published images denotes its significance as a symbol of domestic life in this most personal and intimate location in Le Corbusier's life.

A final example in this sequence of projects is the Petite Maison de Weekend at Celle-St-Cloud in the suburbs of Paris. Kenneth Frampton has referred to Le Corbusier's 'growing ambivalence towards the machine age' in the early years of the 1930s.[25] The Errazuris House, Villa Mandrot and the house at Mathes all support this argument and the Petite Maison de Weekend is, in many respects, a summation of this tendency.

2.22
Apartment at rue Nungesser et Coli, Paris, living room with roof-lit fireplace

2.23
Petite Maison de Weekend, plan

The plan of the Weekend house consists of a simple, south-facing volume wrapped to the north and east by a stone wall (Figure 2.23). Small cells open from the main space containing the bedroom and the kitchen and bathroom. The centre of the plan is occupied by a brick and concrete fireplace that is the only source of heat in the building.

In a telling statement in Volume 3 of the *Œuvre complète*, Le Corbusier wrote:

L'architecture domestique grâce à l'emploi d'éléments standards (voir aussi, ci-devant, la maison de week-end) peut retrouver le chemin des attitudes essentielles qui ont toujours existé dans les époques d'équilibre.[26]
(Domestic architecture favours the use of standard elements (as illustrated in the Maison de Week-end) to discover the path to essential attitudes that always exist in times of stability.)

From this analysis of his work, over almost two decades, we can identify the importance of the fireplace in Le Corbusier's attitude to the domestic environment. Even at the height of his Purist period, when his priority was to apply and demonstrate the principles of the *Cinq points*, fireplaces were present in almost all of his designs, symbolising the essence of domesticity and playing a crucial role in the organisation and inhabitation of space. It would seem that, in spite of his declaration of 'one house for all countries', in his Buenos Aires lecture of 1929, Le Corbusier retained a deep sense of the continuity of tradition alongside of his commitment to *une architecture nouvelle*. In this light, the so-called 'regionalist' projects of the 1930s appear less radical than is sometimes suggested.

Returning to Mies van der Rohe, a review of a series of his house designs in the same period indicates a very different view of the modernist environment. The

2.24
Brick House project, drawing by Werner Blaser

2.25
Wolf House, Gubin, view from east

2.26
Lange and Esters houses, Krefeld, 1927–1930, ground floor plan, drawing in Riley and Bergdoll, 'Mies in Berlin'

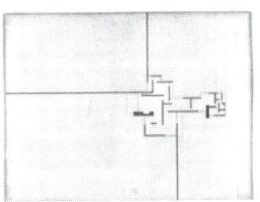

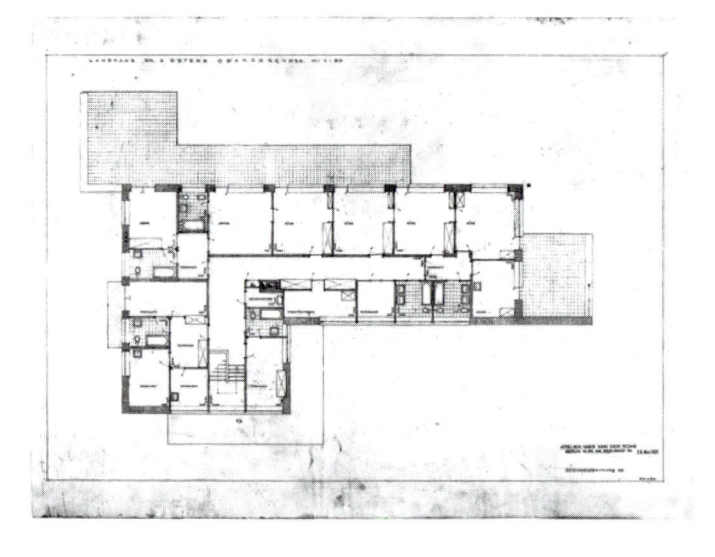

Brick House project (1923) was where he first established the strategy for composition in plan based on free-standing wall planes that extend out beyond the building's enclosure.[27] While there is no specific indication in the original drawing, the solid mass of masonry to the left of centre of the plan is usually taken to be a fireplace and flue and is shown as such in the computer drawing published by Blaser in 1986 (Figure 2.24).[28]

In the Wolf House at Gubin (1925–1927) the fireplace is strongly present in both plan and in silhouette, acting as a pivot in the composition (Figure 2.25). The Lange and Esters houses, built on adjacent sites in Krefeld (1927–1930), take the language of the brick house a further stage in its development, and here fireplaces disappear as Mies makes a move towards an alternative view of the architectural environment (Figure 2.26).

The significance of the Barcelona Pavilion in relation to the Tugendhat House has been discussed above, but its development made another important contribution to the establishment of Mies' vision of the internal environment of buildings. This was one of the first occasions where Mies used the technique of photomontage perspective to depict an internal space (Figure 2.27).[29] In these representations the building is vestigially shown in the form of slender, ink-drawn structural columns, window mullions and perspectival floor grids in relation to collaged images of real materials, landscapes or art works. A similar image, but here purely in pencil on tracing paper, shows the living room of the Tugendhat House.

In their abstraction, these images allude to the possibility of an environment in which the conventional qualities of light and shade, warmth and chill and the visible presence of the instruments of environmental provision, fireplaces, stoves, lamps are omitted in favour of an idealised, uniform environment sustained by invisible machines. In other words, a notion of environment that has cut all links with tradition, and even with advanced contemporary practice, in pursuit of a truly new vision.

2.27
Barcelona Pavilion, interior perspective, photomontage

2.28
Mies van der Rohe, *Die Wohnung unserer Zeit*, Berlin, 1931

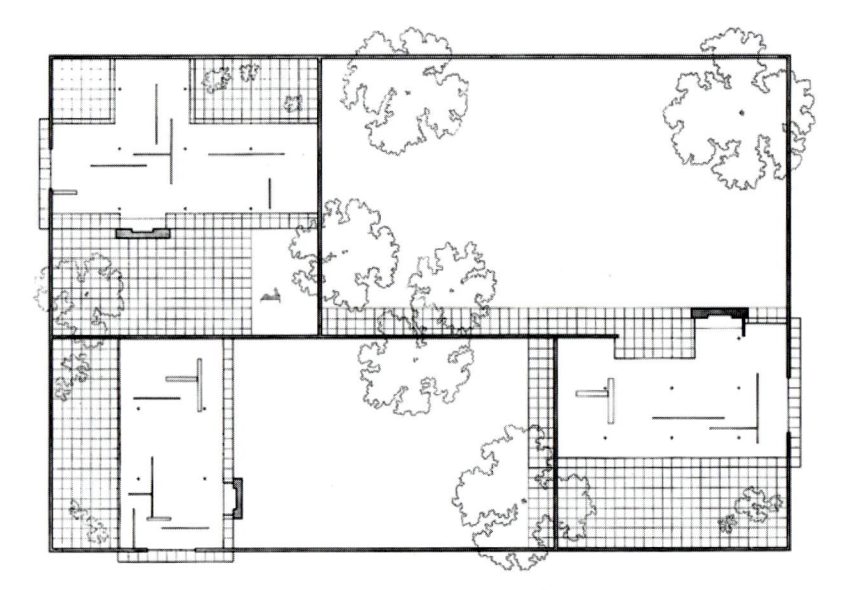

A similarly significant influence on the development of Mies' environmental vision may be found in the Glass Room project that Mies made for the Stuttgart Werkbund Exhibition of 1927. This used a variety of glass types, ranging from clear to opaque, and of varying tones. Under a uniformly illuminated ceiling of white fabric the effect was of shimmering, translucent space.[30]

The Exhibition House constructed at the German Building Exhibition in Berlin in 1931, 'Die Wohnung unserer Zeit', is a particularly effective demonstration of these ideas applied to the design of a full-scale house (Figure 2.28). Within the enclosure of the exhibition hall the project was liberated from all of the conventional demands of environmental shelter, but the beautifully composed image of the living space, without fireplace or light fittings, combines the quality and abstraction of both photomontage and the Glass Room.

In the series of (mainly unbuilt) designs for houses that Mies produced during the 1930s, he consistently applied the principles that he had explored through these earlier projects. The norm was continuous, transparent space, formed and articulated by free-standing screens. The designs for court houses constitute a summation of this process, with their intimate relationships between inside and outside spaces, consistently rendered in montage (Figure 2.29).

In many of these projects fireplaces feature as a point of focus and orientation in the principal living space. The reasons for this are unclear, given their absence in the earlier theoretical projects and, most notably, in the Tugendhat House. The project for the Gericke House, Berlin (1932) one instance where the client's programme explicitly demanded a fireplace, not only in the living room, but also in the principal bedroom, 'for the lady of the house'.[31] In his report describing the design, Mies observes that both fireplaces have been provided and offers a relatively detailed description of the services systems of the house:

The parents' bedroom … provides for a walk-in closet for the husband, a separate dressing room for the wife. The desired fireplace has been accommodated.

The main living room is closed off with large planes of plate glass, some of which can be lowered, some slid to the side and at the outside end of it there is the small winter garden requested.

The fireplace lies at the transition from the main living room to the hall. The desired stove heating is to be combined with the fireplace.

Forced-air heating has been provided for the living area and the main bedroom and can be utilized in summer for ventilation and cooling as well.[32]

2.30
Tugendhat House, the onyx wall as fictive 'hearth'

The pencil perspectives of the house are an interesting departure from the montage images, showing traditional upholstered armchairs by the wide fireplace opening.

In Mies' work, as in that of Le Corbusier, the issue of the architectural environment is a complex affair. It is very clear, from the evidence of the Tugendhat House, and of related projects such as the Glass Room, the Barcelona Pavilion and the Berlin Exhibition design for *Die Wohnung unserer Zeit,* that here were environments that were absolutely dependent on mechanical services, even to the extent that they could be, and were, mechanically cooled in summer, as at Tugendhat, and in the proposals for the Gericke house. But these systems were to provide their services invisibly. In the principal spaces of Mies' buildings we do not find Le Corbusier's almost elaborate display of radiators. Tempered air is supplied from discreet grilles. Sources of artificial lighting are similarly concealed. The smooth soffits of the Barcelona Pavilion and the Glass Room, and the taut fabric velarium of 'Die Wohnung unserer Zeit' would seem to be the objective, rather than the interrupted ceiling of the Tugendhat House.

In the context of this apparently calm, mechanical vision, the status of the fireplace is ambiguous. The conception of these flowing, inter-connected spaces is dependent on central heating. The fireplaces have no practical purpose, but, where they do occur, they inevitably bring a focus to the space by defining the location of the principal seating. But this function is equally well addressed in the Tugendhat House, and even in the non-house of the Barcelona Pavilion, by their respective onyx walls, which assume the status of a fictive 'hearth' (Figure 2.30). The fireplaces, except where they were specifically requested as at the Gericke House, are arguably more significant for their role in the overall composition and massing of the houses than as a component of the environmental strategy. In the Brick House, the tall mass of the fireplace is the fulcrum of the composition.

It can be deduced from these analyses, that both Le Corbusier and Mies van der Rohe regarded the environmental qualities of their buildings to be important in

the development of new architectural language. While they clearly shared much common ground, embracing new technologies and seeking specific ways physically to incorporate and represent these, there are quite significant differences between their environmental thinking that became more apparent in their later works.

2.31
Resor House, living room looking south

If we regard the 1920s as a decade of experiment for each architect, the achievements of, respectively, the Villa Savoye and the Tugendhat House represent points of maturity, of convergence, but also contain the seeds of their subsequent differences.

In the 1930s Le Corbusier, as Curtis argues,[33] moved on to reinterpret the regional and the vernacular in his designs for country houses, Errazuris, Mandrot and Mathes and in the *rus in urbe* proposition of the Petite Maison de Weekend. In all of these, the environmental idea leans heavily on tradition, observing the priorities of good orientation and emphasising the significance of the fireplace as both heat source and symbol. At the same time Mies' designs for houses embraced the theoretical explorations of the sequence of court house projects, in which the idealised environment of the Barcelona Pavilion and the Tugendhat House continued to be demonstrated and the more pragmatic 'real-world' designs, such as the Gericke, Hubbe and Ulrich Lange houses, all unbuilt, in which the ideal was tempered by very explicit references to tradition, most specifically represented by large, in some cases dominant, fireplaces. Mies' first major American design, the Resor House, 1931–1940, in Wyoming, demonstrates this ambiguity in the contrast between two graphic representations, one a pencil-drawn, literal space dominated by a stone fireplace, the other a montage in which a segment of Paul Klee's painting, *Bunte Mahlzeit* (Colourful repast), takes the place of the fireplace (Figure 2.31).

In the post-war years the environmental aspects of the works of Le Corbusier and Mies van der Rohe became markedly distinct. Le Corbusier consolidated his acknowledgement of tradition, of the natural climate as a powerful determinant of the nature and condition of the environment of a building. Mies van der Rohe emphatically embraced the potential of mechanical services, invisibly and silently to provide an 'ideal' and constant environment. The distinction may be characterised as designing, on the one hand, *with* climate and, on the other, *against* climate.[34] Two brief comparative studies now illustrate the end point of this trajectory.

Farnsworth and Jaoul

The Farnsworth House in Illinois (1945–1951) an ideal villa, is a summation of Mies' vision of the essence of the modern house:

> Nature should also have a life of its own. We should avoid disturbing it with the excessive colour of our houses and our interior furnishings. Indeed, we should strive to bring Nature, houses and people together in a higher unity. When one looks at Nature through the glass walls of the Farnsworth House it takes on a deeper significance than when one stands outside. More of nature is thus expressed – it becomes part of a greater whole.[35]

It is curious that Farnsworth proved to be such an environmental failure.[36] As we have seen, the Tugendhat House was judged by its occupants to be an unqualified success and Mies was praised by them as 'not only an aesthete … [but] also … a good engineer'. Unlike the carefully oriented and reportedly well-heated Tugendhat House, the proposition of a completely glazed enclosure is, self-evidently, problematic, compounded by the use of single glazing and an inadequate heating system. The poorly ventilated house also suffered from summertime overheating, receiving insufficient shade from the nearby trees. In addition to the underfloor heating system – perfectly invisible – and a supplementary warm air heater, the house has an open fireplace, located in the central service core (Figure 2.32). There it assumes almost the status of a mechanical service alongside the other systems that are housed there. The artificial lighting is entirely provided by uplighting that reflects off the uninterrupted,

2.32
Farnsworth House, living room with open fireplace in central core

perfect white ceiling, supplemented by free-standing standard lamps. This is reported to work perfectly.

Pushed to such limits, these technical failings inevitably call into question Mies' environmental vision. The fact that they have been redeemed and the house made habitable, by upgrading the heating system installing an air-conditioning plant, demonstrates the technical validity of the idea, but raises many other questions now that environmental consciousness in architecture has taken on other meanings.

By contrast, Le Corbusier's design for the Maisons Jaoul, built in the Paris suburb of Neuilly, 1951–1954, stands as a marked alternative to the modern dwelling. The two houses occupy a restricted site whose long axis is oriented east–west, and share an entrance court close to the centre of the northern boundary: 'The aspect of the sun dominated the lay-out of the plans and sections.'[37]

The simple, rectangular forms of load-bearing masonry and concrete Catalan vaults with grass-covered roofs are punctured by openings containing highly organised elements of glass and timber. These allow the quantity of glass to be calibrated to the dimensions and functions of the rooms. In each house, the living room has a fireplace (Figure 2.33). In house A, this is placed on the gable wall at the point where the double-height volume rises. In house B, where there is no double-height volume, the fireplace occupies the centre of the space. The fireplaces are given absolute priority in the formation and inhabitation of these spaces and are both functional and symbolic.

The Maisons Jaoul clearly refer back to Le Corbusier's youthful experience of the simplicity of vernacular building and this provoked critical response when they were completed. James Stirling wrote of them in 1955:

2.33
Maison Jaoul, fireplace in living room of house B

> If Garches appears urban, sophisticated and essentially in keeping with 'l'esprit parisien', then the Jaoul houses seem primitive in character, recalling the Provençal farmhouse community; they seem out of tune with their Parisian environment … There is no reference to any aspect of the machine at Jaoul either in construction or aesthetic.[38]

But Le Corbusier defended them when he wrote: 'The "meritorious" work is this, that it represents a cogent bringing into focus of elements that constitute an architecture, to wit: the structural system, the choice of materials, the method of ventilation.'[39] These houses are, indeed, a far cry from the pure certainties and universality of Garches and Savoye. They are even further removed from Mies' abstractions and – it must be said – technical failure at Farnsworth. On the other hand, they demonstrate a particular sensitivity to the wider questions of climate response and the realisation of human comfort. Rooms that are sun-filled and well-lit, easy to heat and effectively ventilated could be said to represent the victory of good sense over ideology.

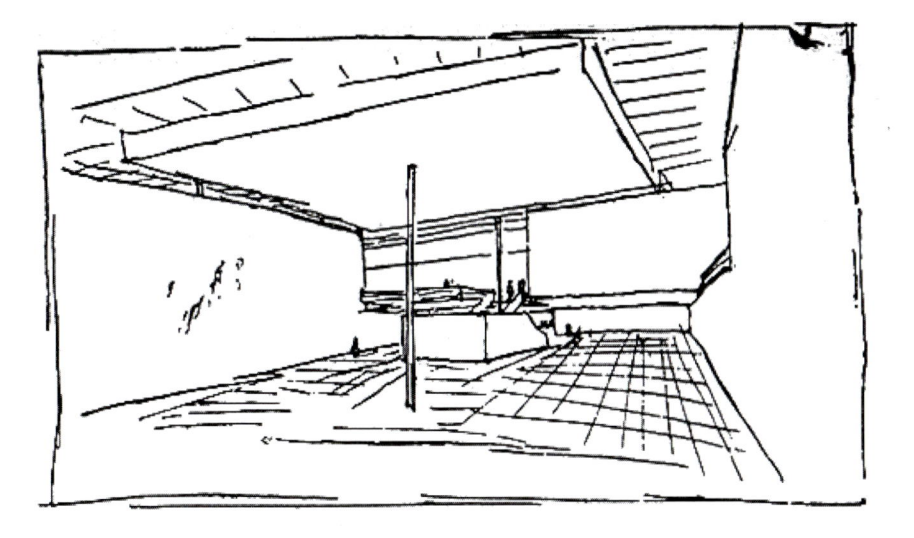

Postscript: two art museums – Berlin and Tokyo

The environmental themes that have been explored through the domestic buildings of
Le Corbusier and Mies van der Rohe are paralleled in their designs for other building
types. This can be illustrated by comparing their approaches to the design of the
art museum. From the outset, these reveal different preoccupations on the question of
the museum environment.

The posthumous, single volume edition of the *Œuvre complète*,[40] collects
together, in a chronological sequence, Le Corbusier's designs for museums. Setting
aside the late Stockholm and Zurich projects of 1962 and 1964–1965, a clear line of
development may be traced in these, running from the Mundaneum and World
Museum project of 1929 to the Tokyo Museum, completed in 1959. All of these, in
some way, explore the idea of the spiral plan as a means of accommodating future
extension,[41] but they equally demonstrate a consistent approach to the design of the
picture gallery that sets them in a particular lineage and tradition (Figure 2.34). This is
the daylit, rooflit picture gallery that has its origins in Soane's Dulwich Picture Gallery
(1811–1814).

Mies van der Rohe's designs for art museums reveal, from the outset,
completely different intentions. In his German years Mies made many designs for
exhibitions, and many of his houses were commissioned by clients who were art
collectors, but his engagement with the art museum as a specific building type began
with the project for a Museum for a Small Town, 1942 (Figure 2.35). This is best
known by the photomontages that depict works of art, including neo-classical and
Picasso's *Guernica*, floating in an undifferentiated neutral space that is devoid of any of
the familiar cues by which we identify the art museum.

Le Corbusier shows a quite specific architectonic condition in which the
elements of the building, specifically of the relationship between the light-giving
rooflight and the wall plane, are instantly identifiable as those of an art museum – even

in the absence of any visible works of art. Mies, on the other hand, concentrates on the works of art, but sets them between a carefully drawn floor grid and a completely undifferentiated ceiling. The floor to ceiling glazing is hardly about the illumination of the art. This could just as easily be an image of one of his house designs.

These differences of principle were translated into practice in two major projects from the end of these architects' careers. Le Corbusier's Tokyo Museum, 1957–1959 and Mies van der Rohe's National Gallery in Berlin, 1962–1968. Both buildings have a square plan, but, in all other respects, could not be more different. In Tokyo, Le Corbusier develops a complex set of relationships between plan and section in solving the problems of circulation and display that are central to the art museum. Mies in Berlin pursues his end of the universal space by making an emphatic separation between the visible representation of the ideal building and the concealed accommodation of the art works.

The contrast between the solid mass of Le Corbusier's building and the transparency of Mies van der Rohe's could not be stronger and the differences become even more apparent when we consider the plans and sections (Figures 2.36–2.38). Le Corbusier's entrance sequence works its way asymmetrically across the ground plane through a complex field of light and within the repetitions of the column grid. Mies offers absolute symmetry set in a column-free, uniformly lit volume. Then, at Tokyo, the journey is upwards towards the light of the sky, whereas in Berlin the route descends to a spatially and environmentally controlled realm.

2.35
Mies van der Rohe, Museum for a Small Town, 1942, photomontage

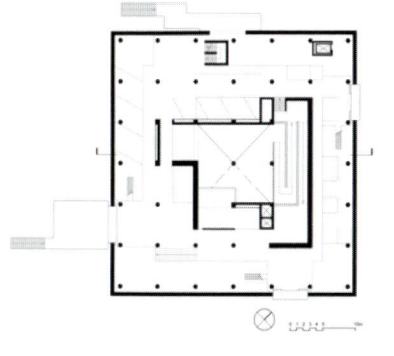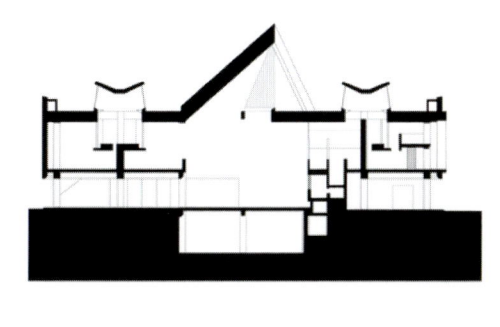

The gallery spaces at Tokyo are dominated by the presence of the *galerie d'éclairage* that hovers above, casting illumination towards the picture walls (Figure 2.39). In addition to the daylight that filters through the outer clerestoreys and the diffusing inner glass panes, the *galerie* also houses electric floodlights that direct artificial light onto the wall below. Compare this with the glass pavilion of the Berlin gallery, in which art, if it is displayed, is artificially illuminated behind the drawn silk curtains. The inaugural exhibition in 1968 of works by Mondrian was shown in just these conditions. In the lower-level galleries the environment is again completely artificial, with artificial light and tempered air issuing from the suspended ceiling. In their mechanical abstraction these spaces are an almost exact translation of photomontage into built reality (Figure 2.40).

Both Le Corbusier and Mies van der Rohe added much to the evolution of the environmental function of architecture. In the designs for houses that stretch across the whole of their working lives they made use of the myriad technologies of heating, lighting and ventilation that the twentieth century brought forth. They brought these technologies to bear in ways that transformed the whole conception of domestic space and the way in which people might live in it. It is possible, in seminal buildings such as the Villa Savoye and the Tugendhat House, to recognise substantial common ground between their thinking. Both houses respect principles of climate response that have their roots in all vernacular building. As a direct expression of this,

2.36
Le Corbusier, Tokyo Museum, plan

2.37
Tokyo Museum, cross-section

2.38
National Gallery, Berlin, cross-section

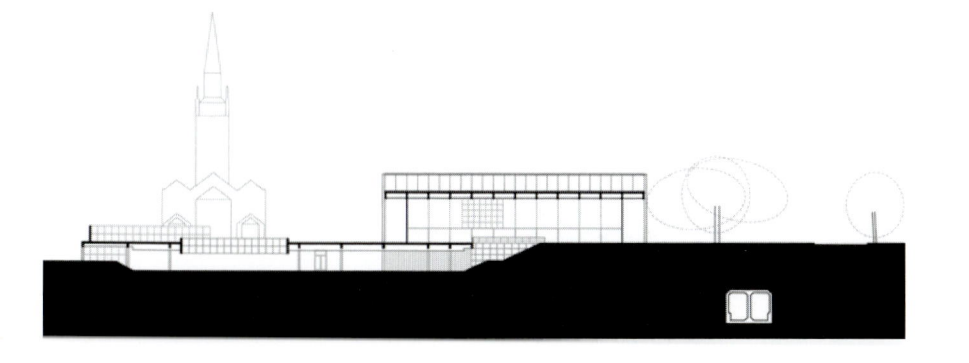

orientation is influential in each design, with the principal spaces benefiting from a southern aspect. On the other hand, in their structures and materials, these houses manifestly depart from the methods of the vernacular. The same can be said of their extensive mechanical installations that allow a fluidity of space that would have been impossible with traditional modes of heating, ventilation and illumination.

But there is a point at which these same buildings reveal a divergence of temperament, or of philosophy, in the work of the two architects. For all of his radicalism, Le Corbusier seems to retain a deep sense of continuity, of tradition held in relation to innovation, that is expressed most potently by the presence of the fireplace, made of brick, in the principal living room of Savoye. At the Tugendhat House, Mies completely eliminates any such reference and combines the elements of exquisitely expressed structure and sub-division of space, with a comprehensive, but totally concealed, system of heating, cooling and ventilation. The balance has tilted decisively from tradition towards innovation.

Nothing is absolutely clear-cut in the complex business of architecture. The recurrence of fireplaces in many of Mies' later house designs, even at the Farnsworth House, is evidence of the latent force of that particular tradition, but it is clear that, by the 1930s, the two architects had established and continued to hold quite distinct positions on the question of environment and that these may be shown to survive throughout the remainder of their work. The contrast between the Maisons Jaoul and the Farnsworth House, the one environmentally concrete, rugged and robust, the other abstract, refined and fragile, and the cases of the Tokyo and Berlin museums show how Le Corbusier's modernism was adaptive, both to time and place, and thus rooted in the environmental tradition that has informed architecture from its origins, whereas Mies' was idealised and universal, and was in that sense attempting to escape from tradition in the search for innovation.

2.39
Tokyo Museum, exhibition hall

2.40
National Gallery, Berlin, lower picture gallery

Notes

1   Le Corbusier, *Précisions on the Present State of Architecture and City Planning*, Crès et Cie, Paris, 1930. English trans., MIT Press, Cambridge, MA, 1991.

2   Le Corbusier, *Les Cinq points d'une architecture nouvelle*, in *Œuvre complète*, Volume 1, 1910–1929, Edition Girsberger, Zurich, 1929.

3   Mies van der Rohe, in *Frühlicht* 1, No. 4 (1922)

4   William Curtis, *Le Corbusier: Ideas and Forms*, Phaidon, London and New York, 1986.

5   Le Corbusier, *Précisions*, op. cit.

6   William Curtis, *Le Corbusier*, op. cit.

7   Wolf Tegethoff, 'The Tugendhat 'Villa': A Modern Residence in Turbulent Times', in Daniela Hammer-Tugendhat and Wolf Tegethoff (eds), *Ludwig Mies van der Rohe: The Tugendhat House*, Springer Verlag, Vienna, New York, 2000.

8   Ibid.

9   Fritz Tugendhat, 'The Inhabitants of the Tugendhat House Give Their Opinion', *Die Form: Zeitschrift für gestaltende Arbeit*, Berlin, 15.11.1931, cited in Daniela Hammer-Tugendhat and Wolf Tegethoff, op. cit.

10 Daniela Hammer-Tugendhat, 'Is the Tugendhat House Habitable?' in ibid.

11 William Curtis, *Modern Architecture since 1900*, Phaidon, London and New York, 3rd edn, 1996.

12 Confirmation to author by Mies van der Rohe Foundation, Barcelona, 26 March 2004, that the pavilion did not have a heating system.

13 Ignasi de Solà-Morales, Cristian Cirici and Fernando Ramos, *Mies van der Rohe: Barcelona Pavilion*, Editorial Gustavo Gili, SA, Barcelona, 5th edn, 2000.

14 H. Allen Brooks, *Le Corbusier's Formative Years: Charles-Edouard Jeanneret at La Chaux-de-Fonds*, The University of Chicago Press, Chicago, 1997.

15 Todd Willmert, 'The ancient fire; the hearth of tradition: Combustion and creation in Le Corbusier's studio residences', arq, vol. 10, no. 1, 2006.

16 See, for example, Geoffrey H. Baker, *Le Corbusier: The Creative Search*, Van Nostrand Reinhold, New York, E. & F.N. Spon, London, 1996, in which he describes the work as, 'disarmingly simple, almost naturalistic and without compositional sophistication'.

17 William Curtis, *Le Corbusier*, op. cit.

18 Tim Benton, *The Villas of Le Corbusier: 1920-1930*, Yale University Press, New Haven, CT, 1987.

19 William Curtis, *Le Corbusier*, op. cit.

20 Ibid.

21 Le Corbusier, *Œuvre complète*, Volume 2, 1929–1934, pp. 48.

22 The house is illustrated in Raymond McGrath, *Twentieth Century Houses*, Faber & Faber, London, 1934. McGrath writes,
    In his other houses Raymond puts the West into adjustment with the East, here he takes the East and gives it that free development which has now been made possible by the experience of the West – 'with some little debt to Corbusier',

as he says. The 'debt' is to Corbusier's South American house for Mme. Errazuriz (sic).

23 Le Corbusier, *Œuvre complète*, Volume 2, 1929–1934, op. cit.

24 William Curtis, *Le Corbusier*, op. cit.

25 Le Corbusier, *Œuvre complète*, Volume 3, 1934–1938, op. cit.

26 Ibid.

27 See, for example, William Curtis, *Modern Architecture since 1900*, op. cit.

28 See Andres Lepik, 'Mies and Photomontage, 1910–38', in Terence Riley and Barry Bergdoll (eds), *Mies in Berlin*, The Museum of Modern Art, New York, 2001, for a detailed account of Mies' use of photomontage in the representation of his buildings and projects.

29 Wolf Tegethoff describes this in detail in, *Mies van der Rohe: The Villas and Country Houses*, 1981, English edition, The Museum of Modern Art, New York, 1985.

30 See Tegethoff, ibid., where the entire programme is reproduced.

31 From Tegethoff, ibid.

32 Ibid.

33 William Curtis, *Le Corbusier*, op. cit.

34 This terminology is derived from the work of Victor Olgyay, the Hungarian/American environmentalist, whose *Design with Climate: Bioclimatic Approach to Architectural Regionalism*, Princeton University Press, Princeton, NJ, 1963, develops a strong argument for climate response in architecture.

35 Mies van der Rohe, cited in Tegethoff, op. cit.

36 See Maritz Vandenberg, *Farnsworth House: Ludwig Mies van der Rohe*, Phaidon, London, 2003, for a detailed technical critique of the building.

37 Le Corbusier, *Œuvre complète*, Volume 5, 1946–1952.

38 James Stirling, 'Garches to Jaoul: Le Corbusier as Domestic Architect', *Architectural Review*, no. 118, September 1955. Reprinted in Carlo Palazzolo and Riccardo Vio (eds), *In the Footsteps of Le Corbusier*, Rizzoli, New York, 1991.

39 Le Corbusier, *Œuvre complète*, Volume 6, 1952–1957.

40 W. Boesiger and H. Girsberger, *Le Corbusier 1910–65*, Les Editions d'Architecture, Zurich, 1967.

41 In *Modern Architecture Since 1900*, op. cit., William Curtis uses the designs for museums to illustrate how 'Le Corbusier would invent a type-form or a motif and then develop it for different purposes and meanings'.

Essay 3
The 'other' environmental tradition
Erik Gunnar Asplund and Alvar Aalto

North and South

Essay 2 explored the relation of environmental concerns with the development of the theories and practices of Modernism in architecture. By comparing the works of Le Corbusier and Mies van der Rohe it was shown how new technologies of environmental management were adopted as instruments in the definition of the new architectural language. An important strand of the critical discourse of the past decade or so has been to articulate the case for an 'other' tradition in twentieth-century architecture that stands in clear distinction from the 'orthodoxy' that may be said to be represented by Le Corbusier and Mies. One of the principal advocates of this position is Colin St John Wilson, who in, first, *Architectural Reflections* [1] and, second, *The Other Tradition of Modern Architecture*, [2] has sought to 'reveal an alternative philosophy that is something much broader than the protest of eccentric individuals and now begins, on the evidence of seventy years of work, to have the authority of an Other Tradition'. In the development of his argument, Wilson gathers together a band of architects whose work exhibits the qualities that, for him, define the nature of this otherness. These include Hugo Häring, Sigurd Lewerentz, Hans Scharoun and, the subjects of the present essay, Erik Gunnar Asplund (1885–1940) and Alvar Aalto (1898–1976). [3]

As a starting point, the distinction between the environmental positions of the 'orthodox' and 'other' traditions of modern architecture might be characterised by a polarity of, on the one hand, generalisation and, on the other, specificity in their relationship to the climatic setting of buildings. For Le Corbusier the 'universal fact' of the sun's path across the sky, and its graphic representation, became an icon of his environmentalism, whereas Aalto would speak metaphorically of the origin of the rooflit reading rooms of the Viipuri Library being informed by, 'some kind of fantastic mountain landscapes with cliffs lit up by suns in different positions' [4] (Figures 3.1 and 3.2).

Curtis has argued that, throughout his career, Le Corbusier's work was suffused by a 'Mediterranean myth', [5] a preoccupation with the conditions of the south: 'Over the years I have felt myself becoming more and more a man of everywhere but always with this firm attachment to the Mediterranean: queen of forms under light.' [6]

Asplund and Aalto were men of the north. With the exception of the small number of late projects that Aalto realised in Germany, France, Italy and the United States, their output was located entirely in Scandinavia. Between the high northern latitudes of 55° and 65°, the entire context of architecture is utterly different from

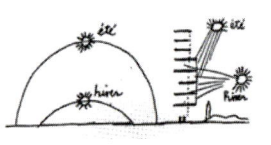

3.1
Le Corbusier, Unité d'Habitation, winter and summer sun angles

3.2
Alvar Aalto, Viipuri Library, 'fantastic mountain landscapes'

that of the Mediterranean, both in fact and in myth. At high latitudes the sense of difference between the seasons of the year is greater than in the south. In Stockholm and Helsinki, both close to 60° north, the sun is above the horizon for barely five hours at the winter solstice, but these cities enjoy virtually continuous daylight at mid-summer. The contrast between the seasons is equally marked thermally, with bitter cold in the dark winter months and pleasant, mild, long summer's days.

Speaking in Vienna in 1955,[7] Aalto emphasised the significance of nature for the outlook and experience of the Finnish people;

> I show here a typical picture of my country. Its purpose is to give you an idea of the landscape that surrounds the buildings I shall discuss. It is a land of forests and lakes, over 80,000 lakes. The people have always been able to maintain their contact with nature in this land.

Later in this lecture, when discussing his work at the Technical University at Otaniemi, Aalto spoke of the importance of the seasons:

> The university has an extensive sports area for the students and a large hall where summer sports can be pursued during the winter. Personally I'm against sports becoming universalized so that summer is turned into winter and winter into summer. I think that one should pursue a sport and change it according to the time of year so that one may experience the natural changes of the seasons.

It was against this background of nature, large in dimension and extreme in climate, that Asplund's and Aalto's work was set and from which much of its essential character was drawn. Aalto's moving 'Memoriam', written on Asplund's death in 1940, captured the ground that they shared, 'the art of architecture continues to have inexhaustible resources and means that flow directly from nature and the inexplicable reactions of human emotions. Within this latter architecture, Asplund has his place.'[8]

Asplund: nature and the city

The vast landscape of Sweden engenders a similar engagement with nature to that experienced in Finland. Stockholm, looking east across the Baltic, shares many characteristics with Helsinki on the opposite shore. Both cities display a deep sense of their respective topography and rural hinterlands. Speaking of Stockholm, in a conversation with James Baldwin, Ingmar Bergman said:

> It is not a city at all. It is ridiculous to think of itself as a city. It is simply a rather large village, set in the middle of some forest and some lakes. You wonder what it thinks it is doing there, looking so important.[9]

Nonetheless, these are cities that are, in their morphology and architecture, profoundly urban. The core of Stockholm, extending inland from Gamla Stan (the Old Town), rests on interlocking urban grids that structure the public and private realms and locate the significant institutions of the city. It is here, as the city extended northwards, that Asplund began work on the design of the Public Library, which occupied him from 1918 until 1927. The elaborate process through which the design was developed is well documented.[10] As built, the library is a clear development of the neo-classical principles and precedents that informed the first design of 1922. The conventions of classical composition establish a strict biaxial symmetry with the axes almost exactly located on the cardinal points of the compass.

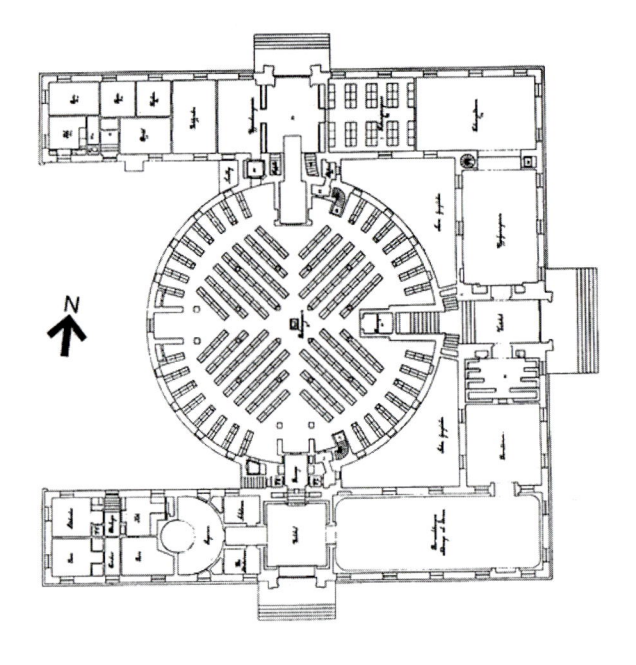

3.3
Asplund, Stockholm Public Library, ground-floor plan as completed in 1928. The children's library is at the south-east corner, with the story-time room to the left of the entrance lobby.

Within these conventions Asplund exhibited sensitivity to questions of orientation, particularly by placing the exquisite children's library, with its own direct entrance, on the ground floor of the south wing. There it enjoys sunlight and a view over the lake and garden that lie on that side of the building (Figure 3.3).

The great circular reading room is at first floor level and is approached from the east by a dramatic staircase, described as a 'ladder to the sky'.[11] In the early design the reading room had a coffered dome with an array of rooflights. But Asplund later rejected this in favour of a ring of twenty tall, narrow windows set high in the drum above the book-lined walls. This was to ensure that direct sunlight would be admitted to the room.[12] The upper walls have a textured, white stucco finish that, struck by light from the windows, works as a bright diffuse reflector, distributing light evenly throughout the room. On clear days at all seasons small, quickly moving

patches of bright sunlight are projected onto the interior (Figure 3.4). Even within the conventions of architectural classicism, this dynamic light transmits a sense of universal nature into the room. During the hours of darkness, and this means for much of the day in winter at this latitude, the reading room receives its primary and symbolic light from a large white glass pendant that hovers, like an inverted representation of the sky vault, above the central desk. Here and throughout the building, where Asplund designed all the light fittings, artificial lighting is an essential element of the architecture.

The combination of urban setting and classical language confronted Asplund again in his work to extend the law courts at Göteborg (Figure 3.5). This project occupied him for even longer than the Stockholm Library, from 1913 until 1937.[13] The design passed through many stages that, crucially, spanned the years during which Asplund made the transition from classicist to modernist.

The city's law courts, located in the heart of the city on Gustaf Adolf Square on the north bank of the Stora Hamn Canal, were housed in a neo-classical building that was begun in the seventeenth century to the design of Nicodemus Tesin and twice had been extended in the nineteenth century. The existing building was centred on an open courtyard and Asplund's design, throughout its many stages, wrapped new accommodation around a second courtyard to the north. This courtyard took a variety of forms and was, variously, open to the sky or rooflit. All the early designs, up to 1925, were neo-classical in manner. At that point the project was delayed for nine years, during which time Asplund developed his particular interpretation of modernism. The effect of this transformed the very essence of the final design and this was no more strongly evident than in the manner in which the building responded to the environmental issues.

3.4
Asplund, Stockholm Public Library, reading room showing projection of sunlight onto the upper walls

3.5
Asplund, Göteborg Law Courts, view across Stora Hamn Canal from the south-east

The masterstroke of the design is the manner in which Asplund juxtaposes the transparency of modernism in the new wing against the solidity of classicism of the existing building. This is immediately evident in the plan, where the mass of the load-bearing structure of the original building contrasts with the delicacy of the extension with its clearly expressed structural frame (Figure 3.6).

By replacing the north wing of the original building with the glazed, skeletal structure of the stair hall, Asplund establishes a direct visual connection between the open courtyard and the new triple-height entrance hall – the great hall. But, more significantly, this brings sunlight into the new heart of the building. When we examine the cross-section we see how the south-facing rooflight that rises above the central hall reinforces the flow of sunlight by illuminating the furthest, northerly edge of the space (Figure 3.7).

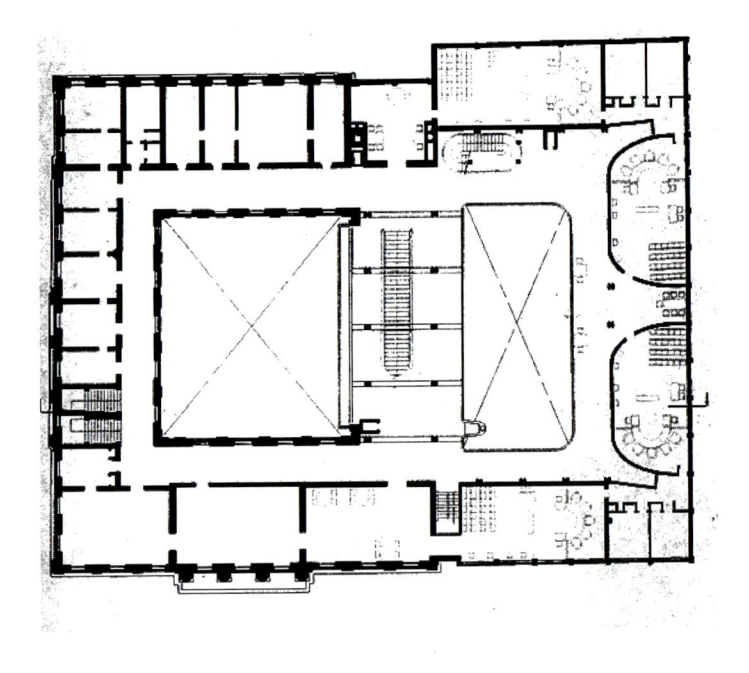

3.6
Asplund, Göteborg Law Courts, first floor plan showing extension to the north of the original building

3.7
Asplund, Göteborg Law Courts, cross-section looking west, showing the transparency of the stair hall of the new wing and the south-facing rooflight

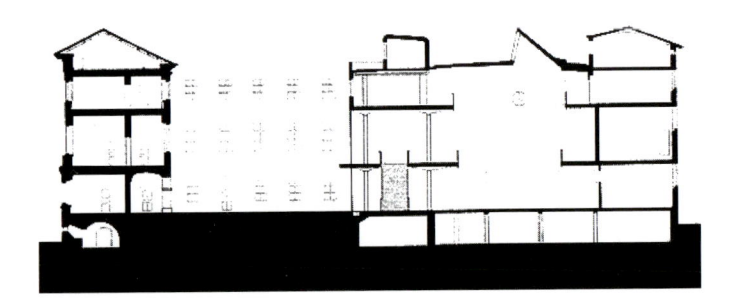

The sun-filled interior speaks eloquently of Asplund's deep sensitivity to the nature of light at this northern latitude. The stair hall is as transparent as can be. The slender mullions hardly interrupt the flow of light, the rounded forms of the encased steel columns are softly modelled, the staircase is delicately suspended from the structure and the balustrades have sparse, polished steel balusters (Figure 3.8).

The great hall further demonstrates Asplund's mastery in organising southerly light. The rooflight is disarmingly simple, a south-facing adaptation of the conventional, industrial north light (Figure 3.9). This admits a flood of unobstructed light to the northern edge of the hall. The rooflight enclosure and the ceiling and walls of the third floor are white-painted to strengthen the illumination by providing strong first reflections. This light then reaches the warmth of the Oregon pine panelling of the balustrades of the first and second floor balconies and lower walls. From these a warm glow is cast throughout the hall and the soft curves of the balcony front and the courtroom enclosures are animated by ever-changing patterns of light and shade as the sun tracks across the sky.

As at the Stockholm Library, the artificial lighting of the building is absolutely integral to its architectural conception. Stuart Wrede has, quite plausibly, suggested that the paired, white glass fittings that are suspended from the columns of the stair hall are an allusion to the scales of justice.[14] They also serve to reinforce the differentiation of the open structure of the stair hall in relation to the enclosure of

3.8
Asplund, Göteborg Law Courts, interior of first floor showing the transparency of the stair hall

3.9
Asplund, Göteborg Law Courts, great hall, showing penetration of sunlight from the south façade and the rooflight

the great hall. After dark, these fittings cast soft, overlapping pools of light into the space. In the body of the hall regularly spaced lines of uplighters are supported on continuous tracks, 'pearls on a string',[15] beneath the white-painted soffits of the galleries and opal disc fittings punctuate the white walls of the third floor gallery. Unlike the 'scales of justice' lamps, that primarily illuminate *space*, these other fittings direct their light towards the enclosing surfaces, towards *material*.

While it is seldom mentioned in the architectural histories, the thermal environment of the building was conceived with as much care as the lighting. A completely new system was installed in the entire building; old and new wings alike.[16] This has both hot water and warm air distribution systems to meet the differing requirements of the diverse spaces and functions. Plant rooms in the basement house boilers, ventilation plant and controls.

In most of the rooms of the old building, and in the basement and attic rooms of the new wing, heating is provided by simple radiators placed beneath the windows. But in the council chamber in the old building and in all other parts of the new, the 'Crittall' system of concealed, hot water, ceiling heating is used. This was clearly an essential component of the architecture of these rooms, particularly of the court rooms, where the integrity of the pine-panelled walls would have been compromised by the visible presence of radiators.

The great hall is heated by warmed air that is delivered through a discreet slot between the edge of the marble floor and the frame of the great south-facing window (Figure 3.10). The duct through which the air flows is formed in the edge of the ground floor slab. From the great hall the heated air passes through grilles to the adjacent rooms and is then evacuated by fans located in the attic.

The thermal environment of the building in winter is finely calibrated to meet the specific needs of the various spaces and their functions, whether these are individual offices, court rooms or the splendour of the great hall. Everywhere the installation is discreetly integrated into the architecture, with no conspicuous display of technology.

At the Stockholm Library, Asplund brought acute environmental sensibility into play within the conventions of classical composition. At Göteborg, the environment is at one with the transformation of architectural language as he moved from classicism to modernism. But this is in no sense a mechanistic environment, it organises environmental qualities to inform the inhabitation of the building, in both public and private areas. Just as the tall windows of the drum project sunlight into the formal cylinder of the Stockholm Library's reading room, at Göteborg the transparency of the stair hall and the clear opening of the rooflight bring rich and complex patterns of light and shade into the building. This becomes a representation of the outside environment – of nature – brought into the heart of the city. This fact establishes a further link between Asplund and Aalto as creators of an alternative environmental vision in twentieth-century architecture.

3.10
Detail of the air inlet slot at the sill of the great window

Aalto's alternative environment

> When you see his buildings in an urban setting you are astonished to find how much of nature's principles he has managed to introduce into the man-made environment, how his lines vibrate with biological life and how his forms follow the complex inner requirements. Yet when you see his creations in country settings you are amazed at the amount of urban culture he succeeds in blending into the virgin landscape … The bridging over of the old gulf between man and nature, the pointing out of what they have in common, is probably the nucleus of Aalto's alternative.[17]

In his Introduction to the first volume of Aalto's *Complete Works*, Göran Schildt beautifully encapsulates the essence of 'Aalto's alternative' as residing in the relation between man and nature. The reciprocities between the 'urban setting' and 'nature's principles' and 'urban culture' and 'virgin landscape' are offered as the key to Aalto's method and, hence, to the interpretation and understanding of his work. In Aalto's specific response to the northern climate of Finland, these qualities are particularly in evidence. The long, light days of summer are celebrated in the forms and details of both urban and rural projects, as are the demands of dark and cold winter.

In considering the environmental qualities of Aalto's works, an essential text is the essay, 'The Humanizing of Architecture'.[18] There, in describing the studies that he conducted during the design of the Paimio Sanatorium, he stated that, 'Architectural research can be more and more methodical, but the substance of it can never be solely analytical. Always there will be more of instinct and art in architectural research.'

Colin St John Wilson has elaborated this point further, observing that:

> we find in Aalto's work from the late 'twenties onward an 'attack' whose freshness, professional rigour and technical imagination amounted to a form of significant innovation in themselves. If we take for instance his analysis and solutions to the needs of the tuberculosis patients at Paimio we find a case-study of a different order from the idealised and abstract models of functionalism proposed by his contemporaries.[19]

Wilson describes how the patients' rooms were designed in their environmental detail to 'respond to the nervous condition and particular needs of a patient'. This intention was translated into a complex installation in which natural light, sunlight and ventilation were supplemented by specially designed light fittings and radiant ceiling heating[20] that together constituted, 'an unprecedented density of relevant detail to sustain the overall generation of novel form'.[21]

3.11
Alvar Aalto, Viipuri Library,
exploratory sketch of the daylighting
of the reading room

3.12
Alvar Aalto, Viipuri Library, artificial
lighting analysis

We have seen how Aalto referred to metaphorical 'fantastic mountain landscapes' when describing the conception of his design for the Library at Viipuri (1927–1935). But he also declared that:

> The main problem connected with a library is that of the human eye … The eye is only a tiny part of the human body, but it is the most sensitive and perhaps the most important part … Reading a book involves both culturally and physically a strange kind of concentration; the duty of architecture is to eliminate all disturbing elements.[22]

Aalto's detailed analyses of the lighting requirements of the reading room at Viipuri, for both natural and artificial lighting, are well known (Figures 3.11 and 3.12). The geometry of the array of rooflights was based precisely on the sun's altitude of 52° at noon at the summer solstice at this latitude. This was the first step in the process of casting a glow of shadowless light throughout the room:

> Theoretically … the light reaches an open book from all these different directions and thus avoids a reflection to the human eye from the white page of the book … In the same way this lighting system eliminates shadow phenomena regardless of the position of the reader.[23]

The artificial lighting installation was designed to reproduce similar conditions during the sunless days of winter. Lamps with parabolic reflectors are set flush into the ceiling and spread light widely onto the white walls above the bookcases. These then become a diffuse secondary light source which illuminates the room.

The 'other' environmental tradition – Erik Gunnar Asplund and Alvar Aalto **69**

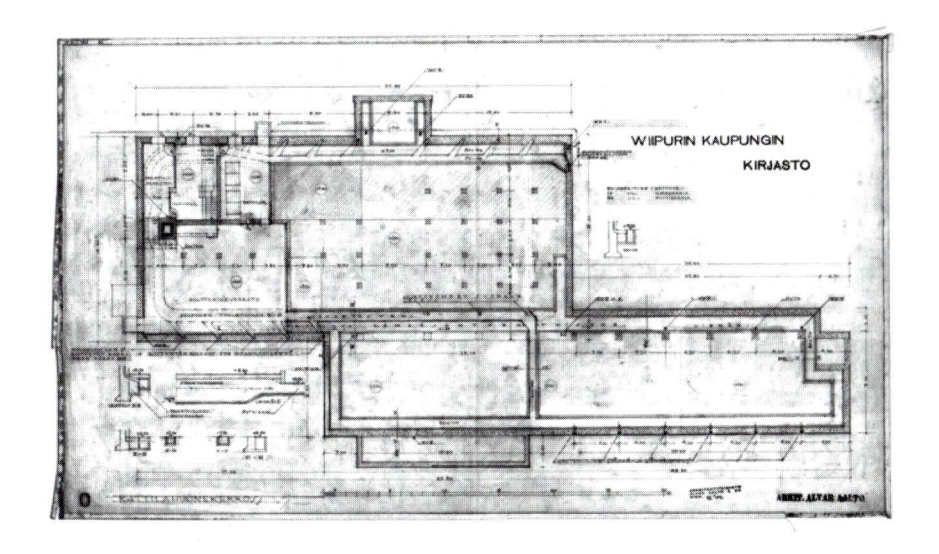

The building also incorporated a sophisticated system of heating and ventilation. A network of ducts runs from a basement plant room to supply warm air and ventilation to all the principal spaces. The extent of these is clearly seen in the working drawings (Figure 3.13). In the reading room, the warm air system that terminates in supply grilles high on the walls was supplemented by a concealed radiant heating system that is clearly visible in photographs of the building under construction. Coils of hot water pipes cover the soffit between the rooflight openings (Figure 3.14).

Marc Treib, among others, has written about 'the landscape within' in Aalto's buildings,[24] the idea that a sense of external nature should be transmitted to the interior. At Viipuri, in particular in the reading room, it is possible to trace the connection between the metaphorical 'fantastic mountain landscapes' and the serene, luminous architecture as it is realised through the medium of building technique, of visible sources of illumination and concealed sources of warmth and air (Figure 3.15).

3.13
Aalto, Viipuri Library, plan showing ventilation ducts

3.14
Aalto, Viipuri Library, reading room under construction showing ceiling heating system

3.15
Aalto, Viipuri Library, reading room. Note the light fittings recessed into the ceiling and the air supply grilles high on the walls.

In August 1936, Aino and Alvar Aalto moved into the house and office that they had designed for themselves at 20 Riihtie in the Helsinki suburb of Munkkiniemi.[25] In his long life as an architect, Aalto built relatively few single-family houses,[26] but, as is so often the case, this building has a significance that belies its modest scale. Juhani Pallasmaa has noted that:

> the humility, understatement, cosiness and relaxed atmosphere of the Aalto House are quite surprising. It clearly reveals his rejection of the ideological, conceptual and formal characteristics of orthodox modernism in favour of domestic comfort and sensuous pleasure. Instead of creating a strikingly formal and visual showpiece, the Aaltos chose to evoke images of deep-rooted tradition and the timeless pleasures of home. No doubt, at the time the house was built in its pastoral setting, it also exuded a utopian and visionary ambience. Presumably it did not appear as humble and reasonable as it does … today. The absence of a roof, the prime symbol of domesticity, as well as the image of the roof terrace … must have evoked both wonder and suspicion … The Aalto House is pivotal in the transition of the Aalto couple from the ideals and aesthetics of rationalism and functionalism towards their personal and idiosyncratic, complex, layered and sensuous expression.[27]

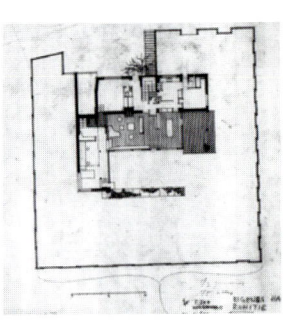

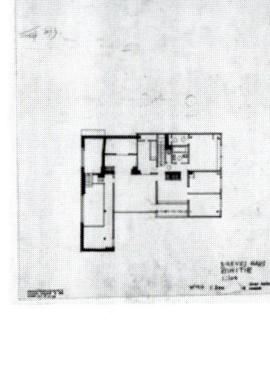

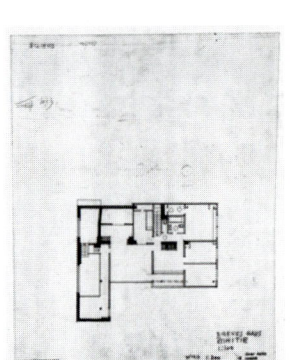

3.16
Aalto House, ground floor plan

3.17
Aalto House, first floor plan

In the context of the present essay the house provides valuable insights into Aalto's understanding of the specific qualities of the northern climate and the manner in which these might inform this 'personal and idiosyncratic' expression.

The site on Riihtie offered the ideal conditions for a climate-related design. It lies to the south of the road and its rocky terrain slopes to the south, looking across an open space that remains clear to this day. This allows the house to make the maximum use of direct sunlight, in illuminating and warming the principal rooms, without compromising privacy. The internal planning beautifully demonstrates this and skilfully organises the relation of house to office by subtle manipulation of floor levels (Figures 3.16 and 3.17).

Pallasmaa has commented on the utility of the L-shaped plan when adopted in the Nordic countries, 'deriving as it does from an attempt to respond to such conditions as basic orientation and sun, the direction of arrival, views and the opposition of public and private realms'.[28] This utility is immediately apparent in the plan of the house, but it is equally clear that this is much more than the simple adoption of convention. The ground floor plan shows the organisation of the house around the east–west oriented spine wall that is made of white-painted fair-faced brick. The rooms to the north accommodate service functions: garage, office, reception, kitchen, maid's room, whereas the principal inhabited spaces, the double height studio, living room and covered terrace face south. Both the studio and the

living room have open fireplaces built into the spine wall. At the first floor the dominance of the spine wall is eroded to some extent as the planning becomes freer, but its presence is maintained by the cores of flues and ducts that rise from below and by the raw brick fireplace of the upstairs hall. A further tiny fireplace is found in the corner of the covered terrace outside the hobby room.

The relationship of the fireplace-filled spine wall and south-facing, sunlit rooms is evocative of the deep traditions of domestic architecture and its response to nature. The house has, as one would expect in Finland at this date, a comprehensive central heating system that is simply and directly expressed by the hot water radiators that are found beneath most of the windows. This is the primary, practical heat source, but the fireplaces are the *symbols* of warmth. In the studio the ensemble of the brick fireplace and steps that lead to the library and the primitive timber ladder to the balcony alludes to the materials and forms of vernacular building (Figure 3.18). The living room fireplace is a simple deep recess in the white brick wall, with a high brick hearth that projects into the room (Figure 3.19).

The south face of the house is elaborately configured to establish a sequence of outdoor extensions of the interior (Figure 3.20). Both the living room and the studio connect to a plateau-like terrace that sits above the natural contours of the site. The dining room also has a door directly opening onto the covered terrace at the south-east corner of the plan.[29] The first floor plan is organised around the open terrace that opens from the upstairs hall. This may also be entered from the balcony of the studio and, via a perilous-looking ladder and a tiny hatchway, from the cul-de-sac of the library onto the covered part of the terrace.[30] This establishes a sequence of diverse, sheltered, sun-warmed places upon which the life of the house may extend to enjoy the precious benefits of the sun as it slants in at the low angles of this northern latitude. One can imagine the Aaltos on long, light summer's nights lingering late in the fire-lit covered terrace; almost recreating the conditions of primitive shelter. The cross-section reveals how the natural contours of the site, sloping upwards to the north, are extended across the terraces, drawing nature and landscape into the building, creating 'the landscape within'.

The year after the completion of Aalto's own house he received the commission that produced one of the great architectural works of the twentieth century, the Villa Mairea that he built for his friends, Marie and Harry Gullichsen, at

3.18
Aalto House, studio showing the fireplace and balcony stair

3.19
Aalto House, living room looking west towards the studio

3.20
Aalto House, view from south-east

Noormarkku, close to the west coast of Finland on the Gulf of Bothnia.[31] Göran Schildt has commented on the relation between the Aalto house and Mairea with respect to their shared materiality 'his love of wood brick, tile and copper'.[32] But it is also possible to trace an environmental lineage between the two buildings.

In their 'Architectural Description' of Mairea, the Aaltos wrote:

> The building is located solitarily on the summit of a hill … It is surrounded and isolated by a continuous conifer forest … The centre is formed by a courtyard lawn and swimming pool surrounded on three sides by the living rooms, balconies and sauna etc.[33]

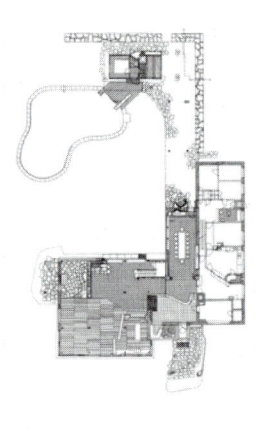

3.21
Villa Mairea, ground floor plan

As we have noted, the site at Riihtie provided precisely the desired conditions for the design of the Aalto's own house. The combination of the road to the north and the south-facing slope of the land were ideal. In the extensive, forest terrain at Noormarkku the selection of orientation was less constrained, but upon examination, it can be shown to be established with equal precision.

The body of the Villa Mairea is, as Pallasmaa observed in connection with the Aalto house, a variant on the Nordic vernacular adaptation of the L-shaped plan (Figure 3.21). This is oriented so that the principal wing, containing, at the ground floor, the living room, library and winter garden, with the master bedroom suite and Marie Gullichsen's studio above, enjoys daylong sunlight through its south-east, south-west and north-west facing façades. The dining room and the terrace above it in the secondary wing receive afternoon and evening sun. The grassy courtyard and the swimming pool, which are sheltered by both the main house and the sauna, face the afternoon and evening sun.

The pavilion that constitutes the principal wing of the house is approximately 14 metres square, with a floor to ceiling height of 3 metres. Its structure and spatial organisation are based on an irregular 3 x 3 grid. Within this simple scheme a sequence of rich and complex spaces is established. The issue of the enclosure of Harry Gullichsen's library has been much discussed.[34] As the question was finally resolved, this is found behind its 'free-standing' partitions at the north-eastern corner, where it overlooks the entrance to the house. Diagonally opposite, at the south-western corner is the winter garden. A white-painted brick wall emphatically defines this – in material, a reminder of the spine wall of the Aalto house, from which grows the remarkable white-plastered chimney with its open fireplace. The remainder of the space falls into two quite distinct territories, which are subtly differentiated by the change in floor finish from tile to timber as one moves deeper in (Figures 3.22 and 3.23).

The relation of the building enclosure, and in particular that of glazed façade, to internal masonry and fireplace that we observed at the Aalto House is further developed at Mairea (Figure 3.24). In addition, the technical apparatus of heating and ventilating moves on to an entirely new level of sophistication. Here,

instead of the straightforward location of the fireplaces in the spine wall, directly opposite the south-facing windows, the fireplaces take up highly specific locations within the topography of the house.

On the ground floor, the living room fireplace forms an L-shaped aedicule with the adjacent white brick wall. The relationship of the fireplace to the courtyard windows is such that the occupant simultaneously enjoys both radiant heat and a view. It is also possible to look diagonally across the internal landscape of the remainder of the room and out into the surrounding forest. As at the Aalto House, a fireplace is also found in the upper hall, next to the master bedroom suite and a further example is in Marie Gullichsen's studio, this has a small hearth set in a tiled surround. The flues for all of these are grouped in the brick wall. At the other end of the house a brick fireplace dominates the end wall of the dining room, where it shares a raking system of flues with the rough stone external fireplace located under the open terrace.

All these fireplaces are practical sources of warmth, but the house has an extensive system of central heating and mechanical ventilation that plays an essential part in its environmental conception and inhabitation. In their published description of the house the Aaltos devoted the majority of their words about the technical design of the house to environmental matters:

> Ventilation in the large living room space has been arranged between the concrete soffit and the suspended pine ceiling below it, where the pine strips act as ventilating filters (52 000 filter-slits), which distribute the purified air evenly over the whole space. Most of the building is air-conditioned, which provides part of the heating for the rooms. Some of the windows are sliding windows, made so that the insulating effect can be increased by various devices during the winter. Part of the external wall is movable on a sliding system so that 'The house can be completely opened to the garden'.[35]

The white brick wall that divides the living room and winter garden is a complex of supply and return ducts serving the living room and the studio.[36] The basement beneath the service wing contains a boiler room and a pump room (Figure 3.25). From these a network of pipes and ducts runs throughout the house. In recalling his first experience of Mairea, as a 7-year-old boy, Kristian Gullichsen has written:

> In truth's name, I must admit what fascinated me most was the boiler room. I would show it proudly to anyone the least bit interested. The murmur of pumps and pipes, together with the two large furnaces, provided the perfect setting for fantastic adventures on the seven seas.[37]

3.25
Villa Mairea, working drawing of the basement showing the boiler room and pump room and the air distribution ducts

3.26
Villa Mairea, working drawing of living room ceiling, showing ventilation slots

3.27
Villa Mairea, working drawing of roof-top fan chamber

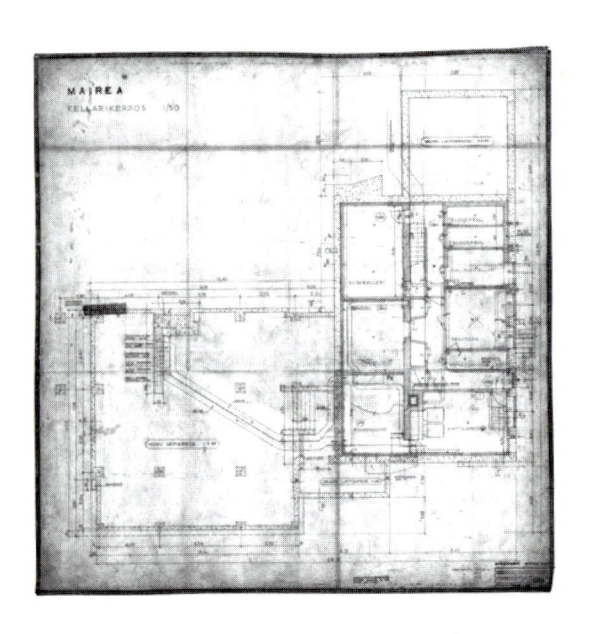

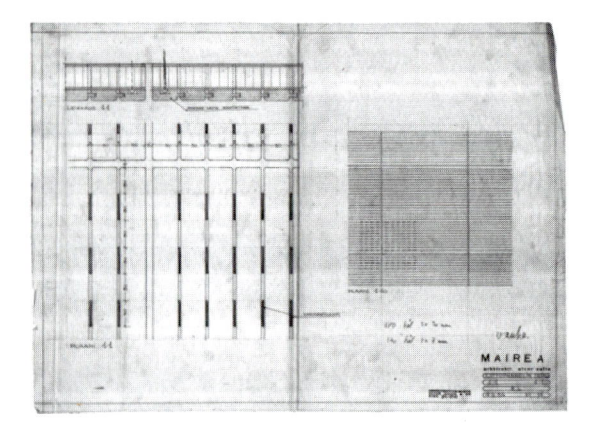

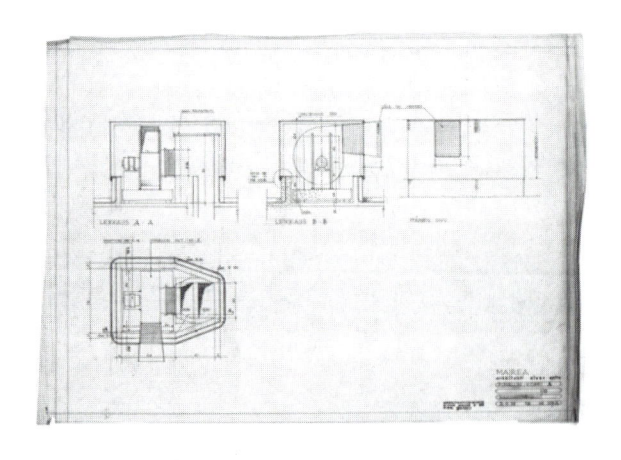

The living room is supplied with warmed air through a plenum above the pine ceiling – the 52,000 slots referred to by the Aaltos (Figure 3.26). Air is extracted through the timber grille set high in the brick wall adjacent to the fireplace, which can be opened and closed using pull chords. Similar grilles are found in the winter garden and the studio. The great fireplace itself is equipped with an elaborate damper mechanism to control the draught.[38] The ventilation system terminates in two roof-top fan chambers that are unassumingly incorporated into the dry Japanese garden (Figures 3.27 and 3.27). In addition the house has a conventional central heating installation that supplies heat to all the rooms through radiators located beneath the window sills. At other points, hot water pipes are set into the floor slab beneath flush metal grilles (Figure 3.28).

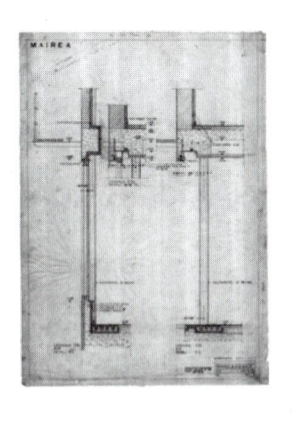

3.28
Villa Mairea, detail of working drawing, showing perimeter heating

In contrast to the calm, relatively conventional, hole-in-wall architecture of the white-painted body of the house, the envelope of the square pavilion is a *tour de force* of environmental devices, mediating, seasonally and diurnally, between the external climate and the interior.

We begin the discussion by considering the configuration and geometry of this remarkable composition. In his essay, 'The Dwelling as a Problem',[39] Aalto wrote,

> A dwelling is an area which should offer protected areas for meals, sleep, work, and play. These biodynamic functions should be taken as points of departure for the dwelling's internal division, not any out-dated symmetrical axis or 'standard room' dictated by the façade architecture.

These principles underlie the design of the Mairea pavilion. Approximately 14 metres square in plan, the pavilion is extremely deep. As a comparison, the Villa Savoye measures overall 19 metres by 21.5 metres,[40] but there the enclosed spaces wrap around the terrace and the *salle*, while being exactly 14 metres in its long dimension, is just 6 metres deep and is lit from three sides. It would seem that a space 14 metres deep and with a ceiling height of 3 metres would be very dark, and that this would be particularly so at a northern latitude. But Aalto's masterly disposition of specific uses, of 'biodynamic functions', around the perimeter of the pavilion ensures that it is always possible to be close to daylight. It also distinguishes between the two conditions of 'window space' and 'fire space' that are found in vernacular houses. The southern prow-like space is, in effect, a giant, sun-filled bay window, equipped with layers of timber-louvred screens to control the sun. Here the warmth of the sun may be enjoyed on clear, cold days and in summer, with the windows thrown open, it may become a verandah. The great fireplace opposite defines a totally different place, whose dimensions are defined by the reach of radiant warmth. This is a kind of ingle nook, a night place and a winter place.

The pavilion space, indeed the whole building, is finely calibrated to the geometry of the sun, which at this latitude – 61.5° N – is only 28° above the horizon at noon at the equinoxes. At midsummer, when the sun is above the horizon from 2.30

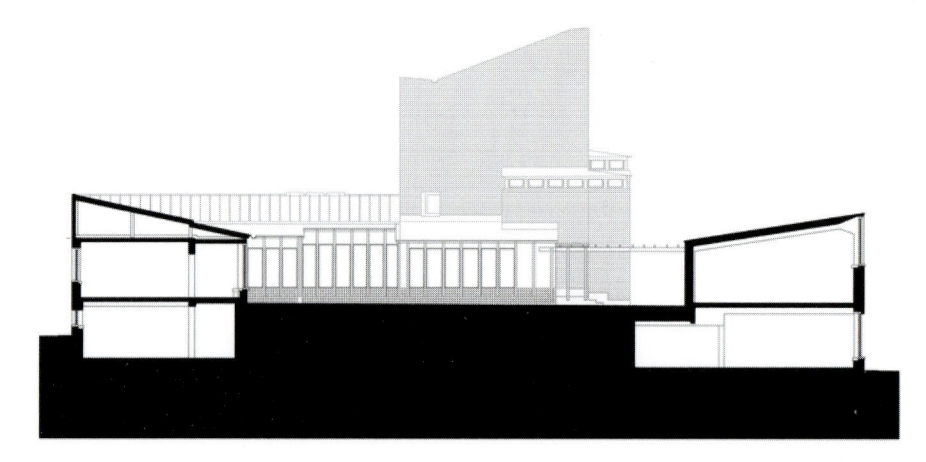

a.m. until 9.30 p.m. and rises and sets just 30° from due north, its altitude at noon is just 52°.[41] This means that sunlight penetrates deep into the space, illuminating the heart of the plan. Here Aalto is revealing and working with his deep understanding of the physical geography of Finland. The angle of the sun is just as important an element of this as the forests and lakes that he spoke of in his 1955 Vienna lecture. On the first floor the house displays a further repertoire of shading devices, adjustable awnings and fixed, pergola-like louvres that protect the various types of bedroom window.

The Aaltos wrote about '[the] deliberate connection to modern painting' that informed the architecture of this house.[42] Richard Weston has further developed this idea, by reference to Braque's invention of collage, to propose an architectural technique of 'collage-composition'.[43] However, as the Aaltos insisted, this is art applied to architecture 'in harmony with the structure … [and] … which by its nature is sympathetic to people'.[44] All the elements of environmental management, mechanical ventilation, fireplace, central heating, fenestration, blinds, awnings, louvres, play their part in this collage, but, in addition, are absolutely central to the creation of a rich environment for domestic life.

The Town Hall at Säynätsalo was completed in December 1951. It was commissioned by the community of 3,000 people who live on this island in Lake Päijänne in central Finland. Aalto described it as, 'a kind of Päijänne Tahiti'.[45] In addition to the civic functions of administration, meeting room and council chamber, the building houses a public library, some shops, apartments and guest rooms. This building beautifully illustrates Göran Schildt's observation on Aalto's ability to bring 'urban culture' to a 'virgin landscape'. Set in a clearing in the forest, it is both building and miniature city. It is also a demonstration of Aalto's mastery of environmental response in the development of its form and in the realisation of its details.

The courtyard form, with its two open corners, is precisely considered in relation to orientation (Figures 3.29 and 3.30). Its axis is slightly rotated relative to true north by some 15° to the west. The material excavated for the foundations was used to

3.29
Säynätsalo Town Hall, section looking east

3.30
Säynätsalo Town Hall, plan at courtyard level

3.31
Säynätsalo Town Hall, courtyard and main entrance pergola

3.32
Säynätsalo Town Hall, cloister

3.33
Säynätsalo Town Hall, detail of
Council Chamber roof

raise the courtyard to first floor level. This was, in Aalto's words, to set the administrative building, 'free, with its accommodation around the patio, of the vulgar influence of the business premises'.[46] But it also produces significant environmental benefits.

By creating this artificial ground level, open to the sky at the centre of the plan, Aalto reduces the obstruction to the sun on the south and west sides of the courtyard, thereby bringing the glazed cloister of the administrative wings barely obstructed sunlight for much of the day. The 10° slope of the library roof, when projected across the courtyard, almost exactly intersects the meeting of the ground and the cloister wall opposite, guaranteeing that the glazed cloister will be filled with sunlight in the depth of the Finnish winter. These dispositions establish a hierarchy of microclimate in which one moves progressively from the open space in front of the building into the shelter of the courtyard, under the pergola above the entrance and, finally, into the enclosed, sunlit and centrally heated interior. The library, which is also entered from the courtyard, occupies the whole of the south-facing block,[47] where it is illuminated by the sun all day long through its tall, timber-mullioned windows.

The building has a straightforward central heating system, served by a plant room at the north-west corner of the lower floor. The chimney from this is seen diagonally across the courtyard as one approaches the main entrance, perhaps a subliminal symbol of the warmth within (Figure 3.31). Throughout the building Aalto took great care to integrate radiators into the fabric in ways that meet the particular needs of each space and its function. In the light-filled cloister the radiators sit beneath a massive brick sill that runs continuously beneath the windows (Figure 3.32). Warm air passes through a gap between sill and window frame and the brick itself becomes warm to act as a secondary heat source. Brick paviors extend part way across the floor and absorb heat from the radiators to extend the sense of the warm perimeter. The rear wall is exposed brick and this absorbs direct sunlight to retain its heat. The whole is a sophisticated environmental micro-system that combines the natural and mechanical with ease.

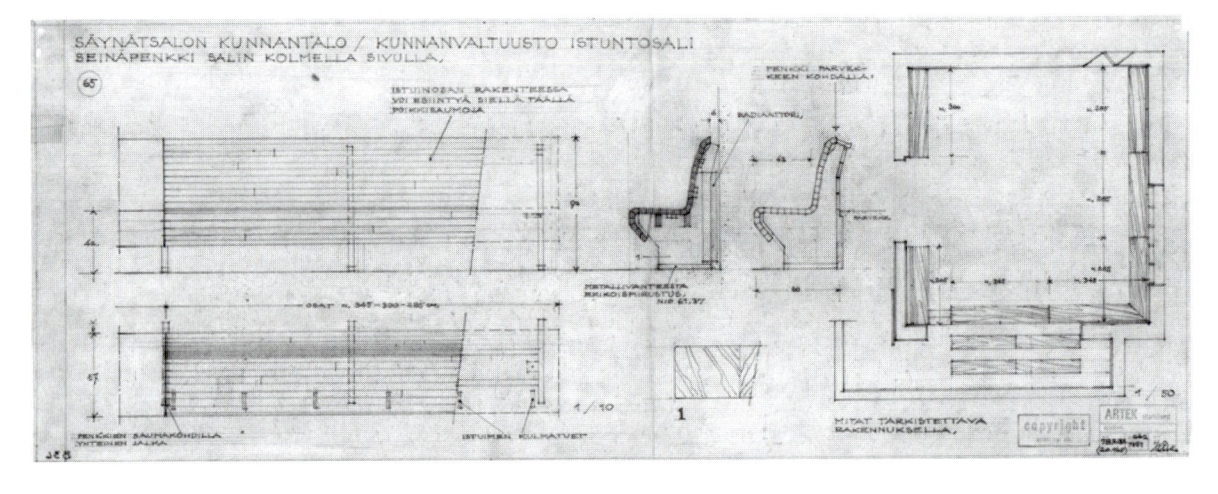

The image of the roof trusses in the Council Chamber at Säynätsalo is one of the most familiar in the whole of twentieth-century architecture (Figure 3.33). These have been interpreted variously as 'upturned hands' – Porphyrios – or as an evocation of a 'great barn' – Quantrill[48] – but they have a significant environmental function in allowing, by supporting the secondary roof framing, unrestricted ventilation between the interior and exterior surfaces of the double roof construction that is necessary in Finland's winter climate.[49] This may be 'prosaic', as Richard Weston suggests,[50] but a crucial part of Aalto's genius was his ability to transform necessity into poetry.

The chamber has a very simple and unobtrusive heating system. Standard steel radiators are concealed behind the fixed seating that lines the walls. Warm air simply circulates from these into the space. In the public gallery a coil of hot water pipe lies beneath a slatted grille in the timber floor under the seats. The room is ventilated through an open brick grille set high in the south wall (Figures 3.34, 3.35 and 3.36).

In contrast to the brightness of the cloister and library below, the Council Chamber is, at all times of day and year, a dark and sombre place. As you rise up the brick stair from the entrance lobby, you are progressively detached from the exterior as light comes either from the high clerestory windows or the lamps that are concealed above the louvred baffle opposite. The entrance to the chamber is directly opposite the large gridded and timber-louvred window that faces north. The only other sources of daylight come from the clerestory of the access passage and the public gallery and the elaborately baffled, small window in the west wall behind the chairman's seat. On most occasions, at whatever season of the year, it is necessary to use the artificial lighting. The lamps used are an adaptation of one of Aalto's mass-production designs. But in this relatively large room – it is approximately 17 metres square – there are only eight lamps. These are arranged in an array ascending and then falling in section on the axis of the chairman's seat and splayed in plan (Figure 3.37). Light, from whatever source,

3.34
Detail of the Council Chamber seating. The relationship of seat and radiator is shown in the cross-section.

3.35
Public gallery.

natural or artificial, is absorbed by the dark brickwork, rendering the room mysterious rather than functional. Juhani Pallasmaa has written that, 'the dark womb of the council chamber … recreates a mystical and mythological sense of community; darkness strengthens the power of the spoken word'.[51] Set against the luminosity of so many of Aalto's interiors, this is a surprising space, detached from external nature, bringing intense focus to the functioning of local democracy.

Speaking more generally, Pallasmaa has described Aalto's works as 'An Architecture of the Senses':

> Aalto is more interested in the encounter of the object and the body of the user than mere visual aesthetics … His elaborate surface textures and details, crafted for the hand, invite the sense of touch, and create an atmosphere of intimacy and warmth. Instead of the disembodied Cartesian realism of the architecture of the eye, Aalto's architecture is based on sensory realism … they are sensory agglomerations.[52]

These qualities are abundantly in evidence in the buildings discussed here. In terms of those qualities that we refer to as 'environmental' we have seen how these buildings consistently make use of all of the tools of modern heating, ventilation and lighting.[53] In many cases the installations were, at the time, at the leading edge of the technology. They were always considered in precise operational and physical relationship to the building's form and its fabric. The aim was service, not technical display. Aalto's metaphor of 'The Trout and the Mountain Stream'[54] referred specifically to the evolution of 'architecture and its details' as biological analogy. But the idea of deep immersion in a stream – a habitat – also serves to define Aalto's own relationship with his habitat in the nature – the environment – of Finland. The outcome is an architecture absolutely of its time and place, but one that achieves a unique synthesis of ends and means – truly an alternative environmental tradition.

3.36
Cross-section through the Council Chamber, showing a detail of the ventilation opening in the brickwork – top left

3.37
Sketch of artificial lighting in Council Chamber

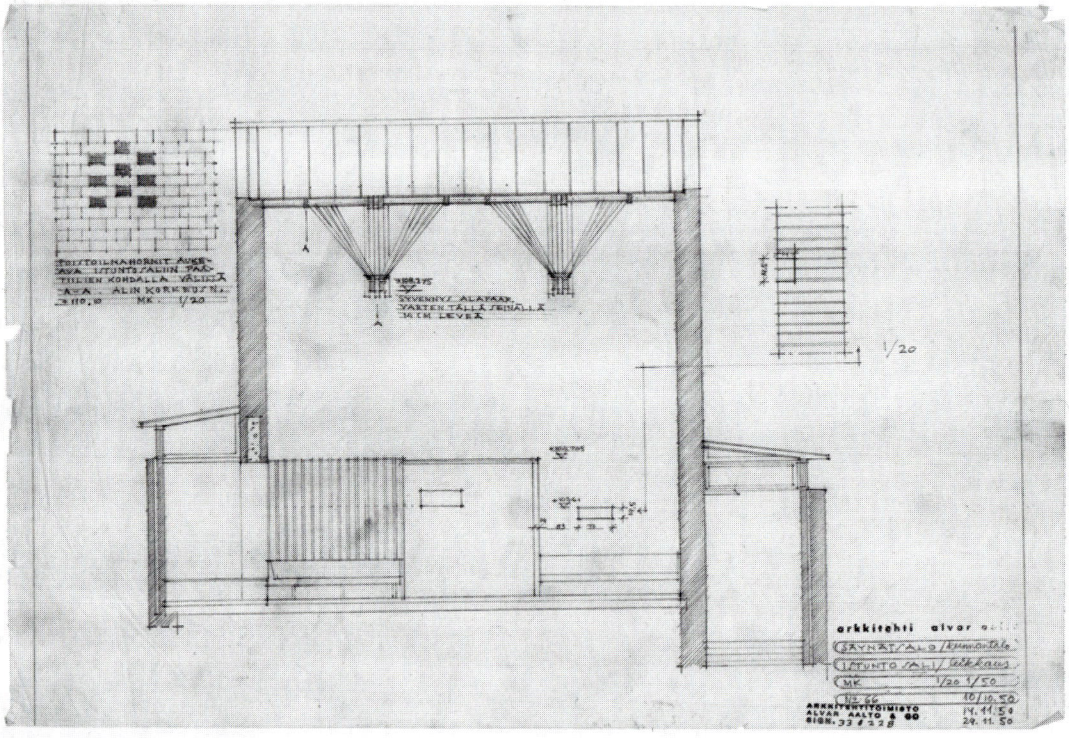

The 'other' environmental tradition – Erik Gunnar Asplund and Alvar Aalto **81**

Notes

1   Colin St John Wilson, *Architectural Reflections: Studies in the Philosophy and Practice of Architecture*, Butterworth Architecture, Oxford, 1992.

2   Colin St John Wilson, *The Other Tradition of Modern Architecture: The Uncompleted Project*, Academy Editions, London, 1995.

3   The environmental qualities of Lewerentz's works are examined in detail, from the specific standpoint of the mechanisms of human adaptation, in Essay 6 below.

4   Alvar Aalto, 'The Trout and the Mountain Stream', *Domus*, 1947, reprinted in Göran Schildt (ed.), *Sketches: Alvar Aalto*, MIT Press, Cambridge, MA, 1985. A wide-ranging, comparative review of the significance of nature in the work of Aalto and Le Corbusier is offered by Sarah Menin and Flora Samuel in *Nature and Space: Aalto and Le Corbusier*, Routledge, London and New York, 2003.

5   William Curtis, *Le Corbusier: Ideas and Forms*, Phaidon, London and New York, 1986. See Chapter 11, 'The Modulor, Marseilles and the Mediterranean Myth'.

6   Le Corbusier, quoted in Curtis, ibid.

7   Alvar Aalto, 'Between Humanism and Materialism', lecture given at the Central Union of Architects in Vienna, 1955, reprinted in Göran Schildt (ed.), op. cit.

8   Alvar Aalto, 'E.G. Asplund in Memoriam', *Arkkitehti*, 1940, reprinted in Göran Schildt (ed.), op. cit.

9   Ingmar Bergman, 1959, quoted in an essay by James Baldwin, 'The Northern Protestant', in *Nobody Knows My Name*, Dial, 1961, reprinted in James Baldwin, *Collected Essays*, The Library of America, New York, 1998.

10 See, for example, Hakon Ahlberg's essay in Gustav Holmdahl, *et al.* (eds), *Gunnar Asplund Architect: 1885–1940*, AB Tidskriften Byggmästaren, Stockholm, 1950, Stuart Wrede, *The Architecture of Erik Gunnar Asplund*, MIT Press, Cambridge, MA, 1983, and Claes Caldenby and Olof Hultin, *Asplund*, Rizzoli, New York, 1986. In addition, Kirstin Neilson and Dan Cruickshank, 'The Fusion of Formalism and Function', in the series of articles on Asplund's works published in *The Architects' Journal*, in 1987 and 1988, later collected in Dan Cruickshank (ed.), *Masters of Building: Erik Gunnar Asplund*, The Architects' Journal, London, 1988.

11 Cited in Kirstin Neilson and Dan Cruickshank, op. cit.

12 Asplund wrote at length about this in an article about the library published in 1928 in the journal *Byggmästaren*, cited by Kirstin Neilson and Dan Cruickshank, op. cit.

13 The works of Wrede, Caldenby and Hultin, op. cit., offer a good background to the genesis of this building. Peter Blundell-Jones provides a particularly detailed account in his essay in Dan Cruickshank (ed.) *Masters of Building*, op. cit. This is reprinted in revised form in Peter Blundell-Jones, *Modern Architecture Through Case Studies*, Architectural Press, Oxford, 2002. The definitive overview of Asplund's life and work is now Peter Blundell-Jones, *Gunnar*

Asplund, Phaidon, London and New York, 2006.

14 Stuart Wrede, op. cit.

15 This term is cited in the pamphlet *The History of the Gothenburg Law Courts*, available at the building.

16 This information is taken from the booklet, *Göteborgs Rådhus*, Rådhusbyggnadskommittén, Göteborg, 1938.

17 Göran Schildt, introduction to Hans Girsberger and Karl Fleig (eds), *Alvar Aalto: The Complete Work*, vol. 1, Birkhäuser Verlag, Basel, Boston, Berlin, 1963.

18 Alvar Aalto, 'The Humanizing of Architecture', first published in *Technology Review*, 1940, reprinted in Göran Schildt (ed.) *Sketches*, op. cit.

19 Colin St John Wilson, 'Alvar Aalto and the State of Modernism', in Kirmo Mikkola (ed.), *Alvar Aalto vs. the Modern Movement*, Proceedings of the International Alvar Aalto Symposium 1979, Kustantja Rakennuskirja Oy, 1981.

20 Was this the origin of Asplund's ceiling heating installation at Göteborg?

21 Colin St John Wilson, 'Alvar Aalto and the State of Modernism', op. cit.

22 Alvar Aalto, 'The Humanizing of Architecture', op. cit.

23 Ibid.

24 Marc Treib, 'Aalto's Nature', in Peter Reed (ed.). *Alvar Aalto: Between Humanism and Materialism*, The Museum of Modern Art, New York, 1998. See also Göran Schildt, 'Comments on Alvar Aalto's Introduction to the Villa Mairea', *Villa Mairea 1937–1939*, Guidebook, Mairea Foundation, Noormarkku, 1982.

25 Information from Rejna Suominen-Kokkonen, 'The Ideal Image of the Home', in Juhani Pallasmaa (ed.), *Alvar Aalto Architect,* vol. 6: *The Aalto House 1935–1936*, Alvar Aalto Foundation/Alvar Aalto Academy, Helsinki, 2003. This volume provides extensive documentation on the conception, construction and inhabitation of the building.

26 The three volumes of Hans Girsberger and Karl Fleig (eds), *Alvar Aalto: The Complete Work*, op. cit., illustrate just the following six completed 'one-family' houses built for private clients: Aalto House, Helsinki, 1935–1936, Villa Mairea, Noormarku, 1938–1939, Muuratsalo Summer House, 1953, Villa Carré, Île-de-France, 1956–1959, Villa Kokkonen, Järvenpää, 1967–1969, Villa Schildt, Tammisari, 1969–1970. In his Introduction to *Alvar Aalto Houses*, A+U, June 1998, Markku Lahti proposes that Aalto 'was able to design almost one hundred one-family houses, more than half of which were built'. This invaluable volume includes early works omitted by Girsberger and Fleig, the houses for industrial managers such as those at Paimio, the Sunila pulp mill and Enso-Gutzeit and, finally, the long series of designs for standard house types. Nonetheless, the houses for private clients, including the two Aalto built for himself and his family, have particular value by virtue of their experimental dimension.

27 Juhani Pallasmaa, 'Rationality and Domesticity', in Juhani Pallasmaa (ed.), *Alvar Aalto Architect*, vol. 6, op. cit.

28 Ibid.

29 This link was modified when the servants quarters were later extended to occupy a part of the terrace.

30 This was allegedly used by Aalto as an escape route to avoid unwelcome visitors.

31 Many writers have studied the Villa Mairea. The principal reference is Juhani Pallasmaa (ed.), *Alvar Aalto: Villa Mairea*, Alvar Aalto Foundation/Mairea Foundation, Helsinki, 1998. Other sources include, by Richard Weston: *Villa Mairea: Architecture in Detail*, Phaidon, London, 1992; *Alvar Aalto*, Phaidon, London, 1995; and 'Between Nature and Culture', in Winfried Nerdinger (ed.), *Alvar Aalto: Toward a Human Modernism*, Prestel, Munich, 1999. Edward R. Ford examines its constructional detail in *The Details of Modern Architecture*, vol. 2, MIT Press, Cambridge, MA, 1996.

32 Göran Schildt, 'Comments on Alvar Aalto's Introduction to the Villa Mairea', op. cit.

33 Aino and Alvar Aalto, 'Mairea', Architectural Description, *Arkkitehti*, no. 9, 1939.

34 See Richard Weston, *Villa Mairea: Architecture in Detail*, op. cit.

35 Aino and Alvar Aalto, op. cit.

36 This installation is described in outline in Edward R. Ford, *The Details of Modern Architecture*, vol. 2: *1928–1988*, op. cit.

37 Kristian Gullichsen, 'Foreword' to Juhani Pallasmaa (ed.) *Alvar Aalto: Villa Mairea*, op. cit.

38 See a detail of this in Richard Weston, *Villa Mairea: Architecture in Detail*, op. cit.

39 Alvar Aalto, 'The Dwelling as a Problem', *Domus*, 1930, reprinted in Göran Schildt, op. cit.

40 See Essay 2. Dimensions taken from published plan in *Œuvre complète*, vol. 2, Les Editions d'Architecture, Zurich, 1934.

41 Compare this with 38° in London and 50° in New York, at latitudes of 51.5° and 40.5° respectively.

42 Aino and Alvar Aalto, op. cit.

43 Richard Weston, *Villa Mairea: Architecture in Detail*, op. cit.

44 Aino and Alvar Aalto, op. cit.

45 Alvar Aalto, 'Kunnantalo, Säynätsalo', in *Arkkitehto*, 9/10, 1953, reprinted in *Kunnantalo/Town Hall, Säynätsalo*, Alvar Aalto Museum, Jyväskylä, 1997.

46 Ibid.

47 The library originally occupied only the upper floor of the south wing. In 1981 it was extended downwards to occupy the original shops at ground level by the construction of a new stair. Information from *Kunnantalo/Town Hall, Säynätsalo*, op. cit.

48 Both cited in Richard Weston, *Alvar Aalto*, op. cit.

49 Hans Girsberger and Karl Fleig (eds), *Alvar Aalto: The Complete Works*, vol. 1, op. cit.

50 Richard Weston, *Alvar Aalto*, op. cit.

51 Juhani Pallasmaa, *The Eyes of the Skin: Architecture and the Senses*, Academy Editions, London, 1996.

52 Ibid.

53 An excellent summary of Alvar and Aino
    Aalto's designs for electric light fittings is given
    in, *Golden Bell and Beehive: Light fittings Designed
    by Alvar and Aino Aalto*, text by Kariina
    Mikonranta, The Alvar Aalto Museum,
    Jyväskylä, 2002.

54 Alvar Aalto, 'The Trout and the Mountain
    Stream', op. cit.

Essay 4
The poetics of 'served' and 'servant'
Louis I. Kahn

I do not like ducts, I do not like pipes. I hate them really thoroughly, but because I hate them so thoroughly, I feel that they have to be given their place. If I just hated them and took no care, I think that they would invade the building and completely destroy it. I want to correct any notion you may have that I am in love with that kind of thing.[1]

4.1
Louis I. Kahn, 'The Room' (inscribed, Lou K '71)

In the company of the great architects of the twentieth century, Louis Kahn (1901–1974) stands out as the first to explicitly acknowledge and address the question of how the ever growing provision for mechanical services might be physically accommodated within the composition and structure of a building. His famous hatred of ducts and pipes was translated into the distinction between 'served' and 'servant' spaces that was a constant strategy in the works of his late period. This invests each of these buildings with a specific and coherent topography that some commentators have identified as 'his main contribution to the history of architecture.'[2]

But Kahn was also the great 'poet' of late twentieth-century architecture and the essence of that poetry may be found in his deep preoccupation with light – *natural* light – and its complex inter-relation with the form and materiality of architecture. This is most succinctly expressed, retrospectively, in his drawing of 'The Room' (Figure 4.1). Here he established the significance of natural light in his work when he wrote:

> A room is not a room without natural light
> [and]
> A great American poet once asked the architect, 'What slice of the sun does your building have? What light enters your room?' – as if to say the sun never knew how great it is until it struck the side of a building.

So, we have, on the one hand, Kahn as one of the great architectural topographers, making clear distinctions between the physical elements and functional dispositions of his buildings and, on the other hand, demonstrating how he could transcend the literal facts of organisation, of structure and services, of 'served' and 'servant', in the realisation of an architecture of immense expressive power. This synthesis of the instrumental and the poetic was central to the universal appeal of his work as he began his rich late period. Vincent Scully has written:

> Kahn's buildings, the very distillation of the twentieth century's later years, are primitive … They are above all built. Their elements – always elemental, heavy – are assembled in solemn, load-bearing masses … Their body is Platonic, abstractly geometric in the essential shapes of circle, square and triangle translated into matter, as if literally frozen into mute musical chords. They shape spaces heavy with light like the first light ever loosed on the world, daggers of light, blossoms of light, suns and moons. They are silent. We feel their silence as a potent thing; some sound, a roll of drums, an organ peal, resonates in them just beyond the range of our hearing. They thrum with silence, as with the presence of God.[3]

The theme of the present essay is to explore the means by which Kahn translated the environmental *technics*, of his buildings, *served* and *servant* spaces, territories of natural light and zones of mechanical systems, into this resonant *poetry*. This is a complex process because, even though consistent principles can be identified in his work, Kahn was never formulaic. Each project was an exploration, an extension and reconsideration, rather than a simplistic application of method: 'When you have all the answers about a building before you start building it, your answers are not true. The building gives you the answers as it grows and becomes itself.'[4]

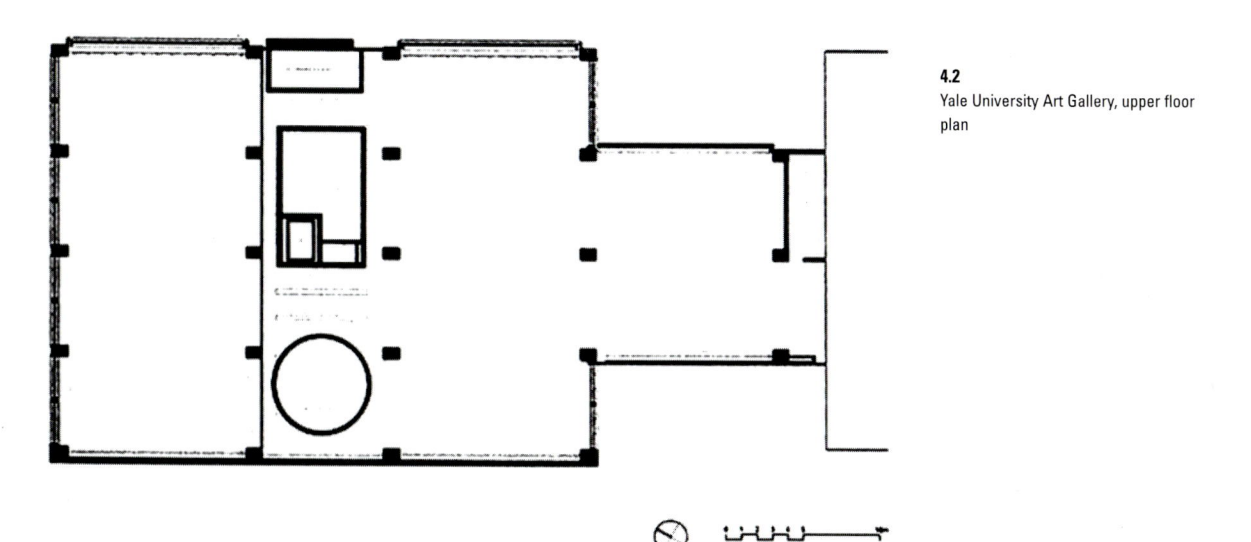

4.2
Yale University Art Gallery, upper floor plan

Yale University Art Gallery, 1951–1953

By general consent, this was the building that defined the transformation of Kahn's work and reputation. Brownlee and De Long have identified the 'Reintroduction of Mass' as lying at the heart of this[5] and Scully referred to the 'sombre and archaic tension' that he detected in the building.[6]

When it first opened in 1953, the building provided studio and other accommodation for the Yale School of Architecture, in addition to exhibition space. Indeed, the project was described in its early stages as 'Design Laboratories and Exhibition Space'.[7] This explains the multi-storey, side-lit arrangement and the absence of rooflit space that had been the norm of art museum architecture since the end of the eighteenth century. The plan of the building could hardly be simpler. The principal, four-storey high volume has an A-B-A configuration in which loft-like gallery spaces flank a central bay containing staircases, elevators and other services, 'served' and 'servant' writ large. A secondary volume provides further gallery space and links the building to the adjacent, existing art museum building. At the upper levels this *'parti'* becomes absolutely clear when the demands of entrance and administration that occupy and sub-divide part of the ground floor are no longer required (Figure 4.2).

In the façades the relation of expressed concrete frame to enclosure conforms to the conventions of modernism, of the separation of structure and enclosure, with the column grid visible through the full-height glazing that faces the enclosed garden. On the street front, storey-high planes of brick are defined and, in appearance, are supported by projecting stone string-courses that also define the floor levels and perform as drip mouldings. These windowless surfaces offer protection from the bustle of the street and from the glare and heat of the morning and afternoon sun at that orientation (Figure 4.3).

4.3
Glazed and brick façades viewed from the west

4.4
Louis Kahn under the Yale ceiling

4.5
Exploded axonometric view of the Yale ceiling, showing the location of mechanical and electrical services

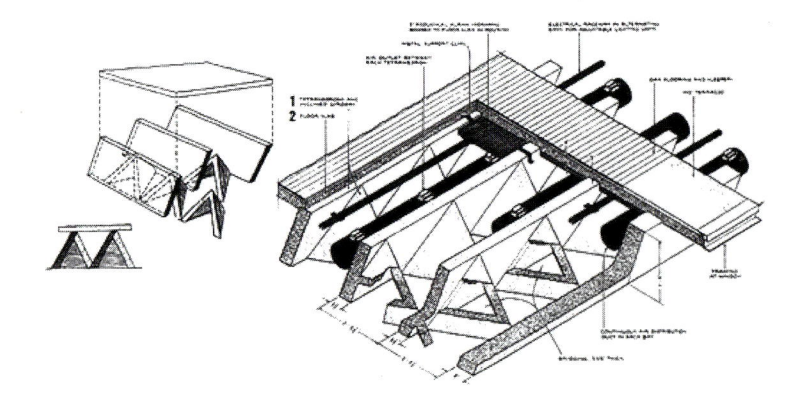

Much critical discussion of the building focuses on the tetrahedral structure of the floor and roof structure.[8] This enabled Kahn to establish a consistent articulation of the ceiling plane in the gallery spaces and to accommodate the horizontal distribution of mechanical services. Acoustic absorbent was incorporated as permanent shuttering to the horizontal slab (Figures 4.4. and 4.5). Kahn explained the virtues of the design as,

> (1) ... lighter construction giving a greater sense of space ...; (2) ... better acoustical properties inherent in the nature of the construction; [and] (3) ... better distribution of the general illumination without any diminishment of the opportunities for specific illumination.

The structure thus became the source of all of the mechanical elements of the internal environment, providing flexible distribution of light and air, whatever the arrangement of temporary partitions or display panels might be. Its specific and original character bestow significance on these normally utilitarian functions. The distinction of 'served' and 'servant' is thereby powerfully declared for the first time in a building with extensive mechanical services.[9]

Richards Medical Research Building, 1957–1965

In *The Architecture of the Well-Tempered Environment*,[10] Reyner Banham proposed the term 'exposed power' to define a category of modern buildings in which the components of mechanical service systems were strongly expressed in the architecture. He cited the exposed ductwork on the ceiling of the foyer of the United Nations Building and the 'heroic and sculptural foul-air stacks' of Le Corbusier's *Unité d'Habitation* as prototypes of the approach that received its first full expression in three contemporary projects: Zanusso's Olivetti-Argentina factory, Albini's *Rinascente* store in Rome and Kahn's Richards Medical Research Building in Philadelphia. Of the latter, Banham wrote:

> Louis Kahn's apparent provisions for environmental services give an immediately striking profile to both plan and elevation, and have been immediately understood and admired. No building of recent years has presented such an air of novelty on the basis of planning methods that were so old – it is worth noting that it was for this ... that *l'Architettura* coined the term *Arcaismo Technologico*.[11]

It was in relation to this building that Kahn made his, according to Banham, 'despairing' statement about ducts and pipes. The modern science laboratory is, of necessity, highly serviced. The delivery of myriad supplies of liquids and gases and the extraction of waste products that are frequently toxic demand machines and the spaces to house them that are far more demanding dimensionally and topographically than the most extravagant of systems for climate control. To give these 'their place' Kahn devised an arrangement where service towers and vertical structure were located on the edges of laboratory floor plates. This provided uninterrupted working space (Figures 4.6 and 4.7).

The pre-cast concrete floor structure offered space for horizontal distribution of services, fed from or leading back to the vertical ducts. These elements were then, by an almost biological system of cellular assembly, grouped into a coherent plan organisation (Figure 4.8). The superimposition of the elements of plan, structure and services ducts, all at face value straightforward necessities, resulted, as Banham recorded,[12] in such widespread admiration and imitation that Colin St John Wilson was compelled to ask, 'Will "servant spaces" be the next form of decoration?'[13]

Vincent Scully and Kenneth Frampton have observed the similarity between the disposition and expression of the service ducts at the periphery of the floor plates and Frank Lloyd Wright's similar strategy in the Larkin Building.[14] The lineage is clear to see, but there is a significant difference of effect between the controlled symmetries of Wright's composition and Kahn's freer order. Larkin is compact and introverted, Richards is dispersed and open. The first phase of design and construction was the group – 'cluster' – of three laboratory towers connected to a shared service tower. This was later extended by the addition of two further towers to the west.

Kahn described the organisation of the first phase in the following terms:

> A central building to which the three major towers cluster takes the places of the areas for services which are on the other side of the normal corridor plan. This central building has nostrils for the intake of fresh air away from exhaust sub-towers of vitiated air.[15]

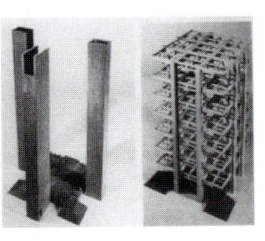

4.6
Richards Medical Research
Laboratories

4.7
Study models of service towers (left)
and structural frame (right)

4.8
Richards Medical Research Building,
ground floor plan, showing first and
second phases

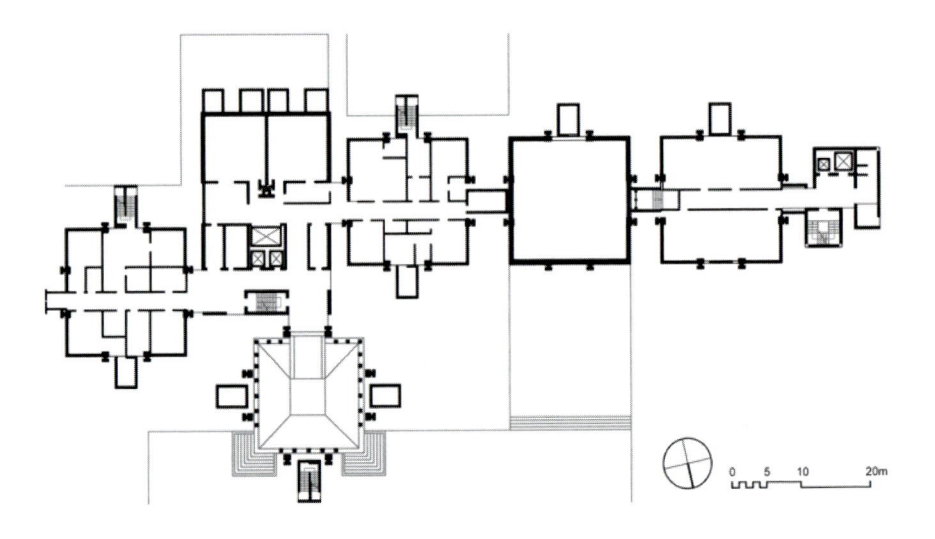

0   5   10   20m

He further insisted that 'a plan should be recognisable as belonging to an era. This handling of our complicated servant spaces belongs to the twentieth century just as a Pompeian plan belongs to its era'.[16] But this is not literal functionality, here the necessities of service are transformed into picturesque silhouette, the functional is made poetic.

It is a sad paradox that, for all Kahn's attention to the organisation of the mechanical service elements and the undoubted status and subsequent influence of the building, the human environment of the Richards Building proved to be unsatisfactory. Kahn originally proposed to install shutters for the south-facing windows, but these were omitted on cost grounds.[17] As a consequence, the south-facing laboratories suffered from glare and solar heat gain and the plan of the towers did not provide the degree of spatial flexibility that scientific research demands. This is particularly poignant in view of Kahn's acute sensitivity to the difference between human and mechanical environments in his statement of the problem, when he wrote:

> Briefly the principles are that the air you breath never comes in to contact with the air thrown away and that men in their laboratories like to work in their studios away from public circulation. These simple realizations give design direction producing true though unfamiliar forms ... I thought what they should have was a corner for thought, in a word, a studio instead of a slice of space. A studio wants to be a place for every man to decide for himself.[18]

It seems as if the demands of the hated ducts and pipes and, perhaps, the complexities of laboratory work distracted Kahn from his acute sensitivity to the human environment. But lessons seem to have been learned and in subsequent works *technics* and *poetics* are unfailingly reconciled, although, as we shall see, servant spaces are never again given such visual prominence. For Kahn himself they did not become 'the next form of decoration'.

Salk Institute for Biological Studies, 1959–1965

The commission for the Salk Institute followed from a visit that Jonas Salk paid to Philadelphia in 1959, when he visited the Richards Laboratories with Kahn. It is, perhaps, not a coincidence that this meeting coincided precisely with the publication of C.P. Snow's well-known critique of the relationship between the 'two cultures' of the arts and humanities. By all accounts this theme underlay much of the conversation between client and architect.[19] From the outset the two men discovered much common ground and, in particular, their shared belief in the need to re-establish connections between the 'cultures'. As is frequently reported, Salk symbolised his ambitions for the project by declaring that he wanted a laboratory to which he could invite Picasso. These aspirations found both literal and metaphorical representation in the building that Kahn designed (Figure 4.9).

4.9
Salk Laboratories, central courtyard

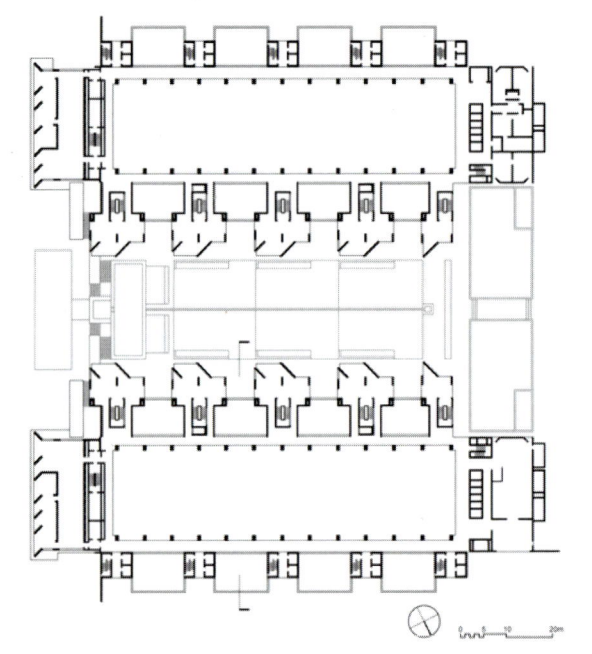

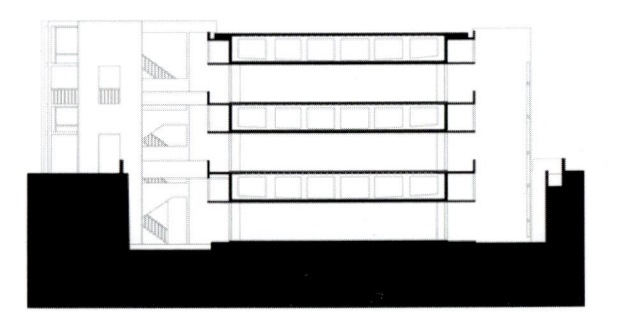

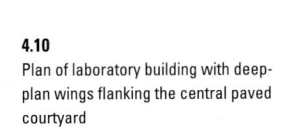

The expansive site, on the edge of a west-facing cliff above the Pacific Ocean, was quite unlike any that Kahn, essentially an urbanite, had worked on before. The design passed through many stages of development before the form of present laboratory building was reached. The early designs proposed laboratory towers on the model of Richards, but this was abandoned in favour of a low-rise alternative. The project, completed under Kahn's direction, is only a fragment of a much larger design that included a 'Meeting Place', very much a symbol of the meeting of the cultures, and a housing group.

The accommodation and organisation of extensive and large-scale services installations were, as at the Richards Laboratories, a key issue. Here the generosity of the site and Salk's direct and intensive involvement in the design process led to a low-rise, horizontal organisation of the laboratories. The final plan of the building takes the form of two parallel wings that define a central, paved courtyard that is overlooked by small study 'towers'. In the laboratory wings, deep service zones alternate in section with the inhabited laboratory spaces (Figures 4.10 and 4.11).

This deceptively simple organisation achieves an effective solution to the problem of servicing the modern science laboratory. The servant zones are 2.7 metres high and the Vierendeel truss structure allows pipe and duct runs to pass the entire length of the building without interruption, while the laboratories remain completely free of internal structure and service elements (Figures 4.12). The problem appears to be solved. [20]

4.10
Plan of laboratory building with deep-plan wings flanking the central paved courtyard

4.11
Cross-section through laboratory wing showing relationship of 'served' and 'servant' spaces

4.12
Laboratory before final fit-out

At the Richards Building Kahn went to some length to attribute studio-like qualities to the laboratories. It was probably the incompatibility of this interpretation with the technical needs of laboratory research that led, at least in part, to the problems that were subsequently experienced with these spaces. At the Salk Institute he suggested that the scientists should have individual studies to which they could retreat for moments of reflection and refuge from the communal space of the laboratories. After overcoming initial resistance from scientists, who were at ease with the laboratory environment, Kahn won the day and the low towers of almost monastic cells that line the central courtyard have become as much a symbol of this institution as were the servant towers at Richards.

Juxtaposed with the industrial scale and nature of the laboratories, the study spaces have the quality of Kahn's house designs. In materiality and ambience they are counterparts to the wonderful aedicule of the fireplace, corner window, window seat ensemble at the Fisher House (Figure 4.13). Environmentally the study towers adopt the strategy of the house, with abundant natural light and natural ventilation, both adjustable by the use of manually operated sliding teak shutters. In his poetic characterisation of these spaces Kahn spoke of 'an architecture of the oak table and the rug' (Figure 4.14).

This differentiation of the mechanical and the natural environments of the laboratories and the studies is, in some ways, as significant for the architecture of the modern building as the idea of 'served' and 'servant'. It questions the portmanteau adoption of mechanical services as the universal answer that became axiomatic in the environmental method of so much late twentieth-century architecture. It allows a finer calibration of *mode* to *purpose* and, crucially, allows the physiognomy of the building to achieve a humanity of scale and texture that the accommodation and expression of the mechanical rarely achieves. In the debate of the 'two cultures', Kahn seems to declare himself for the humanity of the dwelling over the science of the laboratory, but with the concurrence of science. The individual and the institution are practically and formally reconciled.

The most striking difference between the Richards Building and the Salk Institute lies in the shift from the expression of the mechanical, 'servant' elements, to their suppression in favour of the decorum of human inhabitation in the study towers. In a very short period of time – the design and construction of the two buildings overlapped by a number of years – the rhetoric of expressed service was abandoned. Wilson's query about 'servant' spaces as 'the next form of decoration' was answered by Kahn, who, we should remember, concluded his famous statement on ducts and pipes by telling us, 'I want to correct any notion you may have that I am in love with that kind of thing.'[21] This does not mean that the distinction between 'served' and 'servant' is not central to the conception and realisation of the building, but that Kahn was, as ever, responsive to the particularities of context and programme in his search for the correct solution.

4.13
Fisher House, fireplace and corner window

4.14
Study tower interior

Library, Phillips Exeter Academy, 1965–1972

A man with a book goes to the light. A library begins that way.[22]

The architecture of the library revolves around the use and storage of books. In the earliest examples these two functions enjoyed a close and congenial relationship, as is beautifully demonstrated in the medieval library at Corpus Christi College, Oxford (Figure 4.15).

As the number of books and of readers increased, this intimate relationship became ever more difficult to achieve and new configurations had to be found. Christopher Wren's solution at Trinity College, Cambridge (1676) in which he disposed rows of arched windows above high bookcases, was both a logical transformation of the medieval model and a significant architectural invention (Figure 4.16). The projecting bookcases both provided further space for books and defined reading spaces.[23]

The Exeter Library may be seen as a continuation of this tradition of geometry and topography in the architecture of the library. This is particularly so in view of Kahn's adoption of a precise and regular geometrical figure, a near cube, as the determining form of the building.

The diagram of the building is very clear (Figures 4.17 and 4.18). A ring of bookstacks surrounds the central, clerestorey-lit space and reading places are found at the perimeter. In this arrangement readers enjoy natural light and views and the books, on two levels for each reading floor, inhabit the more sheltered, shaded interior, but are usefully close to the readers. A book may be easily 'taken to the light'. Locating the readers at the edge of the building was an explicit requirement of the client's brief.[24] Kahn characteristically restated the requirement in his own words:

> Exeter began with the periphery, where the light is. I felt the reading room would be where a person is alone near a window, and I felt that would be a private carrel, a kind of discovered place in the folds of the construction. I made the outer depth of the building like a brick doughnut, independent of the books. I made the inner depth of the building like a concrete doughnut, where the books are stored away from the light. The center area is a result of these two contiguous doughnuts; it's just the entrance where the books are visible all around you through the big circular openings. So you feel the invitation of the books.[25]

The reading carrels have the intimacy of the medieval library. Set within the giant order of the brick piers, the fine oak joinery offers each reader a private place for study and reflection defined and illuminated by the tiny personal window. The huge undivided pane of glass above lights both the interior space and the way to the

4.15
Library, Corpus Christi College, Oxford, c.1604

4.16
Christopher Wren, Library, Trinity College, Cambridge, 1676

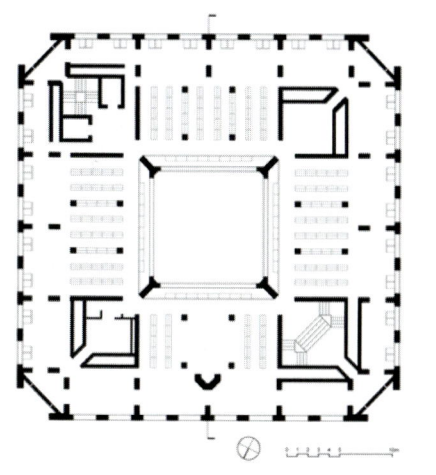

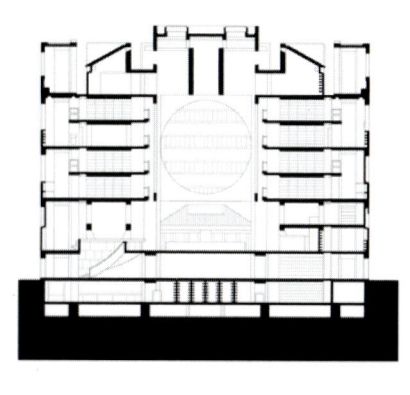

bookstacks. Each carrel provides a microclimate within the more generalised mechanically controlled environment of the building. Local heating solves the problem of downdraughts from the large windows in the cold winters of New Hampshire (Figure 4.19).

The building has a full air-conditioning installation whose presence is visibly expressed by the exposed ducts in the soffit between the brickwork of the reading spaces and the concrete structure of the bookstacks. But the utility and symbolism of older environmental devices are equally on view. As the circular section metal ducts trace their way around the building, they, in places, find themselves in surprising juxtapositions with traditional instruments of environmental service, such as fireplaces. A particularly telling instance is found in the librarian's office, where a cluster of silvery ducts snake across the soffit above a deep, open fireplace, set beneath brick arches (Figure 4.20). Again, on the fourth floor, high above the entrance, a free-standing brick fireplace redefines the reading space, rendering it domestic rather than institutional in character.

As we saw at the Salk Institute, Kahn once again emphasises the human over the mechanical as the basis of the external appearance of the building. The repetition of large windows and human-scale oak carrels, within the framing of the brick enclosure, is a reminder of the historical significance of fenestration in the composition of façades. As Kahn said, 'Exeter started with the periphery, where the light is.'[26] The expressed 'servant' towers of the Richards Building are replaced by the four stair and service elements located at the internal angles of the plan. In this position they efficiently provide service, but play no part in the architectural expression. The distinction between laboratory and library is clearly made.

Kimbell Art Museum, 1966–1972

Fifteen years after he began work on the Yale Art Gallery, Kahn was commissioned to design another art museum for the Kimbell Art Foundation at Fort Worth. In this case, both context and programme were very different from those of the Yale project. In place of the urban setting of downtown New Haven and the, by American standards, northern climate of Connecticut, the site at Fort Worth had an open, suburban character and the bright light and heat of the Texan sky presented a different environmental problem (Figure 4.21). Programmatically the ambiguity of function in the initial brief of the Yale building, part art museum, part architecture school, was replaced by the requirement to house a specific collection of art works. The collection was based on the Kimbell family's existing private collection, but the intention was to show works of art 'of the highest quality' and buying was going on during the design of the building. The aim was to create an 'ideal collection'.[27]

As is usual in most projects of this kind, and certainly in the case of Kahn's late works, the design proceeded through a number of stages of development before it reached its final form.[28] The key to the design lies in the adoption of top-lit vaults of concrete and this element occurred early in the process as preliminary sketches suggest (Figure 4.22). The implications of this can be found in the final design of the

4.21
Kimbell Art Museum, sketch dated March 1967

4.22
Section showing top-lit vaulted galleries and flat-roofed 'servant' spaces

4.23
Detail of vault and light reflector

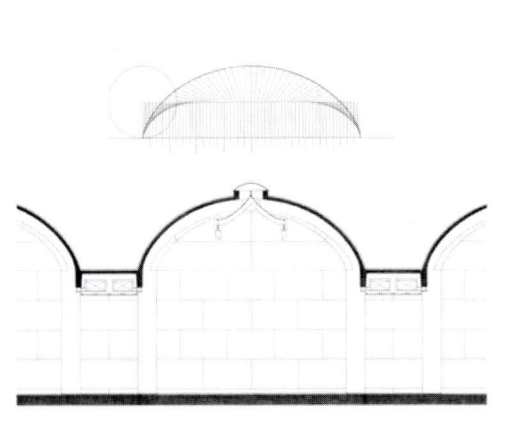

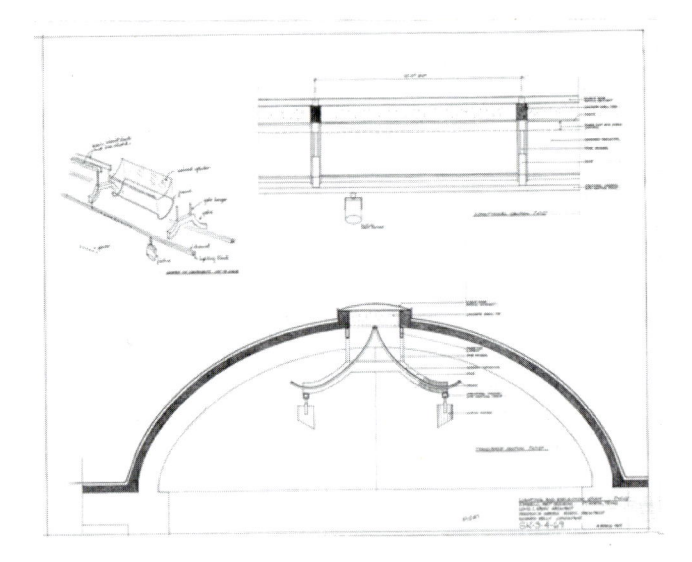

cross-section of the building in which the cycloidal, *in situ* concrete vaults that define the major bays come into a precise relationship with flat-roofed, lower bays; major/minor equating with 'served'/'servant' (Figure 4.23).

This system was the result of a long process of research in which the key consultants played important roles. The structural engineer, August Komendant, devised the cycloidal vaults, supported on only four columns each, that allowed a continuous rooflight at the apex of the roof and an arc of glazing between the soffit and the masonry infill at the gable of each bay. Richard Kelly, the lighting consultant, contributed much to the design of the light reflector that runs beneath the apex rooflight.[29] Kahn considered this to be an important development in the evolution of the architecture of the art museum. He wrote:

> This 'natural lighting fixture' … is rather a new way of calling something; it is rather a new word entirely. It is actually a modifier of the light, sufficiently so that the injurious effects of the light are controlled to whatever degree of control is now possible. And when I look at it I really feel it is a tremendous thing.[30]

4.24
'Natural lighting fixture'

4.25
Gallery level plan

4.26
Cross-section looking south

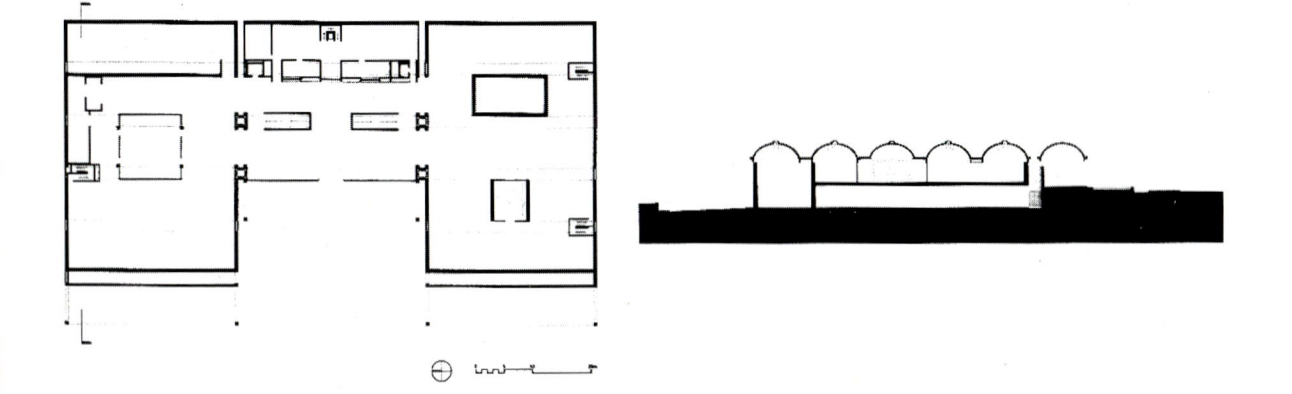

This precisely controls the light that enters the building, working in concert with the form and reflectivity of the concrete vault in an integrated ensemble to produce magical effects (Figure 4.24).

The plan of the building is, with apparent simplicity, a straightforward repetition of these elements to become a pavilion some 97 x 53 metres. The vaults are oriented with their long axis running north/south and the building is entered either from the west directly into the galleries or from the east at the lower, podium level, which also houses administrative offices, laboratories, workshops, storage and utilities, before rising up by stair or elevator to the principal floor. The alternation of major and minor bays, six major vaults and five minor service zones, upon a tri-partite structural grid, regulates the whole building (Figures 4.25 and 4.26).

The elements of the building are disposed on this figure almost as the notes of a musical composition on the staves of manuscript paper. Each of the three courtyards is unique. The dimension of the square north court is the sum of one major and two minor bays and it is glazed on all four sides. The fountain court in the south wing is just one major bay square and is glazed on only its east and west sides. Finally, the double-height conservator's court, also in the south wing, is a double square of the major bay and, enigmatically, is defined at the gallery level by solid walls on all sides. Its nature and function only become apparent at the lower level. These dispositions of the courts result in a rich diversity of space and light within the museum. The north wing is brightly lit from both roof vaults and the large glazed courtyard, whereas the south wing has more distinctly defined spaces and controlled lighting (Figures 4.27 and 4.28).

Another function of the courtyards, that is only apparent by direct experience of the building, is to allow the visitor to enjoy the natural climate as an alternative to the necessarily controlled conditions of the galleries. Beneath the vine-covered wires that criss-cross both the fountain court and the north court – used as an outdoor extension of the cafeteria – the warmth of the sun and gentle breezes may be experienced. Here, just as in the relationship of the natural and mechanical environments of the laboratories and study cells at Salk, Kahn subtly connects the museum environment to nature. The boundary between the two environments can be modified, if needed, by the use of external blinds of fine woven steel mesh.

The double-height conservation studio at the lower level of the building also enjoys a special relationship with its own private courtyard. The studio's entire north wall is glazed, flooding it with copious light to illuminate the work. The blank upper walls of both court and studio are an enigmatic presence in the gallery above.

There are two important spaces within the museum that require specific conditions. These are the library and the auditorium (Figure 4.29). The library is formed by inserting a mezzanine into the 'standard' museum section. The books are stored on the lower level, away from the light, but at the upper level the arrangement brings the scholar into a close relationship with the glowing materiality of the concrete vault. The daylight control device of the museum section is modified to support artificial lighting troughs that span laterally and the arched gables, sheltered by the adjacent bays to north and south, are fully glazed. The result is to provide a general distribution of illumination that is modulated by the special events of the glazed gables and the continuous strip glazing at floor level to the east. In a way Kahn has, again, taken the book to the light.

In contrast to the compression of the cross-section in forming the library, the lecture theatre, which lies at the north-eastern corner of the building, expands the volume as its rake slopes down from the gallery level into the basement void (Figure 4.30). The space that occupies both a major and a minor bay is hardly the kind of volume that acoustic theory would suggest. C. P. Boner, the acoustics consultant, advised the application of acoustic absorbent on the flank walls and the rear wall and projection booth control the reverberation time, but felt that the concrete vault might produce 'weird effects' that might offer 'an interesting atmosphere' that he considered to be acceptable in a museum.[31] The standard light reflector is used to illuminate the lecture theatre and a system of blackout blinds is added to allow the room to be dimmed for projection. But, even here, Kahn remained committed to the principle of natural light as the begetter of architecture:

> When a man says that he believes natural light is something we are born out of, he cannot accept a school which has no natural light. He cannot even accept a movie house, you might say, which must be in darkness, without sensing that there must be a crack somewhere in the construction which allows enough natural light to come in to tell how dark it is. Now he may not demand it actually, but he demands it in his mind to be that important.[32]

In a later modification the slivers of clear glass at the gables and the springing of the vault were replaced by dark red glass in order to reduce the ambient illumination for lectures. Kahn is reported to have sanctioned this, regarding the red light of a photographic dark room as an appropriate analogy for a room in which photographic images are projected.[33]

So, in the sequence of buildings through which Kahn explored the theme of 'served' and 'servant', the design for the Kimbell Art Museum represents a remarkable synthesis of technical means and poetic ends and, in the juxtaposition of gallery space with courtyards, of the mechanical and natural environments. The alternation of vault and service zones is an explicit statement of the principle of 'served' and 'servant', just as clear in its way as the towers of the Richards Laboratory. But here it is seen entirely to support the creation of a setting for the display of works of art that is somehow both mechanically rigorous and visually satisfying. Robert Venturi criticised this building because, in his opinion, it is not clear whether the light is natural or artificial.[34] But that would seem to miss the point. Kahn's aim was precisely to transform natural light into a medium in which art works might be 're-viewed', in a way that is different from that of the traditional daylit gallery and certainly that is different from the absolute uniformity of artificial lighting; as he insisted, 'light is the theme'.

Yale Center for British Art, 1969–1974

Before the Kimbell project was completed, Kahn was given the opportunity to continue his explorations into the nature of the art museum. In 1969, he was appointed to design a building to house Paul Mellon's significant collection of British art that had been given to the university. Unlike his first Yale building this project was, as Kimbell, primarily for the display of an existing and very specific collection, but he was now back in the city (Figure 4.31).

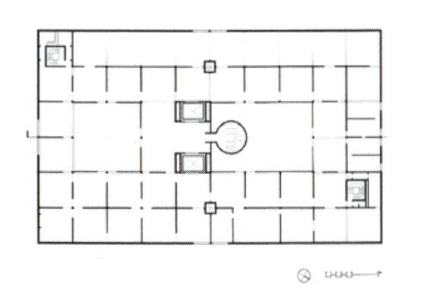

4.32
First-floor plan

4.33
Longitudinal section

4.34
Roof light studies, September 1971

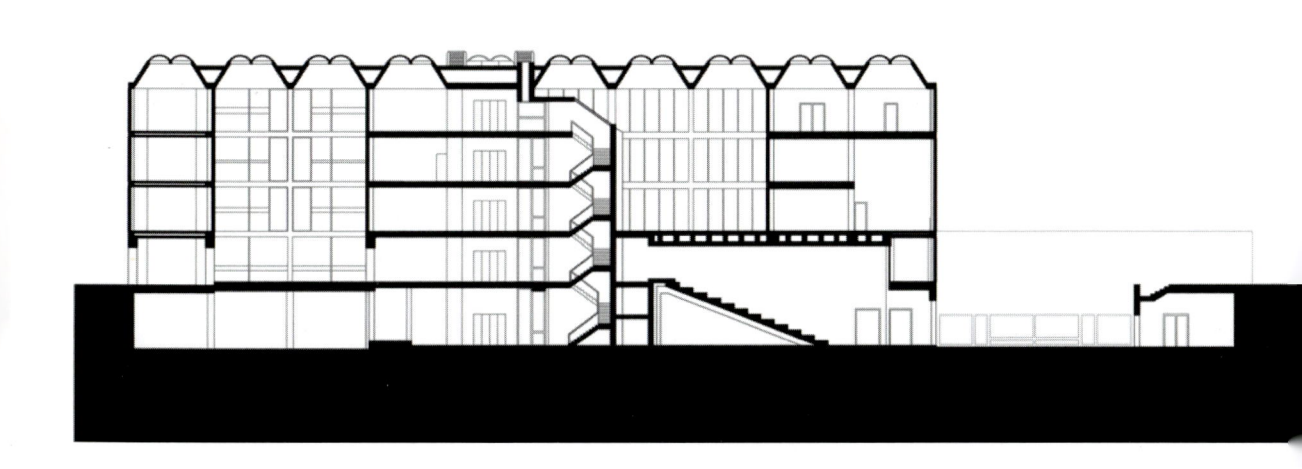

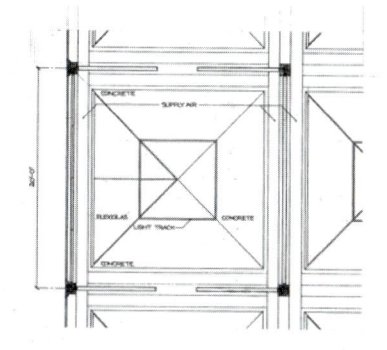

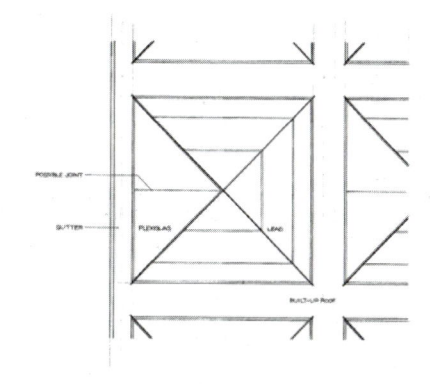

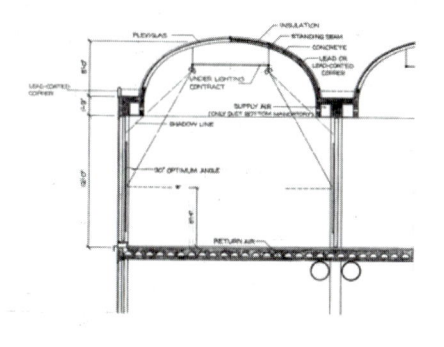

Once again, we can observe a lengthy process of development as Kahn worked his way into the project. Within a compact pavilion form, alternative sizes and conditions of internal courtyards were considered, as were many alternatives for rooflighting systems, until the simplicity of the final design was discovered.[35] In its fundamentals the building could hardly be simpler. An exposed concrete frame defines a Cartesian grid of ten by six bays in plan and four storeys in height. This is penetrated within by two top-lit courtyards, the first containing the entrance is two bays square and rises the full height of the building, the second, whose floor is at first floor level, is three storeys in height and is three bays by two in plan. The cross-section is a simple vertical development of the plan, rising to an array of simple, shallow-domed rooflights that cover the entire roof (Figures 4.32 and 4.33).

The elements of the design are absolutely of their time. The repetitive structural frame with standardised infill panels, stainless steel outside and American oak inside, and the comprehensive air-conditioning installation are the standard technical 'kit' of building technology in the latter half of the twentieth century. The distinction of 'served' and 'servant' is found in the symmetrical disposition of vertical risers about the long axis of the plan and in the horizontal distribution through hollow beams at roof level, ducts incorporated into the concrete floors – he called this an 'air floor' – and, sometimes, exposed ducts on the lower floors. But Kahn transforms all of this in creating a technically sound and poetic setting for the display of art. The rooflight design, as usual, passed through a lengthy process of development.[36] Not surprisingly, in view of the proximity in date of Kimbell, early studies explored the adaptation of vault forms to the new conditions of New Haven (Figure 4.34).

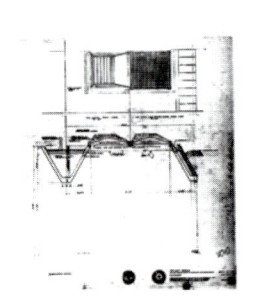

The final design derives simply and directly from the Cartesian grid of the building. The structural bay is subdivided into four equal squares, each covered by a domed rooflight. Above and below these Kahn added controlling devices. Metal louvres are fixed above the rooflights to provide solar control. The building sits diagonally in relation to the cardinal points and the asymmetric louvre system acknowledges this by providing shading in the horizontal plane and to the south-east and south-west and allowing unobstructed north light to enter the building. Below the rooflights, opal glass diffusers further control the quantity and quality of the light (Figures 4.35 and 4.36).

Shortly after Kahn was appointed to design the building, he made a visit, with Professor Jules David Prown, the Mellon Center's first Director, to Mellon's houses at Georgetown, Washington, DC, and to Upperville, Virginia. The object was to view Mellon's collection of paintings in their extant setting.[37] By all accounts, the experience of art in the setting of Mellon's houses made a big impression on Kahn. With reference to Mellon's library, Kahn commented upon, 'the idea of intimacy between book, painting and drawing – this is the room-like quality of the collections'.[38] Kahn and Prown also visited the Philips Collection that is exhibited in a large house in Washington. On these grounds the building at New Haven may credibly be interpreted as a translation of the domestic into the institutional. But, in addition to

the specific influence of Mellon's house, it is also possible to see something of the grand English house in the configuration and qualities of the building. Many of the paintings in Mellon's collection were created to be hung in the rooms of such houses, both in the city and the country, and the galleries of the Mellon Center convey something of the quality of these rooms. In the great houses of England, these paintings are viewed in both grand ceremonial spaces and rooms of intimate scale.

Kahn's topography of central courtyards surrounded by smaller, often side-lit rooms, reproduces just these conditions, but here transformed by the needs of a public museum and by the controlled conditions of environment demanded in the twentieth century. His rooflight design, with its multi-layered system, of solar control and diffusion, simulates the gentle quality of English light that is both found in English buildings and is depicted in the paintings themselves. Whether we consider the great first floor courtyard or the smaller perimeter galleries, the building has the quality of a great house rather than of an institution (Figures 4.37–4.39).

Kahn makes a subtle, but crucial differentiation between the two courtyards. The tall entrance court is not used to exhibit paintings from the collection. It is, therefore, freed of the obligation to provide strict light control. The omission of louvres and diffusers floods the space with vibrant light and this animates the controlled environment of the upper galleries that overlook it.

Although much critical attention has been given to the rooflighting system, it is important to note that, in many respects this is a window-lit building. The complex disposition of window openings in the façades is, in accord with functionalist principles, a direct expression of the location and lighting needs of the rooms within. In the upper galleries, the combination of window and rooflight sustains the illusion of the house as art museum.

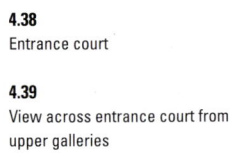

4.38
Entrance court

4.39
View across entrance court from upper galleries

The 'servant' elements of the building are almost completely subsumed into its spatial and constructional systems. Even though the service distribution is logical and hierarchical, it is completely invisible on the exterior and is discreet in the extreme within. The soffits of the V-shaped beams at roof level contain the diffuser grilles of the air-conditioning system, but the beams also function as splayed reveals to the rooflight. They thereby become part of both the mechanical system of the building and of its daylighting strategy. In the library, however, we find Kahn returning to the kind of direct display of mechanical ductwork that he employed at the Exeter Library. There is an almost ironic juxtaposition of traditional oak library furniture and the silver ducts that run along the ceiling and below the mezzanine gallery (Figure 4.40). Perhaps he is at pains to reassure us that this is a building of its time

The quarter of a century traversed by these buildings was the period in architectural history during which the use of mechanical systems of environmental control became commonplace. Their utility and physical presence were, almost axiomatically, assumed in the minds of most architects. This is why Kahn's *cri de cœur* about ducts and pipes had such an influence on both the theoretical debate and practice in the 1960s and 1970s. Viewed over this sequence of buildings, the lesson to be drawn from Kahn is not that these services will come to dominate the appearance of buildings – Colin St John Wilson's 'next form of decoration' – but that they can be incorporated into the body of building with logic, but more importantly, with discretion. This is demonstrated in each of the buildings discussed here, with the notable exception of the Richards Laboratory. The Yale Art Gallery may be seen as a pathfinder, in which Kahn is feeling his way towards the clarity of the later projects. It is a remarkable success in spite of the experimentation in its conception and realisation. Richards stands out for its rhetoric on the subject of servant space, but is, with hindsight, a splendid oddity, rather than an enduring influence – in spite of its numerous progeny.[39] The suppression of servant space into the body of the building that occurred at the Salk Institute marks the priority of human inhabitation over mechanical display and the same emphasis is found in the Exeter Library. The two great, final art museums could hardly be more different. Kimbell deals in the direct expression of method, with its alternating served and servant elements. Kahn's achievement is to transform his 'natural light fitting' into a humane setting for fine art. The Mellon Center seems to be more rooted in allusion to the dwelling as museum, but behind the apparent understatement its tectonic and environmental methods are as rational as those of the Richards Laboratories.

A measure of the significance of an architect's work is the extent to which it reveals principles that add to the body of knowledge that defines and informs the discipline of architecture. Kahn's idea of 'served' and 'servant' long ago achieved that status. But it is important to realise that this is more than a technological distinction between incompatible elements. These buildings show that, without abandoning faith in the modern movement's clarifications of architectural language, it is possible to organise 'served' and 'servant', to mould form, material, light and the other environmental qualities to profoundly expressive ends. Kahn's overriding faith was in architecture itself and that was the source of his method and achievement: 'You realise when you are in the realm of architecture that you are touching the basic feelings of man and that architecture would never have been part of humanity if it weren't the truth to begin with.'[40]

Notes

1 Louis I. Kahn, quoted in *World Architecture 1*, Studio Books, London, 1964.

2 Peter Blundell-Jones, *Modern Architecture Through Case Studies*, Architectural Press, Oxford, 2002.

3 Vincent Scully, 'Introduction', in David B. Brownlee and David G. De Long, *Louis I. Kahn: In the Realm of Architecture*, Rizzoli, New York, 1991.

4 Louis I. Kahn, lecture to the Drexel Architectural Society, Philadelphia, 5 November 1968, in R.S. Wurman, '*What Will Be Has Always Been': The Words of Louis I. Kahn*, Access Press and Rizzoli, New York, 1986.

5 See 'The Mind Opens to Realizations', Chapter 2 in Brownlee and De Long, op. cit.

6 Vincent Scully, 'Sombre and Archaic: Expressive Tension', *Yale Daily News*, 6 November 1953.

7 An extensive account of the development of the project may be found in Patricia Cummings Loud, *The Art Museums of Louis I. Kahn*, Duke University Press, Durham, NC, 1989.

8 Ibid.

9 Kahn asserted that the Trenton Bathhouse (1955) was the first full realisation of the served and servant principle. See John W. Cook and Heinrich Klotz, *Conversations with Architects*, Lund Humphries, London, 1973. In comparison with the Yale Art Gallery, however, the services installations at Trenton were minimal.

10 Reyner Banham, *The Architecture of the Well-tempered Environment*, The Architectural Press, London, 1969.

11 *L'Architettura*, October 1960, cited in Banham, op. cit.

12 Reyner Banham, op. cit.

13 Colin St John Wilson, *Perspecta VII*, cited by Banham, op. cit.

14 Vincent Scully, *Louis I. Kahn*, George Braziller, New York, 1962, Kenneth Frampton, *Studies in Tectonic Culture: The Poetics of Construction in Nineteenth and Twentieth Century Architecture*, MIT Press, Cambridge, MA, 1995.

15 Louis I. Kahn, cited in Heinz Ronner and Sharad Jhaveri, *Louis I. Kahn: Complete Work, 1935–1974*, Birkhäuser, Basel and Boston, 1977.

16 Ibid.

17 Communication to author from Patricia Cummings Loud, 2 December 2004.

18 Louis I. Kahn, letter to William M. Rice, dated 23 December 1959, cited in Ronner and Jhaveri, op. cit.

19 C. P. Snow delivered the annual Rede Lecture in Cambridge in 1959. His subject was 'The Two Cultures and the Scientific Revolution'. The lecture was published under the same title, Cambridge University Press, Cambridge, 1959.

20 See James Steele, *Louis I. Kahn: Salk Institute, La Jolla, 1959–65*, Phaidon, London, 1993, for a detailed description of the services installation of this building.

21 Louis I. Kahn, *World Architecture*, op. cit., 1964. It is interesting to note that Banham omitted this last sentence when he cited Kahn's statement in *The Architecture of the Well-tempered Environment*. This omission subtly, but radically, shifts the

meaning of the statement.

22 Louis I. Kahn, "The Continual Renewal of Architecture Comes from Changing Concepts of Space', *Perspecta*, No. 4, 1957.

23 See David McKitterick (ed.), *The Making of the Wren Library, Trinity College, Cambridge*, Cambridge University Press, Cambridge, 1995, for the most extensive account of the creation of this remarkable building.

24 Peter Kohane, 'Library and Dining Hall, Philips Exeter Academy', in Brownlee and De Long, op. cit.

25 Louis I. Kahn, lecture given at Phillips Exeter Academy, 15 February 1970, quoted in 'The Mind of Louis Kahn', *Architectural Forum*, July–August 1972. Cited in Kohane, op. cit.

26 Ibid.

27 Communication to author from Patricia Cummings Loud, 2 December 2004.

28 As is the case with all of Kahn's designs for art museums, Patricia Cummings Loud's *The Art Museums of Louis I. Kahn*, op. cit., is the definitive source of information. For Kimbell, see also Michael Brawne, *Louis I. Kahn: Kimbell Art Museum, Fort Worth, Texas, 1972*, Phaidon, London, 1992.

29 Ibid.

30 Louis I. Kahn, interview with Marshall D. Meyers, Philadelphia, 11 August 1972, cited in Nell E. Johnson (compiler), *Light is the Theme: Louis I. Kahn and the Kimbell Art Museum*, Kimbell Art Foundation, Fort Worth, 1975.

31 C. P. Boner, letter, dated 24 April 1970, cited in Patricia Cummings Loud, op. cit.

32 Louis I. Kahn, interview with Marshall D. Meyers, op. cit.

33 Patricia Cummings Loud in conversation with the author, Kimbell Art Museum, Fort Worth, 21 April 2004.

34 Robert Venturi, news conference, National Gallery, London, 1 May 1991, cited by Dean Hawkes, 'The Sainsbury Wing, National Gallery, London', in Dean Hawkes, *The Environmental Tradition: Studies in the Architecture of Environment*, E & FN Spon, London, 1996.

35 As before, Patricia Cummings Loud's *The Art Museums of Louis I. Kahn*, op. cit., is the definitive source for a detailed account of the development of Kahn's design.

36 Ibid.

37 Information from Patricia Cummings Loud, op. cit.

38 Patricia Cummings Loud, 'Yale Center for British Art', in Brownlee and De Long, op. cit.

39 The extreme mechanical expression of Piano and Rogers' Centre Pompidou or Rogers' Lloyds Building would, perhaps, have been impossible without Kahn's proposition and the critical attention that it engendered in the 1960s and the 1970s.

40 Louis I. Kahn, Lecture to the Drexel Architectural Society, Philadelphia, 5 November 1968, in Wurman, op. cit.

Essay 5

'I wish I could frame the blue of the sky'
Carlo Scarpa

Carlo Scarpa (1906–1978) spent the whole of his working life in Venice, the city of his birth, or in the surrounding region of the Veneto. When he was two years old his family moved to Vicenza, the city of Palladio, where he came to know the countryside around the city, with its remarkable villas. Following the death of his mother in 1919, the family moved back to Venice, where Scarpa received his diploma at the Accademia Reale di Belle Arte in 1926. He remained in Venice until 1962, when he moved home and office to the beautiful hill town of Asolo, near Treviso, working both in architectural practice and as a teacher at the school of architecture, Istituto Universitario di Architettura di Venezia, where he became a full professor in 1964. In 1972, he became head of the architectural faculty and moved once more, this time again to Vicenza, where he lived and worked until his death while on a visit to Sendai in Japan in 1978.[1]

Scarpa's built works are, with a few exceptions, concentrated in this fertile landscape between the Adriatic and the Dolomites and in its fabulous cities, Venice itself and, to the west, Vicenza and Verona. While Scarpa's work has received international recognition, and his extensive personal curiosity about matters artistic, cultural and social brought numerous other influences to bear upon his thinking, it is clear that, in its deepest fundamentals, the work is rooted in the conditions of culture, history, climate and building traditions of the Veneto; the landscape of Palladio.

In *The Four Books of Architecture*[2] Palladio explains the basis upon which the size of windows should be determined in response to the climate of the Veneto:

> It is to be observed in making the windows, that they should not take in more or less light, or be fewer or more in number, than what necessity requires: therefore great regard ought to be had of the largeness of the rooms which are to receive the light from them; because it is manifest that a great room requires more light to make it lucid and clear, than a small one: and if the windows are made either less or fewer than that which is convenient, they will make the places obscure, and if too large, they will scarce be habitable, because they will let in so much hot and cold air, that the places, according to the season of the year, will either be exceeding hot or very cold, in case the part of the heavens which they face, does not in some manner prevent it.

This statement is followed by a mathematical formulation that precisely relates the size of windows to the dimensions of the room that they serve. The effect of this is seen in Palladio's designs, where the ratio of window to wall is finely balanced to provide adequate light without suffering the penalty of over-heating in the hot summer months, nor excessive loss of heat during the cold winters of the region. The environmental priority in such a climate would be to achieve comfort – coolness – during the hot months with winter warmth being a secondary, but not unimportant concern. This view is supported by Holberton[3] who observes that Palladio's villas were conceived to be occupied from spring, 'since it was cooler and more salutary out of town during the heat of mid summer', until late autumn, when the harvest and hunting seasons were finally over.

> It is an obvious consequence that Palladio's villas were built against the heat rather than against the cold, although one finds fireplaces invariably provided, because the spring is usually cold in Italy; anyway the weather might be vagarious, and the owner would probably also visit the villa … at other times of the year.

Writing about Scarpa's architecture, Francesco Dal Co has observed: 'The sensitivity Scarpa reveals in, for instance, his treatment of light and its handling of colour tones is the outcome of … his profound affinities with Venice.'[4]

> Sergio Los further expanded on this theme:

> one compositional technique introduced by Scarpa may, I think, be derived from the architecture of the towns of the Veneto. For this purpose it is sufficient to recall Scarpa's projects of the 1950s, with their corner windows … He translated the corner-windows of the new spatial concept into the vocabulary of the Veneto.

> > The light produced by the corner-windows becomes a chromatic luminosity full of transparency, typical of the region's visual arts for centuries … His rooms have a luminosity which, apart from the manifestly different vocabulary generates the flowing light of Palladio and his 17th and 18th century successors.[5]

Other commentators have also illustrated the key role that is played by light in Scarpa's work. Boris Podrecca writes:

> In Scarpa's work it is not just the physical presence of things that transfigures tradition, but also the light, which is a *lumen* not of tomorrow but of the past – the light of the golden background, of the glimmering liquid, of the ivory-coloured inlay, of luminous and shimmering fabrics recreated in marble. It is the light of a reflection of the world.[6]

Museo Canoviano at Possagno

The influence of this regional tradition of environmental response is extensively revealed in Scarpa's mature projects. In 1955, he began work at the Museo Canoviano, at Possagno, where, in commemoration of the bi-centenary of Antonio Canova's birth, he added an extension to the existing nineteenth-century gallery.[7]

This is a key building in Scarpa's *œuvre* and demonstrates fundamental aspects of his environmental intentions. Speaking about the project in 1976, Scarpa expressed the nature of his approach when he said, 'I really love daylight: I wish I could frame the blue of the sky!'[8] Sergio Los has written at length about the narrative function of light in Scarpa's approach to the display of Canova's sculptures, 'bringing them to light'.[9] In the same essay he goes on to suggest that, 'It is precisely the light that shows the illuminated sculptures and "translates" Canova, giving them a new interpretation and constituting – together with the organisation of space and construction – the typological content of the museum.'

Scarpa's building takes its place in an ensemble consisting of Canova's former house and garden and the neo-classical basilican gallery by Francesco Lazzari (1832–1836). Scarpa's contribution is, in effect, an extension to Lazzari's building,

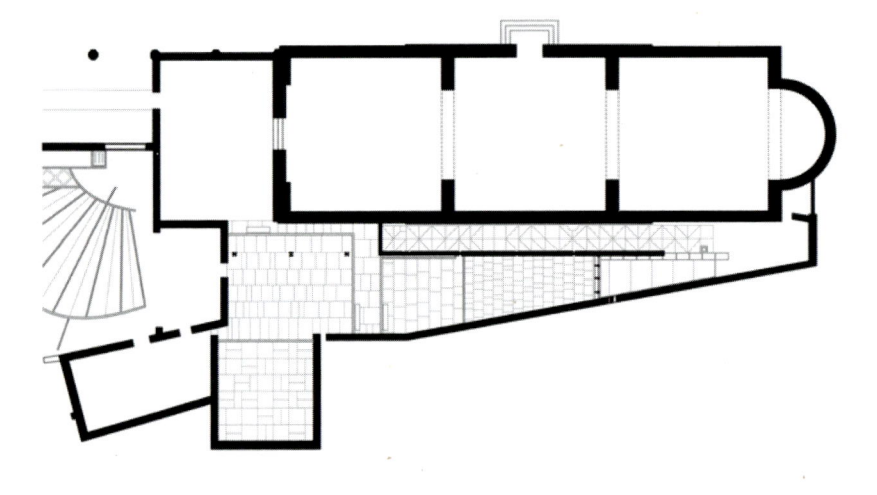

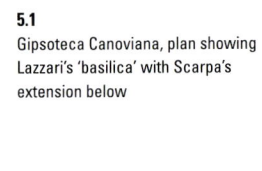

5.1
Gipsoteca Canoviana, plan showing Lazzari's 'basilica' with Scarpa's extension below

through which it is entered (Figure 5.1). The emphatic juxtaposition of Lazzari's neo-classical symmetry and conventional architectural language with Scarpa's free compositional system lies at the heart of the project. The formal differences between these distinct modes of architectural composition are reinforced by their fundamentally different environmental qualities.

Lazzari's basilica, whose long axis is orientated north–south, is lit through small rooflights set at the apex of the coffered barrel-vaulted ceiling, one in each of the three bays. These shed a generalised light within the space, although direct sunlight enters with dramatic effect when the sun is high in the summer months. The diurnal symmetry of the light is quite different from that of a basilican church, where the east–west orientation demanded by Christian orthodoxy creates a strong contrast between north and south aspects. Here the uniformity of the light emphasises the geometrical axiality of the space. Scarpa's light couldn't be more different. From the vestibule of the basilica the eye is led into a dazzling white volume in which sculptures are freely disposed in a complex field of light, some in silhouette, others brightly illuminated.

In his 1976 lecture, Scarpa described how this space originated in a requirement to house a large statue.[10] As the project developed, 'however, I happened to think that, all in all, a high hall was alright. But that it should not be used to house the famous statue, because otherwise the space would have been misused, it would have turned into a mere receptacle for a large object, a high case for a high object.' He went on to propose to his clients,

> why not leaving (sic) this big statue where it is instead of bringing it here where there are plenty. We'd better remove some important statues from among those standing here and arrange them following an inspired principle of composition of elements which should be the most important thing to a museum.

This is the basis of the design as realised. Individual works by Canova are disposed in both the 'high hall' and in the sequence of spaces that open from it, descending southwards, in step with the contours of the site. The light works in concord with the individual works of art, defining their locations relative to each other and to the space they inhabit. As Sergio Los has observed:

> Each statue has a very precise place, with respect to the overall space and to the light that pours in – at times with glaring violence, at other times softly and faintly – modelling the plasters on display, modifying them over the course of the day, with the changing seasons and the variations in weather.[11]

Los cites Giuseppe Mazzariol describing the sculptures as, 'personalities in stone'. The extreme contrast between the Lazzari and Scarpa spaces, set adjacent to each other and, therefore, in exactly the same field of ambient light, derives from the totally different conceptions of architecture and its method that they represent, the one conventional and formal, the other inventive, specific and intuitive.

Scarpa's invention of the trihedral corner windows, simultaneously window and rooflight, that illuminate the 'high hall' is, environmentally and tectonically, the most remarkable element of the building (Figure 5.4). To the west, they are tall and concave and to the east, where they are partly obstructed by the mass of the basilica, they are cubic and convex. Their configuration admits light from all orientations and, unlike a conventional window set within a wall, casts light across the walls themselves. This apparently simple device is the source of the magical quality of light that binds art and architecture into a complex unity. Los has proposed that the Modernist invention of the corner-window, as Scarpa adapted it, lies in lineal succession of the principles outlined by Palladio as the basis of *his* Veneto architecture of the sixteenth century.[12] The ratio of solid to void in the 'high hall' at Possagno is as constrained and disciplined as Palladio's dimensioning of openings in the walls of both villas and palazzos.

Looking west into the 'high hall', the afternoon light of an early summer's day is cast directly on the floor, the northern wall and the sculptures. In addition, it is reflected onto the other wall surfaces by the trihedral windows. From a west-facing viewpoint the figure of George Washington, in senatorial costume, is silhouetted against the light, but is fully illuminated and modelled when viewed from the other side.

These images demonstrate the variety of conditions under which the sculptures are simultaneously illuminated (Figures 5.3 and 5.4). George Washington is strongly modelled by direct sunlight, 'Amor and Psyche with Butterfly' stand in relative shade, against the projection of the light of the corner window upon the wall, and the bust of Napoleon is softly modelled against the shadow by reflections transmitted from the adjacent sunlit wall (Figure 5.5).

5.2
'I wish I could frame the blue of the sky': trihedral window, east facing

5.3
George Washington in silhouette

5.4
George Washington in bright sunlight

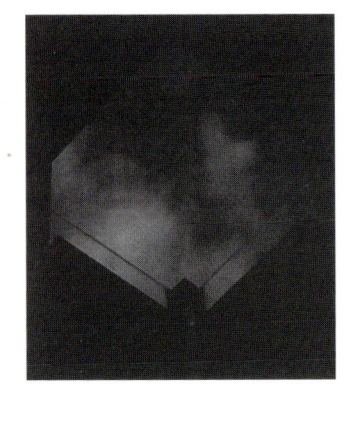

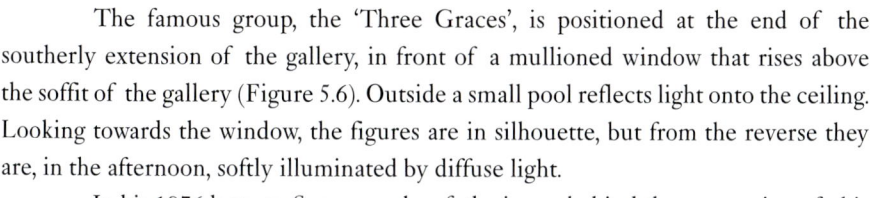

The famous group, the 'Three Graces', is positioned at the end of the southerly extension of the gallery, in front of a mullioned window that rises above the soffit of the gallery (Figure 5.6). Outside a small pool reflects light onto the ceiling. Looking towards the window, the figures are in silhouette, but from the reverse they are, in the afternoon, softly illuminated by diffuse light.

In his 1976 lecture, Scarpa spoke of the issues behind the conception of this arrangement:

> I wanted to give a setting to Canova's 'The Graces' and thought of a very high wall: I set it inwards because I wanted to get the light effect of a bay. That sort of dihedron getting into the room produces that fineness of light which makes that point as well-lit as the other walls.[13]

It is clear from Scarpa's descriptions that light was the primary element of the environmental vision of the project. Sculptures, by their nature, are environmentally robust and are not subject to the strict demands for conservation that apply to the design of spaces for the display of paintings and drawings. They are similarly unaffected, in relative terms, by the thermal environment in which they are kept.

It is rarely observed that the Gipsoteca has no heating system. It simply shelters its priceless contents from the elements by the methods adopted by all pre-industrial architecture, by the organisation of form and material, of solid and void. In the true sense of the term this architecture is *primitive*, 'relating to … the character of an early stage in the evolutionary or historical development of something'.[14] But this only enhances the profound quality of the building by maintaining the essence of the issue. By rejecting the implicit technological expectations of mid-twentieth-century building, with its extensive apparatus of environmental services, Scarpa is able to

5.5
Amor and Psyche with butterfly and bust of Napoleon

5.6
The 'Three Graces' in silhouette

5.7
Castelvecchio, Verona, plan of main courtyard

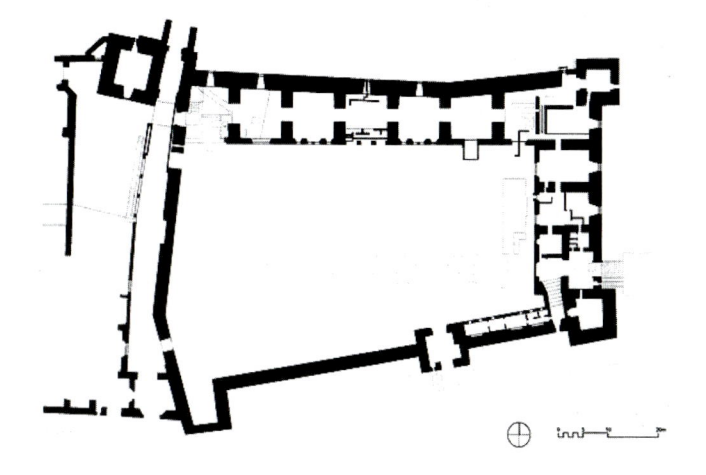

focus on the fundamentals of the architectural environment. The ambience of the interior, luminous, thermal and acoustic, is the direct product of the interposition of the enclosure within the ambient climate. In this way, whatever the consequences in terms of modern notions of environmental comfort, there is an absolute unity of the internal environment in all its dimensions. This building is a supreme instance of the environmental imagination.

Castelvecchio at Verona

In 1956, the year after he began work at Possagno, Scarpa embarked on his lengthy engagement with the rebuilding of the Castelvecchio at Verona.[15] Here the principles that underlie his work at Possagno are applied to the very different circumstances of the transformation of this ancient military building into an art museum that houses a much more diverse collection of art and in which the relation of intervention and existing structure occurs at a more intimate scale (Figure 5.7).

On entering the castle from the street, one's first impressions are of the transition from the brightness and bustle of the street, as one passes over the timber drawbridge, through the archway and into the courtyard. Arriving in the shadow of the fortified wall, the sounds of footsteps on white gravel paving and, then, of running water from the two fountains to the right establish a clear sense of a new calm and orderly environment. The gravel paving is bright, almost glaring in the sunlight. The green hedge that defines the boundary between the gravel and the lawn beyond almost instantly moderates this effect. The façade of the museum faces almost due south and, on the abundant sunny days of Verona, is brightly lit with strong shadows cast in the deeply modelled loggia. The recess of the Cangrande statue to the left is also deeply modelled with a complex rhythm of light and shade (Figures 5.8 and 5.10).

5.8
Loggia

5.9
Cangrande Space

5.10
Enfillade view through sculpture galleries

5.11
Sacello with clerestory above

Moving towards the entrance of the museum, the visitor passes from the irregularity, brightness and looseness of the gravel paving to the firmer platform of the stone paving. The 'threshold' between the two surfaces is marked by a drinking fountain to the left, with its stepping stone set in the slightly agitated pool, and the calm, shallow pool to the right that lies in front of a larger fountain. As one proceeds towards the entrance, the pavement is poised between the inaccessible water to the right and the open space of the lawn to the left. Proceeding further towards the entrance the detail of the wall of the 'Sacello', made from Prun stone, standing to the left of the entrance becomes visible. The entrance itself is declared by the projecting, steel-framed, concrete wall that leads one into the interior. In comparison with the exterior, the interior presents a strong contrast of all three environmental elements: thermal, visual and acoustic. The entrance hall is dark, but adequately lit, cool, but comfortable and quiet. This allows the visitor to adapt in preparation for entry to the 'enfillade' sequence of the ground floor sculpture galleries to the left.

Standing at the threshold of the first gallery, the spaces, with their careful differentiation of old fabric and new surfaces, are relatively dimly lit, with the array of sculpture modelled by light that enters from the, as yet, unseen windows to the left-hand, southerly side of the building (Figure 5.10). At the end of the axis, the lower part of the Cangrande space is seen through a characteristic Scarpa metal grille. The strongly directional quality of the light is enhanced by the texture of the plaster and neutral colour of the walls and the lateral banding of the marble and slate floor. The darker tone of the smooth plaster ceiling adds to the calmness of the space and focuses attention on the human-sized territory defined by the sculptures. The serenity of the space is reinforced by the contrast of its coolness on a hot summer's day.

Moving on into the first gallery, attention is immediately drawn to the south, where the cavern-like interior of the 'Sacello' stands beneath the gothic arch of the clerestory (Figure 5.11). The clerestory brings light into the principal volume and strongly models the sculptures there. The 'Sacello' contains light of an entirely different nature. Its black plastered walls and dark brown clay-tiled floor are strongly illuminated by the flood of light that enters through a full-width rooflight, creating a strong contrast with the calm light of the main gallery. From the gallery the clerestory frames a view of the tower above the entrance to the courtyard. The juxtaposition of vertical and horizontal light powerfully reinforces the distinction between the two spaces. Scarpa's intentions for the lighting of the Sacello in relation to the main gallery were stated with absolute clarity in the sketches that he made during the development of the project.

In this linear sequence of spaces, the location and orientation of the individual sculptures is absolutely integral with the entire architectural composition. These occupy the 'light field' in a manner that reveals and interprets their individual qualities as works of art, but which, reciprocally, demonstrates the character of the architectural space through the inter-relation of material, form and light. Most of the sculptures stand freely in space, but a small number are precisely located. For example, the 'Madonna Incoronata' and the 'Madonna con Bambino' in the third space, are placed in specific relationship to the architectural intervention of the steel-framed, blue and red plastered screen that stands in front of the north wall of the space (Figure 5.12). By its dimensions, material and position, this screen reconstructs the nature of the space and its light and thereby emphasises the significance of these quite small sculptures. The qualities of these rooms and of the works displayed in them support Sergio Los' hypothesis, made with particular reference to the Canova Gipsoteca, 'The architect makes room for the sculpture and places them in the correct

5.12
Detail of 'Madonna Incoronata'

5.13
Paintings in the Reggia

light, in such a way that they "constitute" the space which they occupy.'[16]

Scarpa's spaces for the display of paintings, in both the Reggia and the upper galleries of the fortress, are consistent with his treatment of the sculpture galleries (Figure 5.13). But the requirements for the display and conservation of paintings lead to an intervention that is apparently simpler than that of the sculpture galleries. Here the architectural system becomes a relatively simple background to the works of art, with subdued light filtering in through screened openings.

As in the case of the Museo Canoviano, there is again clear evidence that Scarpa was deeply aware of the thermal properties of the building. The fabric of the existing structure at Castelvecchio, with its massive masonry walls and small apertures is as much a thermal response to the climate of the Veneto as it is to the defensive requirements of military structures. The explicit codification of thermal response in Palladio's 'Four Books' is evidence of this.[17] The intention and effect of these characteristics of construction and form are to give primacy to the prevention of overheating during the warmth of the summer. It is precisely this contrast between the warmth of the courtyard and the coolness of the interior that is felt on a summer's day at Castelvecchio.

In winter, however, the climate of the Veneto is often cold and damp and buildings must be heated, as is attested by Palladio's attention to the design of fireplaces and chimneys. A striking feature of Scarpa's work at Castelvecchio is the attention paid to the nature, location and expression of elements of the heating system. In the entrance hall, a large cast-iron radiator prominently occupies the floor

5.14
Radiator in entrance hall

5.15
Sketch of relationship of window and radiator in second gallery

between the entrance and exit doors (Figure 5.14). In this location it will effectively neutralise the effect of opening and closing doors and its presence suggests that the transition from the cold of the courtyard in winter will be immediately sensed, both physiologically and psychologically. The apparatus is both instrument and symbol.

In the sculpture galleries the radiators are, in general, discreetly located in recesses formed in the dividing walls between the apartments. But at two significant points the heat source enters into a complex relationship with the architecture. In the second gallery, Scarpa inserted a large rectangular window frame behind a Gothic window. In a recess beneath this he placed a cast-iron radiator. This is a relatively conventional arrangement, but here it liberates the sidewalls of the gallery to act as uninterrupted backdrops for the free-standing sculptures (Figure 5.15).

In the third gallery, Scarpa inserted a complex composition of wall and window, solid and void, into the three bays of the gothic loggia (Figure 5.16). The loggia is a relatively modern intervention created in 1923, when the original military structure was converted into a palazzo by the addition of gothic elements. Speaking of this Scarpa declared that, 'Castelvecchio was all deception. I decided to break up the symmetry as the gothic demanded: gothic, especially in its Venetian form, is not very symmetrical.'[18] Scarpa disturbed the symmetry of the loggia by inserting a clerestory with a syncopated rhythm of mullions that hovers above an asymmetrical screen of glass and solid panel. On the interior, this screen locates the two radiators that serve this space in a precise relationship to the windows and, hence, to the principal point of heat loss. The entire assembly, contained within the gothic arcade, thereby becomes a complex device for the admission of natural light and supply of artificial heat to the room.

At the end of the sequence through the galleries we discover Scarpa making use of a suspended ceiling, one of modern architecture's standard elements. Above it, there is, apparently, a relatively conventional ventilation system that serves the space below through grilles. As ever with Scarpa, the conventional is transformed through his attention to form and material. Here the chrome yellow grille is set within a cobalt blue ceiling of *stucco lucido* (Figure 5.17).

Scarpa's work at Castelvecchio is, correctly, represented as one of the supreme instances of investing an historic structure with new life and meaning. Richard Murphy has drawn attention to the similarity between Scarpa's approach and the philosophy of William Morris in defining historical continuity as 'perpetual change'.[19] Conventionally, the conservation debate is concerned with questions of material, structure, construction and spatial organisation, but close analysis shows that, for Scarpa, the nature of the architectural environment, both natural and mechanical, was close to the heart of the matter. As at Possagno, his masterly manipulation of daylight is a primary element in the presentation and interpretation of the works of art that it houses and in the parallel narrative on the building itself. Furthermore, his approach to the incorporation of the components of the heating installation is conceived as much as a question of conservation as of modernisation and raises this frequently mundane function to a new level of architectural representation.

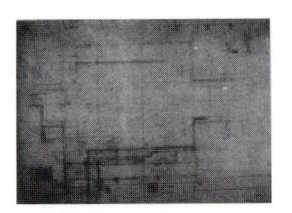

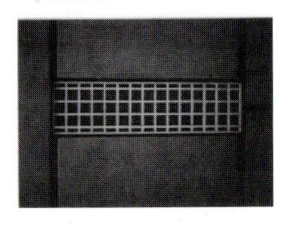

5.16
Sketch plan showing the location of the radiators

5.17
Detail of ventilation grille in plaster ceiling

Querini Stampalia, Venice

At the Querini Stampalia Foundation in Venice (1961–1963),[20] Scarpa again shows his originality in integrating elements of twentieth-century environmental systems (Figure 5.18). The principal exhibition hall runs through the entire depth of the historic building and links the water gate leading from the canal with the courtyard garden. The space, which is used for a variety of exhibitions and functions, is heated by two radiators, each differently incorporated into the architecture of the room. At the entrance from the water gate there stands a travertine stone and glass enclosure inlaid with gold leaf. This contains a large cast-iron radiator, open to the room, in elaborate celebration and containment of the heat source (Figure 5.19). Opposite, in the fenestration to the garden, we find an installation that is reminiscent of the loggia screen at Castelvecchio. But here the radiator stands on a steel angle frame in front of the glazing, where, unlike the Verona design, it is seen silhouetted against the light of the garden (Figure 5.20). The radiator 'cabinet' is an entirely original invention and, in its compactness and intensity, transforms the modern heat source into something more akin to a fireplace in traditional building.

The room is beautifully daylit from either end, in the manner of the Venetian palazzo, but its modern system of artificial lighting is another of Scarpa's inventions. The existing side walls are lined with travertine marble that are punctuated along their length by flush panels of diffusing glass that cover fluorescent lamps. These cast a glare-free light throughout the room. These lamps run at eye level so that they are perceived as horizontal; as the eye line or horizon of perspective construction.

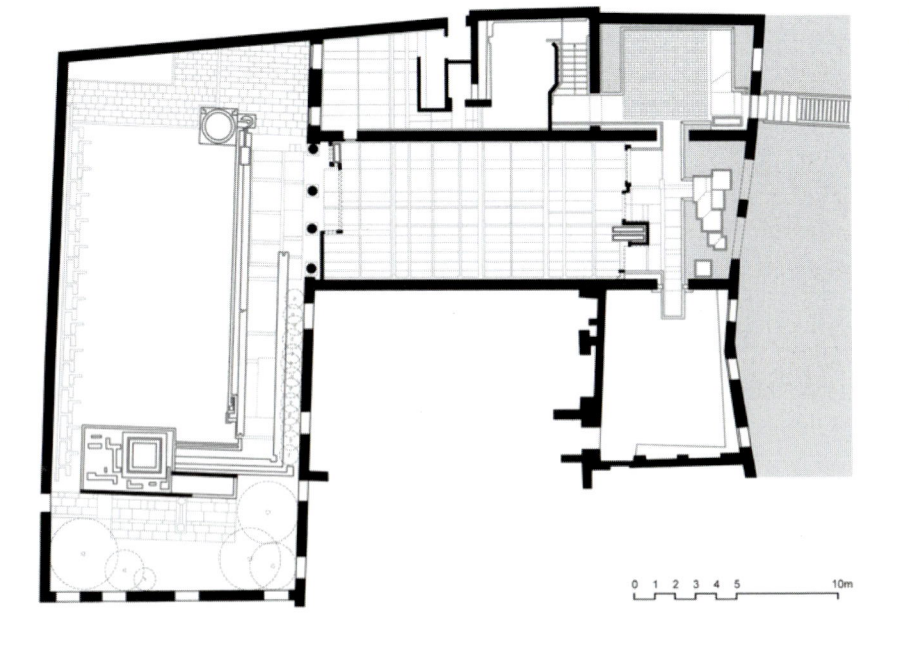

5.18
Querini Stampalia, Venice, ground floor plan

5.19
Querini Stampalia, radiator cabinet

5.20
Radiator in glazed screen and flush lighting set into travertine marble wall

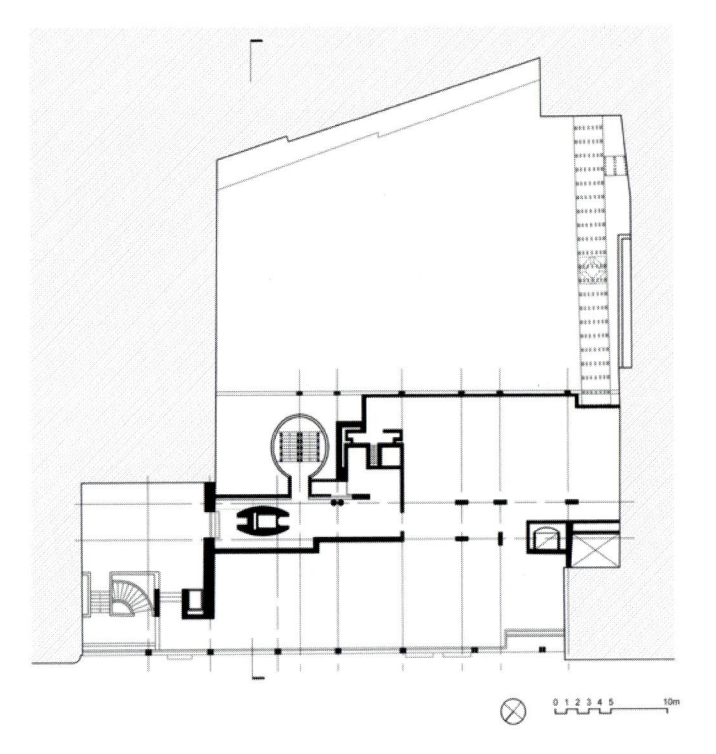

5.21
Banca Popolare di Verona, plan at
+9.70 m. This is the open plan *ufficio
fidi* on the top floor of the building.

Banca Popolare di Verona

The office building is, perhaps, the most ubiquitous building type of the twentieth century. The accommodation of the prosaic functions of commerce and administration has led to the evolution of a technologically based building type, in which utility and consistency are usually given priority over poetry and diversity. Cities throughout the modern world are dominated by these structures providing identical environments for identical functions and representing the triumph of globalisation over local identity. In 1973, Scarpa was commissioned to extend the head office of the Banca Popolare di Verona on a site in the historic centre of the city. Almost inevitably his response was to challenge the conventional assumptions about the modern office building in almost every respect.[21]

Two buildings adjacent to the existing bank in Piazza Nogara were demolished to make space for the extension. The main entrance remains in the existing building and the extension is entered from this by a half level rise up a short staircase, the *servizi speciali per il pubblico*. The floor above this contains the offices of the *Direzione Generale* of the bank and the top floor is the open plan *ufficio fidi*.

The plans show that the building provides both open plan and enclosed offices (Figure 5.21). The structural and spatial organisation is based on a simple layout with a central spine defined by structural columns that also contains vertical circulation by lift. This clear logic is, however, adapted to the specific conditions of the site, where the adjoining walls demand a slight deviation from the orthogonal to accommodate the new structure.

The design of the fenestration rejects the repetition of most modern office buildings in favour of a more specific response to both the context and conditions of the medieval city. On both the northern and southern elevations, to the piazza and the internal cortile respectively, the cellular rooms of the *Direzione Generale* on the middle floor of office space are lit by circular openings in the concrete envelope (Figure 5.22). This window is an instance of Scarpa's method of reinvention and exploration of even the most conventional elements of architecture. The design consists of an unglazed circular opening behind which is a larger rectangular opening containing a glazed timber frame.[22] The inter-reflection of light in the void between the outer façade and the inner frame, and the softness of the rounded marble lining to the circular opening, achieve a transition from the bright exterior to the subdued illumination of the office. Scarpa's sketches clearly explain his intentions. It should be noted that the inner timber window frames contain casement opening lights.

In two places on this floor Scarpa disregards this solution where he lights two small offices at the western end of the façade with frameless projecting glass bays (Figure 5.23). This departure seems to be more a matter of compositional than environmental logic, since these windows are grouped with a corresponding pair to serve the open plan floor below, but the effect of the windows on the quality of illumination of the rooms that they serve was studied carefully in a sketch. Otherwise, on the floor below the *Direzione Generale*, the windows, in both north and south façades, are simple openings with metal frames in the masonry wall, but here they are located tautly in the external plane. On the upper floor the building is crowned by a system of continuous windows that are set behind the external steel structure that supports the roof. Scarpa acknowledges the difference between northern and southern orientations by incorporating a system of individually controlled blinds on the south façade (Figure 5.24).

5.23
Detail of the façade to Piazza Nogara

Throughout the building Scarpa's inventiveness provides an alternative to the standardised office environment. His attention to the detail of fenestration, to the relationship of windows to the space they illuminate, brings diversity and richness to the office environment that is rarely encountered in the standardised solution of the corporate office building. A particular quality of the interior of the Banca Popolare lies in the surface finishes that Scarpa employs. Polished and coloured *stucco lucido* is applied to many surfaces and is particularly associated with elements of vertical circulation – stair and lift enclosures. This is not merely a decorative device since the specular reflections from this conjunction of form and material act to convey light deep into the heart of the building (Figure 5.25).

The modern office building, almost inevitably, has comprehensive systems of heating, cooling and ventilation. Banca Popolare is no exception, but Scarpa's originality of mind allows him to avoid the conventional solutions to the physical incorporation of the systems into the fabric of the building. A number of vertical risers carry services up the building from the basement plant room and a large horizontal duct runs at roof level connecting these to a rooftop plant room (Figure 5.26). The relationship of the structural and environmental systems of the building is given expression in the design of the ceilings at all levels. Unlike the vertical layering of the continuous suspended ceiling found in most modern office buildings, Scarpa establishes a clear horizontal differentiation between the structural and servicing zones. The ceiling plane thereby alternates between exposed concrete structure and plastered surfaces beneath service voids. This organises and disciplines the position of artificial light fittings and air-conditioning grilles (Figure 5.27). As Kenneth Frampton observes:

> The suspended nature of the plaster ceiling is made manifest through its subdivision into fairly large areas by seams that not only impart scale to the expanse of the overall soffit, but also return the eye to the salient points at which the concrete column heads come through the plaster to lie flush with the ceiling.[23]

5.24
Detail of south façade to the courtyard

5.25
Spiral staircase at the junction between the old and new buildings

5.26
Cross-section looking west through the staff staircase. Note the horizontal service duct at roof level.

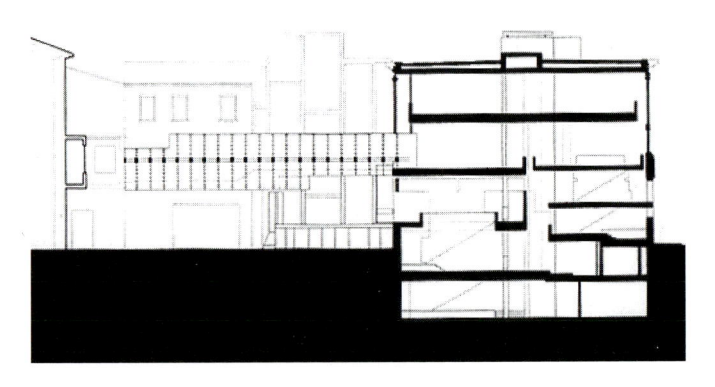

All these buildings demonstrate Scarpa's acute sensibility to the environmental dimension of architecture. This sensibility is founded upon his understanding of the potentiality of the historical precedents, of both vernacular building and the high architecture of Palladio, as models for contemporary design in the climate of the Veneto. Relationships of volume, material, solid-to-void that derive from these are acknowledged and reinterpreted in his deeply satisfying designs. At Possagno, the inspired invention of the convex and concave corner window brings Canova's sculptures to life in a field of natural light that is entirely modern. The transformation of the Castelvecchio links both works of art and the historic building in a collaboration that re-presents and interprets them for a new age. The new services installations at Castelvecchio and at Querini Stampalia show how these may contribute to the historical continuity of ancient buildings by providing modern levels of comfort by frankly expressed means. The addition to the Banca Popolare shows how the environment of commerce may be invested with the same level of invention that is usually reserved for the buildings of cultural institutions.

Speaking in Vienna in 1976, Scarpa said, 'Architecture is a very difficult language to understand – it's mysterious, unlike the other arts … The value of a work lies in its expression – when a thing is well expressed its value is high.'[24]

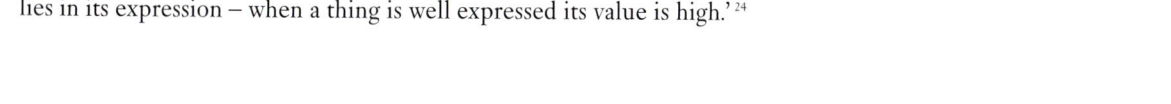

5.27
Cross-section looking west through the staff staircase. Note the horizontal service duct at roof level.

Notes

1   Useful biographies of Scarpa can be found in the following: Sandro Giordano, 'Biographical Profile', in Francesco Dal Co and Giuseppe Mazzariol, *Carlo Scarpa: The Complete Works*, Electa/The Architectural Press, Milan and London, 1986, Sergio Los, *Carlo Scarpa*, Benedikt Taschen Verlag, Köln, 1993, and Giuseppe Mazzariol and Francesco Dal Co, 'The Life of Carlo Scarpa', in Dal Co and Mazzariol, op. cit.

2   Andrea Palladio, *The Four Books of Architecture*, First Book, Chapter XXV, Isaac Ware edition, London, 1738, reprinted with Introduction by Adolf K. Placzek, Dover Publications, New York, 1965.

3   Paul Holberton, *Palladio's Villas: Life in the Renaissance Countryside*, John Murray, London, 1990.

4   Francesco Dal Co, 'The Architecture of Carlo Scarpa', in Dal Co and Mazzariol, op. cit.

5   Sergio Los, op. cit.

6   Boris Podrecca, 'A Viennese Point of View', in Dal Co and Mazzariol, op. cit.

7   This building is comprehensively described and beautifully illustrated in Judith Carmel-Arthur and Stefan Buzas, with photographs by Richard Bryant, *Carlo Scarpa: Museo Canoviano, Possagno*, Edition Axel Menges, Stuttgart/London, 2002.

8   Carlo Scarpa, 'I wish I could frame the blue of the sky', from a recording of a lecture given on 13 January 1976, published in *Rassengna*, *'Carlo Scarpa, Frammenti, 1926/78*, 7 June 1981.

9   Sergio Los, 'Carlo Scarpa – Architect and Poet', in *ptah: architecture design art*, 2001: 2.

10 Carlo Scarpa, op. cit.

11 Sergio Los, op. cit.

12 Ibid.

13 Carlo Scarpa, op. cit.

14 *New Oxford English Dictionary*, Oxford University Press, Oxford, 1998.

15 For the most detailed published description and analysis of this work, see Richard Murphy, *Carlo Scarpa and the Castelvecchio*, Butterworth Architecture, London, 1990.

16 Sergio Los, op. cit.

17 Andrea Palladio, *The Four Books of Architecture*, op. cit.

18 Carlo Scarpa, op. cit.

19 Richard Murphy, op. cit.

20 See Kenneth Frampton, *Studies in Tectonic Culture: The Poetics of Construction in Nineteenth and Twentieth Century Architecture*. MIT Press, Cambridge, MA, 1995, for an analysis of the tectonic qualities of Querini Stampalia.

21 A detailed description of the building (in Italian) may be found in *La Sede Centrale della Banca Popolare di Verona*, Arrigo Rudi and Valter Rossetto (eds), published by Banca Popolare di Verona, 1983.

22 Sergio Los, *Carlo Scarpa*, Benedikt Taschen, Köln, 1993, offers a good account of the design of the fenestration at Banca Popolare.

23 Kenneth Frampton, op. cit.

24 Carlo Scarpa, 'Can Architecture Be Poetry?', in Dal Co and Mazzariol, op. cit.

Essay 6
Architecture of adaptive light
Sigurd Lewerentz

Adaptation

One of the most remarkable attributes of human vision is our ability to see in levels of light that vary from the darkness of a moonless night to the vivid glare of a sunlit summer's day. This phenomenon is known as adaptation and the mechanisms by which it occurs and its implications for building design have been the subject of much study.[1] The construction of a building enclosure inevitably limits the range of illumination that exists under the open sky. The amount of light that enters an interior is determined by the size and position of windows and rooflights and the reflectance of the materials that line internal space. In principle, the range of possibilities is almost infinite, but in common practice empirical conventions impose limits that ensure adequate lighting for practical purposes.

But, as other essays here illustrate,[2] there are many circumstances in architecture where light takes on a more profound role than to sustain practical needs. Writing about the nature of light in Sigurd Lewerentz's designs for the churches of St Mark's at Björkhagen near Stockholm (1956–1964) and St Peter's at Klippan (1962–1966) Colin St John Wilson has observed:

> Instead of the coloured radiance of the Gothic or the dazzling luminous white of the contemporary tradition from Bryggman to Leiviska, we are invited into the dark. Enveloped in that heart of darkness that calls on all the senses to measure its limits, we are compelled to pause. In a rare moment of explanation, Lewerentz stated that subdued light was enriching precisely in the degree to which the nature of the space has to be reached for, emerging only in response to exploration. This slow taking possession of space (the way in which it gradually becomes yours) promotes that fusion of privacy in the sharing of a common ritual that is the essence of the numinous. And it is only in such darkness that light begins to take on a figurative quality – the living light of the candle flame or, as at Klippan, the row of roof lights which forms a Way of Light between sacristy and altar.[3]

This eloquent analysis is, in effect, a poetic description of the mechanism of adaptation. The 'slow taking possession of space' is the outcome of the eye's gradual transfer from the 'cones' of the retina, by which we enjoy bright, daylight vision, to the retinal 'rods', that come into play in low light levels. In a different, but also poetic, interpretation of this process the psychologist Richard Gregory suggests:

> It might be said that moving from the centre of the human retina (cones) to its periphery (rods) we travel back in evolutionary time, from the most highly organised structure to a primitive eye which does no more than detect simple movements of shadows. [4]

A further, and specifically architectural, insight into the poetics of adaptation is offered by Juhani Pallasmaa in *The Eyes of the Skin*, [5] where he writes:

> The eye is the organ of separation and distance, whereas touch is the sense of nearness, intimacy and affection. The eye controls and investigates, whereas touch approaches and caresses. During overpowering emotional states, we tend to close off the distancing sense of vision; we close our eyes when caressing our beloved ones. Deep shadows and darkness are essential because they dim the sharpness of vision, make depth and distance ambiguous and invite unconscious peripheral vision and tactile fantasy.

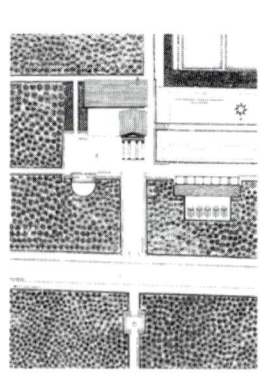

6.1
Resurrection Chapel, planometric projection from the north

Lewerentz made designs for sacred buildings throughout his long life [6] and it may be suggested that the two masterpieces of St Mark's and St Peter's stand in relation to his earlier works in a way that is analogous to the sudden deepening of substance and idiom that occurred in Beethoven's late string quartets. In their specific organisation of form, material and light, and in particular in their appropriation of darkness, these churches are unanticipated in the earlier work, but, on the other hand, the masterly organisation of light to expressive ends is demonstrably present from Lewerentz's earliest projects.

In 1915, Lewerentz, in collaboration with Erik Gunnar Asplund, was awarded first prize in the competition for the extension to Stockholm's South Cemetery at Enskade. Within a landscape that juxtaposes meadow-like open space and deep forest, the architects located a sequence of chapels and other buildings that they executed both in partnership and individually. The first significant building was Asplund's Woodland Chapel, completed in 1920, followed in 1923–1925 by Lewerentz's Chapel of the Resurrection.

Chapel of the Resurrection, Stockholm (1923–1925)

The Resurrection Chapel stands at the southern end of a long axial path that is cut from north to south through the forest (Figure 6.1). The chapel is entered, from the north, through a remarkable detached portico that is slightly rotated in relation to the body of the building. The geometrically regulated interior [7] is orientated east–west. The interior of the chapel is an austere white box, with its wall surfaces articulated by minimally projecting pilasters (Figures 6.2 and 6.3). At the east, a severe baldachino echoes the great portico, before which is placed the bier. The chapel is lit by a three-light window, high in the south wall and precisely aligned to light and model the baldachino and bier (Figure 6.4). As the termination of the journey through the dark forest and the entry through the shaded, windowless northern façade, this warm light has powerful significance. Following the committal ceremony, mourners leave the chapel through a second doorway to the west. Ahlin offers the following description of this sequence:

6.2
Resurrection Chapel, plan

6.3
Resurrection Chapel, section

6.4
Exterior showing south window

> The mourners would wait along the shaded north side. They were then led in through the portal, turning their attention to the east, toward the sunrise. At the ceremony's end they would go out through a low door which opened up on the landscape to the west. Here the ground was sculpted out to a lower level and the pine trees were sparse. Light flooded in, the field of vision was opened out and one's pupils would contract. One's gaze returned to the living.[8]

This analysis reveals Lewerentz precisely manipulating the potential of visual adaptation, from shaded exterior, to controlled, subfusc, directional interior, finally to temporary glare and rapid adjustment to the full light of the forest clearing.

Light is clearly the principal environmental instrument in the chapel. But Lewerentz's sensibility was alert to the importance of both heat and sound. The slightly undulating, grey marble mosaic floor of the chapel conceals a hypocaust-like heating system. Lewerentz described the heating arrangements as follows:

> The chapel is warmed in part by free-standing radiators as well as by a canal system of hollow brick which heats the floor. With regard to this system of canals the finished floor has been made as thin as possible through the use of mosaic stone.[9]

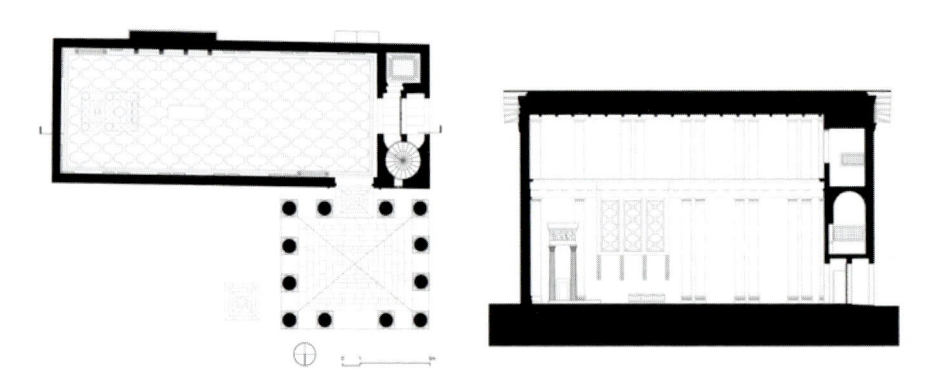

The shallow coffers of the stencilled ceiling serve an acoustic function in diffusing sound and the roof void above has an absorbent layer of cloth and cotton wool, 'To avoid the disturbing sounds of automobiles during speeches and singing'.[10]

6.5
St Mark's, plan

6.6
St Mark's, cross-section

The complex relationship of this building to the conventions of orthodox classicism has been extensively discussed.[11] Viewed from an environmental perspective, it is clearly a work of great originality, in which precise control of quantities and qualities of light lies at the heart of its narrative strategy. The experience of this is unobtrusively, but equally precisely, supported by the thermal and acoustic conditions that Lewerentz realises. The two late churches adopt an entirely different language of form and material, but it may be possible, beneath their differences, to recognise a continuation of the same complex environmental sensibility and, in particular, the same understanding of the scope of visual adaptation in fashioning sacred places.

St Mark's Church, Björkhagen, Stockholm (1955–1964)

In 1955, thirty years after the completion of the Chapel of the Resurrection, Lewerentz won the competition to build St Mark's Parish Church at Björkhagen in the southern suburbs of Stockholm. The site is a small birch wood lying low in relation to the surrounding terrain. Lewerentz's design consists of two buildings, a low wing containing offices connected to the belfry and an L-shaped block in which a series of rooms for parish activities are linked to the church itself. The offices and parish rooms stand opposite each other, defining a courtyard. The principal approach to the building is from the west, drawn onwards, through the birch wood and past the cubic belfry, to the threshold of the courtyard from where the body of the church comes into view.

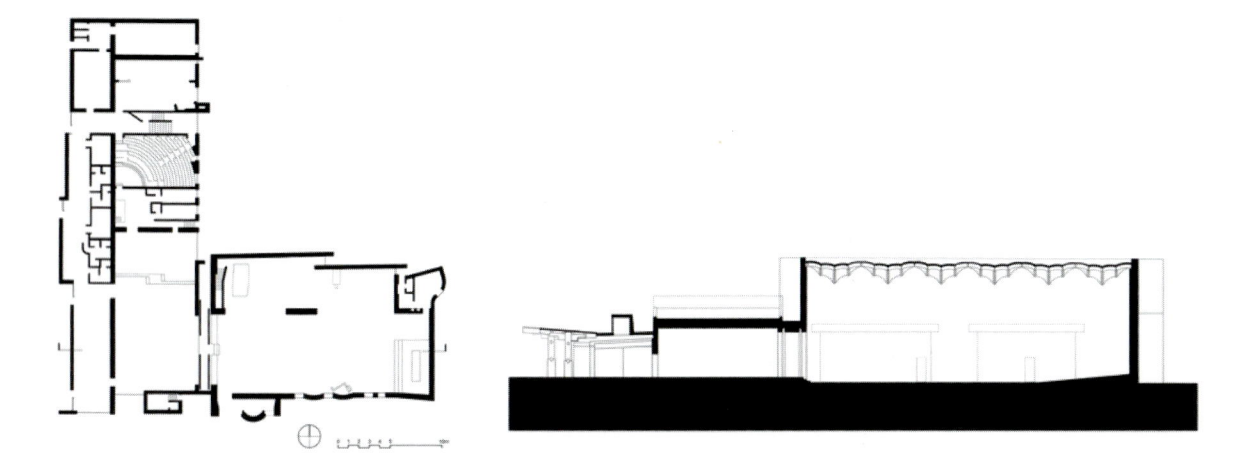

In the intervening decades Lewerentz's work had passed through many stages of evolution.[12] With regard to the specific transformation of Lewerentz's design for sacred buildings, Colin St John Wilson has identified the chapels of St Gertrud and St Knut, built at the Malmö Eastern Cemetery in 1941, as the moment of the 'turn':

> at which Lewerentz spoke out with a voice entirely his own. Up to that time, his invention had gone into the manipulation of a received language, be it neoclassical or, from the time of the 1930 Stockholm Exhibition, Rationalist. But at this point we can speak of a 'turn' or fundamental shift in his work.[13]

St Mark's was the first building in which Lewerentz used brick as the primary material. The interior of the church has walls of fair-faced brickwork and is covered with a series of brick vaults that span, supported by iron beams, from south to north across the plan. The floor is made of clay tiles with inserts of brick. In was here that Lewerentz first adopted the rule of allowing no cut bricks using wide, 'bagged' mortar joints. The church is entered at the south-west corner through a door that is protected by a tall, free-standing brick screen. The plan consists of a nave with a single 'aisle' to the north. Here are the baptismal font, carved from a single block of North Swedish limestone, and the organ, housed in a timber case designed by Lewerentz (Figures 6.5 and 6.6).

Against obvious expectation, Lewerentz compounds the dark materiality of the interior by casting only minimal quantities of daylight upon it (Figures 6.7 and 6.8). The body of the nave is lit through only five openings, all in the south wall. The largest are a pair of windows, separated by a narrow brick pier, that rise from floor level to illuminate the sanctuary. To the west of these are two square openings with high sills and high in the wall close to the entrance is a window that is shaded by the

curved brick screen at the entrance. The 'aisle' is lit by two slots of light that are formed by the positions where the north wall breaks in echelon, casting oblique east light at 'grazing' incidence along the rich texture of the brickwork.

The outcome of this configuration of volume, material and light is a complex field of luminance that highlights specific points in the space, the altar table, the pulpit, font and organ within the low ambience of the whole. Lewerentz's use of frameless sheets of glass, attached to the inner face of the brickwork of the south wall, emphasises the contrast of brightness between outside and inside (Figure 6.9). On entering the church the darkness is first tempered by the presence of the arrays of polished copper and brass light fittings that float in the space. These provide artificial illumination to supplement that from the windows, but their specular surfaces also pick up and inter-reflect light from the windows, adding an additional element to the visual field. Small candelabra and carefully sited spotlights bring yet more diversity of light, as do the glittering gilt and silver of the cross and candlesticks that adorn the altar.

In the north aisle artificial light is used to illuminate both the baptistry and the organ. A glittering brass chandelier hangs above the font, drawing the eye to this significant locus of the church and symbolising the importance of the act of baptism

(Figure 6.10). The timber organ case, in effect a miniature building-within-a-building, receives general light from the high, east-facing window, but is itself a source of light, when the bright light from its music stand floods out into the body of the building (Figure 6.11).

At the conclusion of a service the congregation leaves the church through the sliding timber screen leading to the more brightly lit Fellowship Hall, in a reenactment of the sequence found at the Chapel of the Resurrection.

A particular property of visual adaptation is that the general level of light to which we are adapted determines how and what we see. This means that, at low levels of ambient light, specific objects appear brighter than they would in brighter surroundings.[14] It is precisely this effect that Lewerentz exploits at St Mark's. In the general darkness of the interior the intense patches of natural and artificial light stand out in ever shifting relationships. The space is not merely lit, but becomes a composition of lights. The other significant property of adaptation is the process by which we gradually become adapted to low levels of light. As Gregory explains,[15] so-called 'dark' adaptation takes place in the first few minutes of darkness, but rod and cone cells adapt at different rates. The cones complete their adaptation in about seven minutes, but rod cells continue to adjust for over an hour. This means that the worshipper at St Mark's will gradually perceive more detail of the space as the church service progresses, a powerful metaphor of revelation. This is a continuation of Lewerentz's sensibility to the nature of human sight that was shown in the Chapel of the Resurrection, transformed by the different conditions of weekly worship and by the implications of Lewerentz's new, strikingly original language.

6.10
St Mark's, font with polished brass chandelier

6.11
St Mark's organ

The undisguised raw brick construction of the church led Lewerentz to invent a method for the suspension of the light fittings in which cables span across the space to carry the individual lamps and their electricity supply. Conduits, cables and switches are fixed to the brickwork at just the places they are needed, not as clumsy afterthought, but as essential expression of the materiality of the building. However, while these services are so explicitly displayed, Lewerentz continued to be as discreet about heating and ventilation systems as he had been at the Chapel of the Resurrection. The cavities of the thick enclosing walls of the church accommodate a forced air system that discharges warmth through clusters of open perpends in the brickwork, particularly in the south wall of the nave. These small voids also perform an acoustic function by acting as absorbent cavities to control the reverberation of the otherwise highly reflectant materials. The undulating rhythm of the brick vault will also help the acoustics by diffusing reflected sound, in a similar manner to the shallow coffers of the ceiling at the Chapel of the Resurrection.

So we may see that environmental themes played a major role in the late 'turn' that occurred in Lewerentz's work. The acute sensibility to the function of light in sacred ritual that he evinced at the Chapel of the Resurrection was intensified at St Mark's church by the manner in which he fused natural and artificial light into a rich and original unity. Lewerentz's understanding of the mechanism of visual adaptation, almost certainly intuitive rather than scientific, allows a particular kind of vision in the darkness of the church that reflects and sustains the mystery of religious ritual.

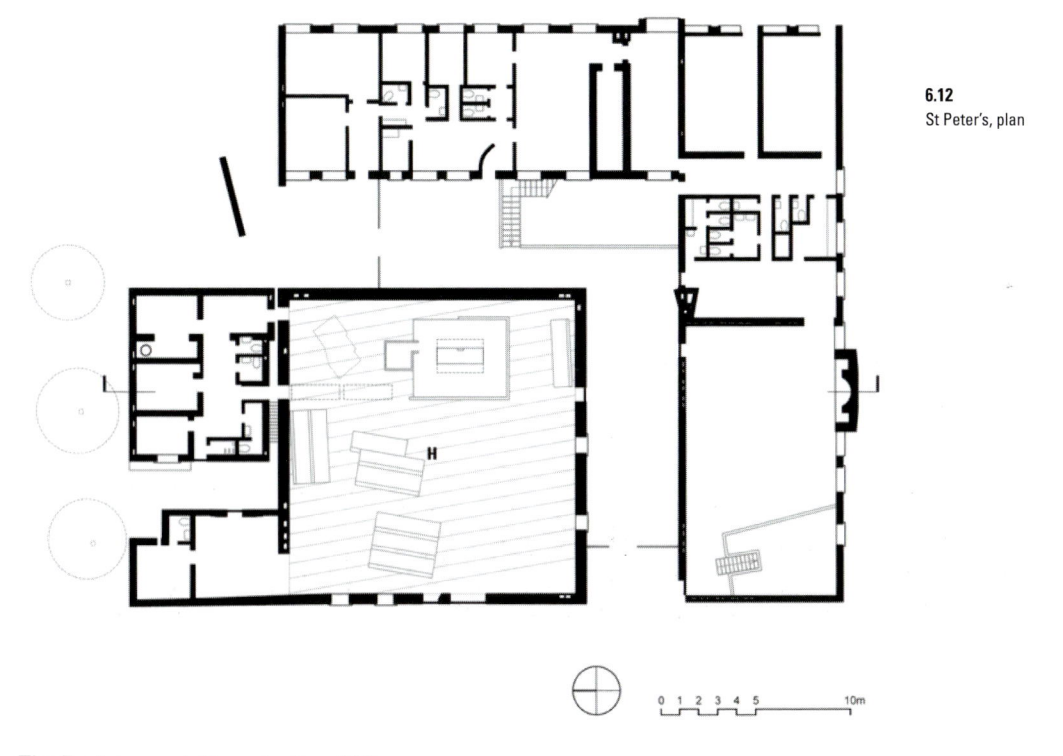

6.12
St Peter's, plan

0 1 2 3 4 5   10m

The Environmental Imagination **136**

St Peter's church, Klippan (1962–1966)

St Peter's church at Klippan near Helsingborg followed soon after St Mark's, when Lewerentz was 78 years old. It, self-evidently, continues the themes first explored at Björkhagen, and most critical opinion regards it as an intensification of these. The plan is, again, extremely simple, but more condensed, with the rectangular block of the church held within the angle of an L-shaped building that houses the parish functions. The church is a precise square in plan, with two small wings projecting from its north side (Figures 6.12 and 6.13). Unlike the aisled plan of St Mark's, the church is a single volume. A brick-vaulted roof, similar to that at Björkhagen, is now oriented east to west and the span is reduced by a secondary steel structure – although that is hardly an appropriate term. Pairs of steel sections make up a T-shaped support that stands at the centre of the space. This holds two transverse beams that carry the vaults. The whole enclosure is made of dark Helsingborg brick, now also used for the floor, which slopes gently from west to east, and is penetrated by even smaller openings than at St Mark's. The square windows, two in the west façade and two facing south, are, in detail, an inversion of those at St Mark's (Figure 6.14). Here the glass is fixed to the external face of the wall with a simple detail of steel plates and mastic pointing. This shift brings the deep brick reveals within the interior and conveys an even more acute sense of the enclosing presence of the walls. But, unlike St Mark's, windows are not the only source of natural light to be found in the church. In another tectonic invention, perhaps even more remarkable than the window detail, Lewerentz constructs a series of rooflight

6.13
St Peter's, cross-section

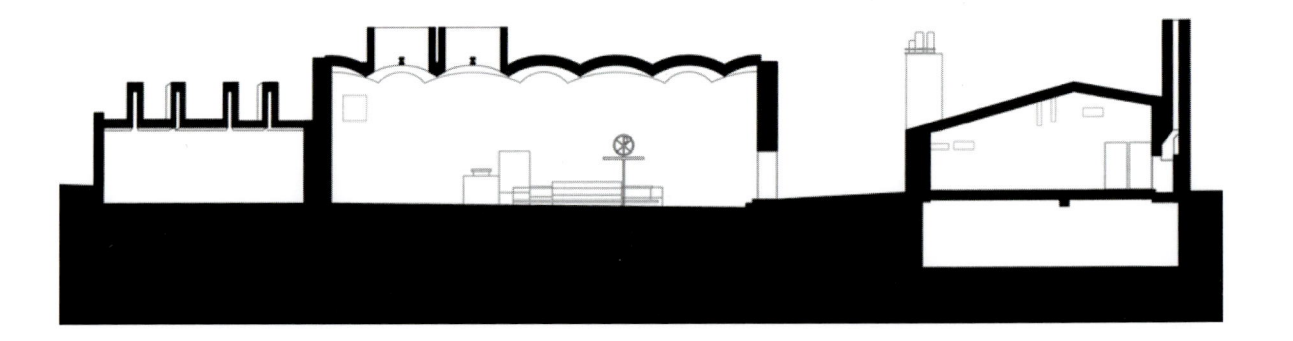

shafts that rise above and illuminate key places. Two of these are in the church; elsewhere they bring light to the wedding chapel and waiting room and to the sacristry. Apparently similar at first sight, they are subtly differentiated in relation to their orientation and materiality.

The relation of windows and rooflights to volume and material means that the interior of the church is even darker than St Mark's (Figure 6.15). The sequence of entrance leads from the north, between the projecting wings of the wedding chapel and the belfry. The actual entrance lies through the dimly lit wedding chapel and begins the process of adaptation that prepares the eye for the broad vista of the church, first seen from the north-west corner. This threshold is illuminated by the paired, square windows in the west wall immediately to the right. These cast light onto the remarkable baptismal font, just to the left, with its giant, white, reflectant seashell suspended, on a black metal frame, over a fissure in the brick floor. Looking beyond the font the visual field is a complex combination of dark brickwork. Here walls, roof and floor are all of Helsingborg brick, against which pools of daylight sparkle from the south-facing windows and are projected down from the rooflights (Figure 6.16). Mapped over this tectonic background, the artificial lighting uses the same polished copper and brass lamps as St Mark's, emitting and reflecting multiple light sources as before. At key points on the east and north walls, pinpoints of naked light from candelabras flicker against the brickwork. The pair of rooflights above the church are glazed horizontally. They are oriented north–south and capture the brightest light of the high sky, projecting it precisely onto the priest's path from the sacristy to the sanctuary, signalling his entrance and the beginning of the service. The orientation means that direct sunlight enters the space at midday. Ahlin suggests that the image of slanting shafts of light from above, which he calls 'bundles of light', was drawn by Lewerentz from the old brick factory at Helsingborg; the source of the bricks for both St Mark's and St Peter's (Figure 6.17). [16]

Light and lighting, darkness and shadow have been essential elements of Lewerentz's work since the earliest projects. At St Peter's, these are brought together in a complex composition that is progressively revealed as the eye adapts and as the light

6.14
St Peter's, exterior from south-west

6.15
St Peter's, detail of south wall showing pools of daylight cast on interior.

6.16
St Peter's, interior showing rooflights

itself changes with the passage of time. In contrast to the brightness that prevails in so much architecture of modern times, the literal and metaphorical darkness of this building uncannily makes the nature of light more apparent.

Lewerentz uses a system similar to that adopted at St Mark's to support and supply the hanging lamps. But here the supporting cables pass from east to west over the intervening steel structure. The space between the sloping brick floor and the brick vaulted roof is thereby vertically layered, primarily by the steel structure, then by the web of dark wires and cables and the polished metal lamps that they support.

The heating system is also a development of that used at St Mark's. A basement plant room beneath the parish block houses the boiler and air-handling units from which air is ducted to the church (Figure 6.18). Air is supplied through ducts to open joints within the brickwork of the walls. Return air is collected high on the north wall.[17] In the parish rooms air is supplied through wide openings in the window sill detail. The warmth to be expected within the building is strongly expressed by the mass of the brick flue, capped by three large chimney pots, that acts as a pivotal element in the composition of the space between the church and the parish building (Figure 6.19).

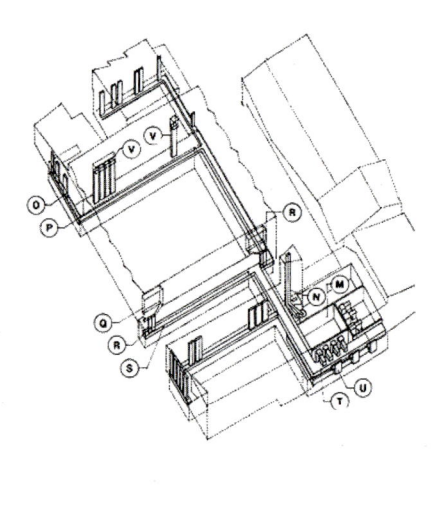

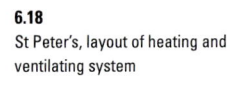

6.17
Interior of the old brickworks at Helsingborg

6.18
St Peter's, layout of heating and ventilating system

Acoustics are the final element of the environmental ensemble at St Peter's. As we found at St Mark's, the darkness of the church is complemented by a calm acoustic that, at first sound, seems at odds with the apparent hardness of the brickwork and the volume of the space. This calm is the result of the acoustic absorption of the cavities in the brickwork and of the diffusing effect of the roof vault. Most important of all is the intermittent sound of baptismal water as it drips from the shell font into the fissure in the brick floor. Quietly insistent, this sound reinforces the inwardness of the church and clinches its separation from the everyday world without.

In 'The Epiphany of the Bindweed', the concluding chapter of his study of Lewerentz, Janne Ahlin describes the architect's last workroom, constructed for him by his landlord, Klas Anselm, at Kävlingevägen 26 in Lund (Figure 6.20):

> It was shockingly simple, even for Lewerentz. With nervous exertion, Anselm had designed something he believed was in the spirit of Lewerentz. The result was a box smelling of tar with plain deal flooring of common pine, walls of asphalt-impregnated woodfiber sheathing, and an aluminium-clad roof. Three acrylic skylights set on the diagonal allowed in light but no view. In one corner was a door which opened onto the garden. His meagre form was warmed by a couple of rusty radiators mounted on the walls. [18]

6.19
St Peter's, boiler house chimney and flues
6.20
Lewerentz's last workroom, Lund, 1970

This captures the combination of simplicity of physical means with complexity of environmental ends that runs through Lewerentz's life's work. We read about dim light refracted by aluminium foil, elemental heat sources directed precisely towards the human form to be warmed, of the smell of tar and the texture of the plain deal floor. This is, at face value, a far cry from the qualities of the three churches that we have been considering here. But they, with their knowing tectonics and sophisticated services installations, strive to reach a similarly direct representation of the human environment. Most particularly they teach us that this environment is a complex overlapping of sensations, of natural elements, particularly of light and mechanical provisions, of all-enveloping warmth in the cold of the northern winter and of subtle acoustics. Quantitatively and qualitatively these sensations change almost imperceptibly as time passes and as our bodies and minds assimilate and respond to the rich ambience of the spaces that Lewerentz created.

Notes

1   See Richard Gregory, *Eye and Brain: The Psychology of Seeing*, Weidenfeld and Nicholson, London, 1966, for a clear exposition of the physiological and psychological bases of adaptation. On the specific implications of adaptation in building science, see R.G. Hopkinson *et al.*, *Daylighting*, Heinemann, London, 1966.

2   See instances in the works of Soane, Essay 1, Kahn, Essay 4, Scarpa, Essay 5, Holl, Siza and Zumthor, Essay 9.

3   Colin St John Wilson, *Sigurd Lewerentz and the Dilemma of Classicism*, The Architectural Association, London, 1989. This essay may also be found in *Architectural Reflections: Studies in the Philosophy and Practice of Architecture*, Butterworth Architecture, Oxford, 1992.

4   Richard Gregory, op. cit.

5   Juhani Pallasmaa, *The Eyes of the Skin: Architecture and the Senses*, Academy Editions, London, 1996.

6   For comprehensive descriptions of Lewerentz's works, see Janne Ahlin, *Sigurd Lewerentz: Architect*, Byggförlaget, Stockholm, 1985, English edition, Byggförlaget/MIT Press, Stockholm and Cambridge, MA, 1987 and Nicola Flora, Paolo Giardiello and Gennaro Postiglione (eds), *Sigurd Lewerentz: 1885–1975*, Electa, Milan, 2001.

7   Hans Nordenström made a detailed analysis of the geometrical order of the entire building in his book *Hus*. Janne Ahlin reproduces this in full in *Sigurd Lewerentz*, op. cit.

8   Ahlin, op. cit.

9   Sigurd Lewerentz quoted in ibid. It is interesting to note that a tall cast-iron radiator placed in the east corner of the south wall, that is visible in early photographs, has been removed.

10 Ibid.

11 Colin St John Wilson, op. cit. and 'Sigurd Lewerentz: The Sacred Buildings and the Sacred Sites', in Nicola Flora, *et al.*, op. cit., and Nicola Flora *et al.*, 'Journey to Italy', in the same work.

12 This is mapped comprehensively by Nicola Flora *et al.*, op. cit.

13 Colin St John Wilson, 'The Sacred Buildings and the Sacred Sites', op. cit.

14 See R.G. Hopkinson *et al.*, op. cit., for a detailed explanation of this.

15 Richard Gregory, op. cit.

16 Janne Ahlin, op. cit.

17 The installation is described in detail by Edward R. Ford in his *The Details of Modern Architecture*, vol. 2: *1928 to 1988*, MIT Press, Cambridge, MA, 1996.

18 Janne Ahlin, 'The Epiphany of the Bindweed', in Ahlin, op. cit.

Part III

Image and Environment

Essay 7
The Sheltering Environment
Fehn and Zumthor

Fundamentals of environment

As we have seen in the early parts of this book, around the middle of the eighteenth century a process began by which the nature of architecture was fundamentally transformed. Progressively the environmental functions of the form and construction of a building were supplemented by the addition of mechanical devices. By various means and in varying measures these brought supplies of heat, light, ventilation and cooling that could not normally be delivered by the unaided building. In the so-called developed world, this had, by the end of the twentieth century, wide consequences for the nature of buildings as physical artefacts, as social containers and as economic instruments. Whatever the purpose, location or scale of a building it would be assumed that it would be an ensemble of structures, materials, spaces and mechanical systems. These would operate in concert to allow year-round, 24-hour-a-day occupation and use.

These are the attributes of almost all of the buildings that are discussed in this book. They almost entirely benefit their purposes, whatever they might be, and they have in many ways added to the experiential and aesthetic qualities of architecture. It would be unusual for a modern building to be conceived that did not make use of the full technical 'kit'. This expectation is almost invariably implicit in the statement of the problem. But occasionally we find circumstances in which the nature of the problem, or its particular interpretation, reopens the question. When this happens we find that it casts a new light – or perhaps rekindles useful old light – on by now conventional and unquestioned assumptions.

At the Gipsoteca Canoviana at Possagno,[1] the cold plaster casts of Canova's works stand in a luminous environment made magical by Scarpa's masterly organisation of the solids and voids of the enclosing envelope and whose thermal qualities are the outcome of the interaction between the building's form and materials and the climate of the Dolomite foothills. By their nature the sculptures are relatively immune to fluctuations in temperature and the visitor, tourist or scholar, must make do with what she or he finds, inhabiting the environment of the sculpture. Scarpa's building has its roots in the environmental traditions of Veneto architecture, reaching back to the strategies of Palladio and beyond. While it is absolutely a building of the twentieth century, it reinterprets and adapts the qualities and properties of the masonry buildings of the region to the particular conditions of its modern purpose. It is simultaneously historic and contemporary. It is this that invests it with its particular effect.

The modern museum is one of the building types that would seem, *prima facie*, to depend on the full repertoire of mechanical systems in order to meet the ever-greater technical demands for the preservation of works of art and historic artefacts. The vulnerability of the materials – wood, canvas, paper, cloth, pigments, lacquers – that these are made from has led to the establishment of extremely precise specifications of levels of illuminance, temperature, humidity and air quality. To satisfy these, the modern museum has, almost always, a sealed envelope within which extensive plant installations and controls quietly whirr away. But there are occasions when these conditions do not apply, when it is possible to return to an architecture of pure enclosure unaided by mechanical systems. When this occurs, architecture re-establishes contact with its fundamental nature. This quality is found in two other significant buildings; Sverre Fehn's Archbishopric Museum at Hamar in Norway (1967–1970) and Peter Zumthor's Shelter for Roman Archaeological Excavations at Chur in Switzerland (1985–1986).

Fehn at Hamar

The architecture of Sverre Fehn demonstrates a particular sensibility to questions of context, in both the physical and cultural senses of the term. In writing about his house at Norrkoping, Fehn also invoked the shade of Palladio:

> In this house I met Palladio. He was tired, but all the same he spoke: 'You have put all the utilities, bath, toilets and kitchen in the center of the house. I made a large room out of it, you know, and the dome with the opening was without glass. When I planned the house it was a challenge toward nature – rain, air, heat and cold could fill the room.'
> 'And the four directions,' I replied. [2]

Fjeld elaborates on the qualities of this house when he writes about its intimate relationship with the 'continuous rhythm of day and night'.[3] These themes of nature, day and night, winter and summer, are expressed and interpreted in diverse ways throughout Fehn's work. This is particularly shown in the Nordic Pavilion at the Venice Biennale site, where a structure of disarming simplicity provides a setting for the display of works of art, finely tuned to the late summer climate of Venice and to the unique physical presence of a fine existing tree. Concrete structure and fibreglass roofing are organised, with precision and poetry, to form a canopy to provide shade from the heat of the sun and shelter from the occasional rain of the season. That is all there is. It is purely a shelter, simultaneously primitive and sophisticated.

The issues at the Archbishopric Museum at Hamar (1967–1970), on the shore of Lake Mjosa, two hours north of Oslo, were quite different, but were addressed with a consistency of thought that produced a necessarily different, but equally appropriate outcome. The ruins of a fourteenth-century bishop's manor have been

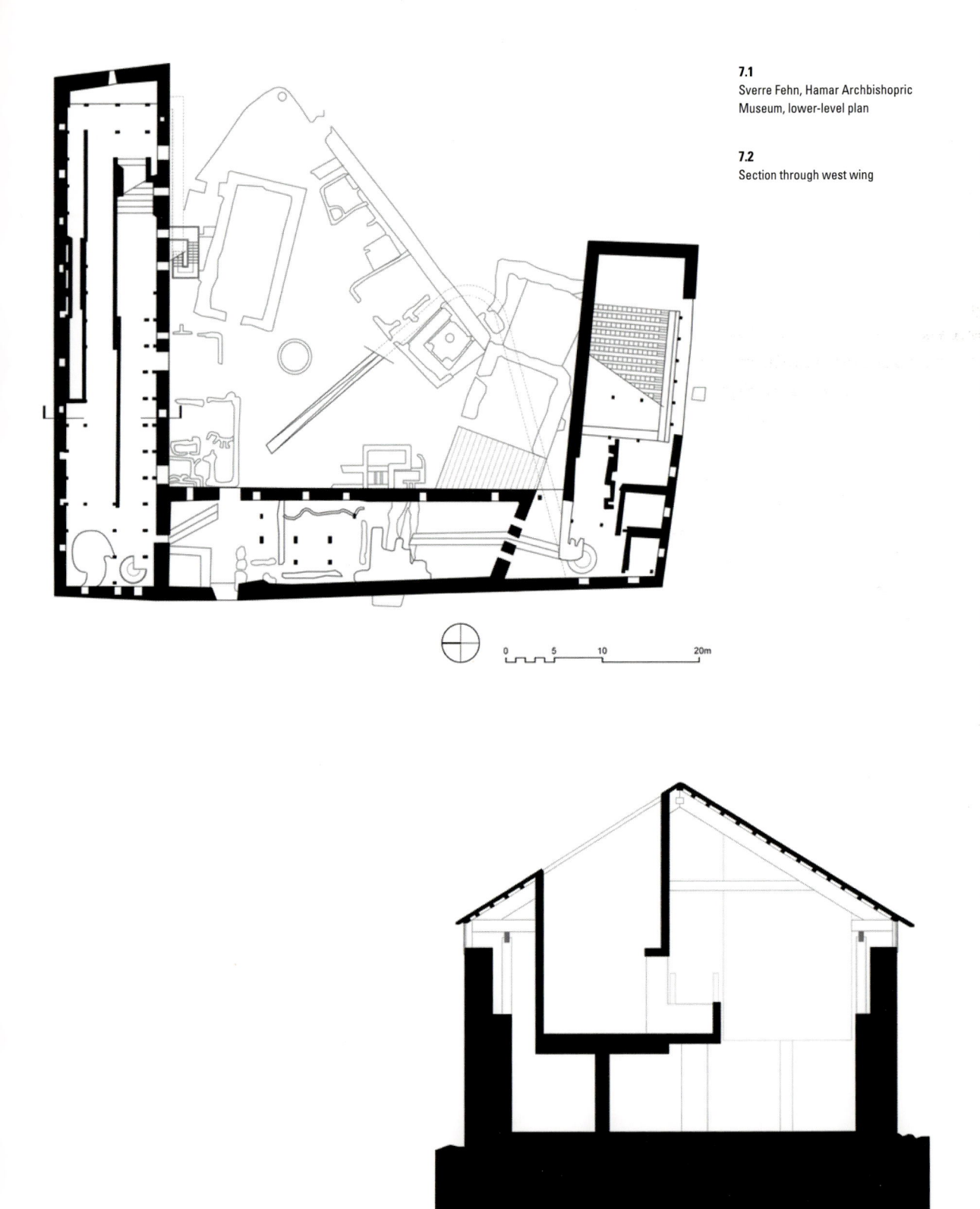

7.1
Sverre Fehn, Hamar Archbishopric
Museum, lower-level plan

7.2
Section through west wing

transformed into a museum that records and represents the history of the site and displays a collection of historic artefacts from the surrounding region. Fehn juxtaposes new structures of concrete, timber and glass with the found remains of the manor house in a way that absolutely declares the modernity of the one and antiquity of the other (Figures 7.1 and 7.2). There is no attempt to restore the old fabric; it is a visible record of its six centuries of construction, occupation and decay. The interventions enclose, surround and inhabit the remains and thereby enter into a rich relationship with them. Concrete ramps, platforms and rooms-within-rooms order the route in and through the museum and the presentation of the artefacts. A timber structure, tiled roofs and traditional boarded cladding stand clearly separated from the original stone walls. The building is completed with an array of metal-framed glazed structures and sheets of frameless glass, fixed to the face of the masonry, that complete the last degree of enclosure[4] (Figure 7.3).

Within the topography of the ancient structure and its modern additions Fehn fashions a complex and compelling environment. The principal instrument of this is light. Working with the given condition of the existing fabric, he manipulates the distinctions between north and south light, top light and side light, fully formed apertures and caesurae between old and new to conjure a whole series of conditions. These literally and metaphorically illuminate the journey through the museum and the objects that are displayed. Fehn also makes judicious use of artificial light, not as a mere night-time substitute for daylight, but as a specific element bringing its own qualities to the environment.

There are three distinct locations for display. The first is the mezzanine of the south wing in which precious objects are housed in spotlit showcases. The large space of the north wing, in which a free-standing concrete structure accommodates a collection of folk art and agricultural implements, is top-lit by glass tiles set into the north-facing slope of the new roof and side-lit through surviving window openings in both north and south faces (Figure 7.4). Here there is a combination of relatively generalised illumination of the principal volume and specific locations of artefacts in relation to light sources, as in the setting of glass vessels in the deep reveals of the south-facing windows (Figure 7.5).

It is in the west wing that the design is most intense. Here the original fabric is more fragmented and its archaeology is most visible (Figure 7.6). This fabric is in effect the prime exhibit. All the elements of Fehn's strategy are brought into play: the

7.3
East face, showing glass skins and lean-to structure

7.4
North wing upper level

7.5
South-facing window in north wing

timber-framed structure of the roof, the concrete of the ramp and three enclosures and the glass skins and structures that sail over the openings in the masonry. Light flows through the jagged outlines of the ruined walls and its projection into the interior is, as Fehn has said,[5] a kind of representation of the building's history. The warm tones of the timber roof hover above the cool grey of the original stone and the concrete of the ramp and the three small chambers. These are capped with glazed ceilings that receive light through glass tiles in the roof above. The exhibits are individually lit by artificial light sources that model and dramatise them within the uniform field of the daylight (Figure 7.7).

The manner in which the play of ancient and modern fabric is used to create the unique qualities of the museum and settings for the artefacts that it contains, is one of the most telling examples of environmental poetics in late twentieth-century architecture. Fehn works purely with the physical tissue of architecture in interpreting and consolidating the essence of the site and its content. He works almost exclusively with the environmental material of the past, organising climate and fabric in making a place that is outside conventional time. Fjeld has observed: 'The building is a reflection of time through material. The nature of both the new and old construction, the natural colour of wood, concrete and stone, are a complement, thus no age favours another.'[6]

7.6
West wing looking south

7.7
Medieval crucifixion, artificially lit beneath glazed roof

The museum is open to the public in the summer months, from May to September. For the remainder of the year it stands as a simple shelter for its contents. With the exception of the south wing, the exhibition spaces are unheated. They simply provide primary protection from the elements, but no more. The more delicate exhibits in the south wing are served and preserved by an electric underfloor heating system. These thermal arrangements are less physically manifest than the illumination of the building, but they are an equal part of an absolutely consistent environmental philosophy. The fabric of the building simply stands as a shelter from the natural climate. In winter it keeps out the snow and wind, but the temperature within falls close to that outside. The cold is matched by the dark of the northern winter. In summer the temperature rises and the visitor moves around the dynamically lit interior passing from zones of relative brightness and warmth to darker and cooler places as the route winds in and out and up and down.

A note should be added concerning the auditorium in the south wing. The rake of seating rests upon a concrete structure that stands detached from the walls of the enclosure. The space is lit by large south-facing window that is sheltered from the glare of the sun by a stand of fine trees. Louvred blinds provide blackout when needed. The roof structure supports auditorium and stage lighting, in the manner of many modern auditoria. Ventilation and heating are provided by a discreet mechanical system that declares its presence by a louvred air intake structure that stands before the window.

Zumthor at Chur

At Chur in Switzerland, Peter Zumthor has made a building that also adopts the fundamentals of the architectural shelter. In 1985–1986, he built a protective housing over the excavated remains of two Roman buildings and a fragment of a third. In Zumthor's own words:

> [the building] was conceived as a kind of abstract reconstruction of the Roman volumes: a lightweight framework of walls, made of timber lamella which admit light and air, [it] exactly follows the Roman outer walls, thus producing a package-like effect which gives a visible form to the location of the Roman buildings in today's city landscape. The spaces inside the shell refer to Roman interiors … mellow zenithal light enters through black skylights. Inside the building, the sounds of the town penetrate the lamella structure of the walls. Enclosed in historical space, one senses the sounds of the 20th century city, the position of the sun, and the breath of the wind.[7]

The form of the building could hardly be simpler (Figures 7.8 and 7.9). Its timber-framed volumes are directly mapped onto the remains of the three Roman buildings; one consisting of two bays, one of a single bay and, finally, a triangular sliver encloses the fragment of the third. The cross-section is a direct vertical development of the plan. The timber-framed structure rises to support a zinc-clad roof through which three welded steel rooflights are cut, whose internal surfaces are painted matt black.

     The building is found in a semi-industrial zone, at the foot of a north-facing slope and close to the centre of the city. To the north is a street and modern buildings and to the south a tiny meadow of grasses and wildflowers (Figure 7.10). The entrance is from the east through an enigmatic, cantilevered steel porch. Once inside, the visitor traverses the interior on a steel bridge that spans each space from east to west. From this, cantilevered stairs lead down to the Roman floor level.

7.8
Peter Zumthor, Shelter for Roman Remains, Chur, ground plan

7.9
Cross-section looking east

7.10
South face from the meadow

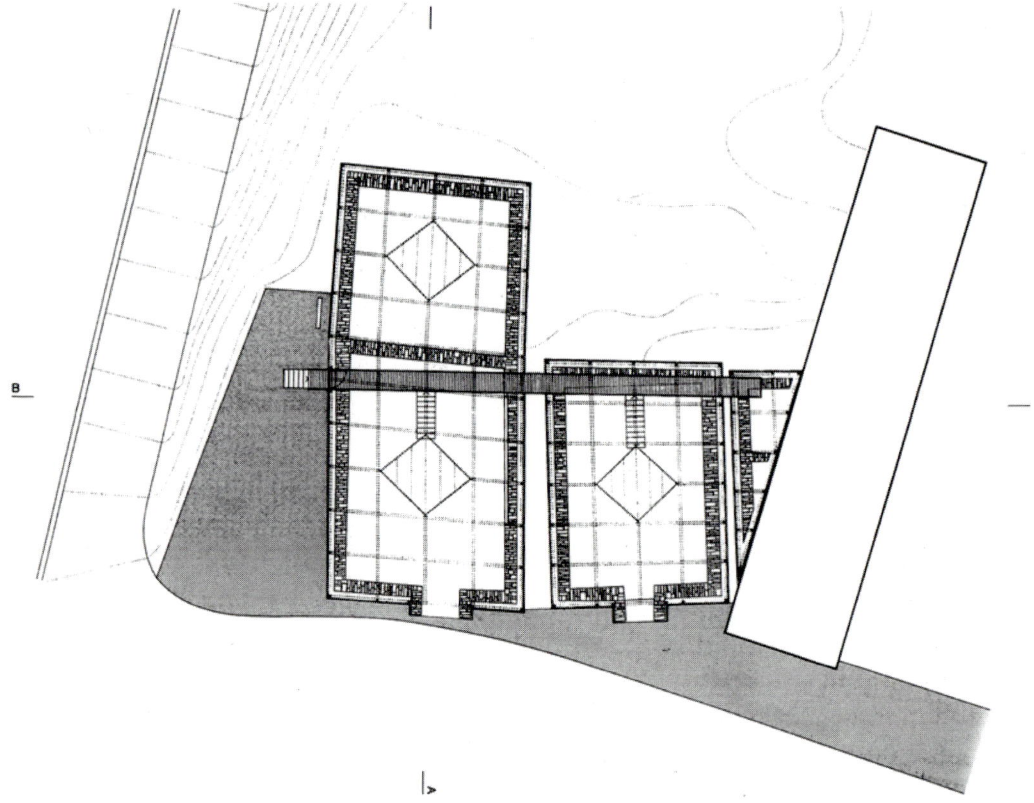

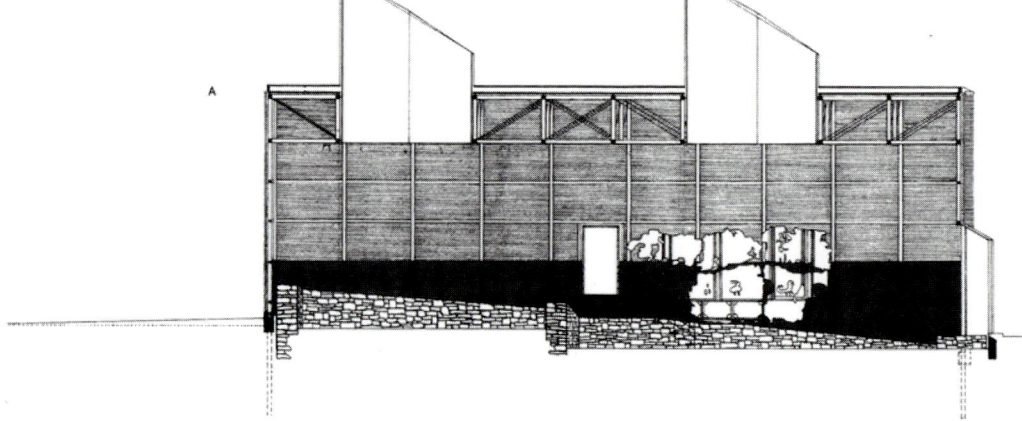

The skylights are cut to slope to the north and these flood the interior with strongly directional light from above, set against diffuse illumination that enters through the lamella of the walls. The effect of this contradicts the expectations that are suggested by the subfusc materiality of the exterior. The rooflights are the primary source of natural light, but, as Zumthor has observed, light also enters by inter-reflection through the warm timber of the lamella. The envelope thus becomes a diffuse and magical light source, neither opaque nor transparent, neither wall nor window. The effect is to invest the space with a surrounding glow within which the stronger zenithal illumination is tempered and focused (Figure 7.11). The defining walls of the Roman remains are set against black cloth backdrops that absorb the light and, by contrast, make the ancient stones luminous. Under bright sunlight the black painted interiors of the rooflight enclosures appear brightly reflectant. Looking to the north they are patterned by shadows cast by the glazing bars and to the south they glow with diffuse light (Figures 7.12 and 7.13).

The enclosure to the street is penetrated by two black metal-clad window openings that mark the location of the entrances to the Roman buildings. These allow passers-by to glimpse the interior and, at night, they may turn on the light of an array of suspended metal lamps by pressing a switch mounted on a stainless steel post. From the interior the windows strongly frame a prospect of the ordinary world outside (Figure 7.14). The louvred skin is opaque from most points within the building, but at the point where the bridge is adjacent to the envelope at the southern edge of the second chamber, a stratified glimpse of the meadow appears (Figure 7.15).

Apart from these specific and precisely calibrated points of contact, the interior is disconnected visually from the exterior. It does, however, establish connections that are atmospheric and acoustic. The permeable skin is a technical device to provide natural ventilation and it achieves this effectively. But it is also the source of air movements that transport the scents and sounds of the exterior. Here city and countryside meet. Industrial noise and bird song merge and a palpable, gentle sun-warmed breeze of a spring day flows into the cool interior.

One of the paragraphs of Peter Zumthor's essay, 'A Way of Looking at Things'[8] is entitled 'Chinks in sealed objects'. The argument concerns the significance of the joint in building construction, 'Details express what the basic idea of the design requires at the relevant point in the object: belonging or separation, tension or

7.11
Interior of large chamber looking south, showing Roman walls set against black fabric background

7.12
Skylight looking north with cast shadows of glazing bars

7.13
Skylight looking south showing diffuse illumination

lightness, friction, solidity, fragility.' But the idea of the 'chink' in the 'sealed object' also operates in considering the environmental qualities of this building. The idea of the sealed envelope is a very recent development in the technical repertoire of architecture. It depends on the capability, first to achieve air-tight junctions between components and, then, to deliver, of necessity by mechanical means, the well-tempered environment that technical function requires. Sheet materials, synthetic gaskets and mechanical plant, the products of the industrialisation of construction, make this possible, often to useful effect. But before this all buildings were to some degree permeable. This was a consequence of the materials from which they were made and of the methods by which they were assembled. Timber construction is, of its nature, an assembly of chinks and is inherently permeable.

Achleitner has suggested that the shelter for the Roman remains might have its roots in memories of the old drying barns found in the Graubünden countryside surrounding Chur.[9] This is highly plausible, but Zumthor has commented: 'If a design works only out of tradition and what is already there, repeating that which the site presents, the confrontation with the world, the feeling of contemporaneity is missing for me.'[10]

The point at issue in this essay is that giving priority to the building enclosure over mechanical systems as the primary instrument of 'climate modification', 'environmental control' – or whichever of these contemporary clichés one chooses to apply to this fundamental purpose of building – re-establishes contact with deep themes of architecture. The works of Scarpa, Fehn and Zumthor, different from each other in many ways and located in very different cultural and physical contexts, all arrange the elements of material, form, construction, solid and void to make buildings that are alert to the specific conditions of their locations, appropriate to their contents and, most significantly, original. In this, they help to challenge the received wisdom that modern architecture is inevitably and primarily a technological enterprise.

7.14
View to street through north window

7.15
View of meadow through lamella

Notes

1   See Essay 5, 'Carlo Scarpa: "I wish I could frame the blue of the sky".'

2   Sverre Fehn, cited in Per Olaf Fjeld, *Sverre Fehn: The Thought of Construction*, Rizzoli International Publications, New York, 1983.

3   Per Olaf Fjeld, op. cit.

4   The overall topography of the project is illustrated in Christian Norberg-Schulz and Gennaro Postiglione, *Sverre Fehn: Opera completa*, Electa, Milan, 1997. English edition, Monacelli Press, New York, 1997. An extended interpretation of the building may be found in Per Olaf Fjeld, op. cit.

5   Sverre Fehn speaking in *Architect Sverre Fehn: 4 Buildings*, video recording, Spinning Globe Studio, 1997.

6   Per Olaf Fjeld, op. cit.

7   Peter Zumthor, *Peter Zumthor Works: Buildings and Projects 1979–1997*, Lars Müller Publishers, Baden, Switzerland, 1998.

8   Peter Zumthor, 'A Way of Looking at Things', in *Thinking Architecture*, Birkhäuser, Basel, Boston, Berlin, 1999.

9   Friedrich Achleitner, 'Questioning the Modern Movement', in *Architecture and Urbanism: Peter Zumthor*, Extra Edition, February 1998, A+U Publishing, Tokyo.

10 Peter Zumthor, 'From Passion for Things to the Things Themselves', *Thinking Architecture*, op. cit.

Essay 8

The art museum: art, environment, imagination
Moneo, Siza, Caruso St John, Zumthor

Tradition and transformation

The art museum is one of the most significant institutions in modern culture and has, throughout its history, enjoyed a close and mutually influential relationship with architecture. In his encyclopaedic, *A History of Building Types*,[1] Pevsner locates the beginning of art collection, in its modern meaning, in the Italian Renaissance and proposes that the first 'special setting' for the display of antiques was Bramante's open cloister adjacent to Innocent VIII's Belvedere Pavilion in the Vatican, dated about 1508. This was quickly followed, throughout Europe, by the construction of buildings specifically for the display of statuary. As a typical example Pevsner illustrates Scamozzi's long gallery at Sabbioneta (1583–1590). In addition to sculpture, paintings were also collected and special rooms for their display were commonplace in palaces and country houses throughout Europe during the seventeenth century. By the beginning of the eighteenth century the museum had become a specialised building type, separate from the house, and soon after collectors began to open their museums to the public, creating the conditions of the modern institutional museum that was to emerge at the end of the eighteenth century and to flourish in the nineteenth. At this time the museum became increasingly specialised as distinctions between categories of knowledge – art, science, natural history and so forth – were increasingly institutionalised. As a consequence of this process, the *art* museum acquired particular architectural characteristics that derived from its purpose to display works of art, increasingly collections of paintings to a wider public.

In Essay 1 we identified Soane's Dulwich Picture Gallery (1811–1814) as one of the first buildings to be constructed specifically for the presentation of paintings to the public. There the relationship of the work of art, the viewer and the rooflight – the primary agent of display – lies at the heart of the design. The cross-section with, in its original form, the gallery walls illuminated by the vertical glazing of the monitor rooflights is an exact analogue of the problem. The picture 'sees' the light and is thereby rendered visible to the viewer, but the light is outside the viewer's field of view, thus avoiding glare in the field of vision. This set of geometrical relationships were quickly established as the basis for the design of the art museum and can be traced throughout the subsequent history of the building type in the nineteenth and twentieth centuries. Just in relation to other buildings that appear in the present book, Le Corbusier's suspended 'Lighting Galleries' at Tokyo are a variant on this theme – although Mies van der Rohe conspicuously eschews any reference to the daylighting tradition at the National Gallery in Berlin.[2] Louis Kahn, with his insistence that 'light is the theme', is very evidently located in this lineage. This is absolutely clear at Kimbell, where the top-lit vaults are a geometrical transformation of the Dulwich section, calibrated to the light of Texas and to the late twentieth-century's notions of the necessity to control the illumination of pictures. The Mellon Center's grid of zenithal rooflights stretches the Soanian model towards its limits, but, after the superimposition of louvres above and diffusing membranes below, the result still preserves the essential qualities of the original model.[3]

By the latter decades of the twentieth century, art museum design was becoming dominated by concern for the conservation of the works on display, even at risk of rendering their display difficult. Uncontrolled exposure to high levels of light had been proved to cause irreversible damage to colour pigments and the effect of this was to look for ways to reduce both light levels and duration of exposure, perhaps a retrospective validation of Mies' artificially lit basement at Berlin. As a small aside it is worth noting the paradoxical – perhaps more appropriately 'contradictory' – strategy adopted by Robert Venturi in the Sainsbury Wing of the National Gallery in London, where an explicit *homage* to Soane and Dulwich is cocooned within a wrapping of machinery for environmental control, creating the illusion, but hardly the reality of natural light.[4]

Many recent designs have continued to apply the forms and devices of the daylit tradition while adapting these to meet the demands of conservation. The art museum designs of Renzo Piano are a consistent demonstration of the tradition's continuing validity and vitality in projects such as the Menil Collection at Houston (1982–1986), the Cy Twombly Gallery (1993–1995) also at Houston and the Beyeler Foundation near Basel (1994–1997). At Fort Worth, adjacent to Kahn's Kimbell Museum, Tadao Ando's Museum of Modern Art (1997–2002) adopts the linear discipline of the clerestory-lit gallery space for its upper floor, but with such exaggeration of protective overhangs to render these rooms, for all practical purposes, permanently artificially lit.

But, alongside the persistence of tradition, there have been a number of important, recent designs that have seized the opportunity fundamentally to reconsider the nature of the art museum. In most cases the essence of these new directions may be found, to a significant extent, in new interpretations of the issue of the museum environment. The present essay examines a number of these.

The Pilar and Joan Miró Foundation, Palma, Mallorca (1989–1992)

8.1
Rafael Moneo, Fondación Miró, Palma, Mallorca, plan at entrance level

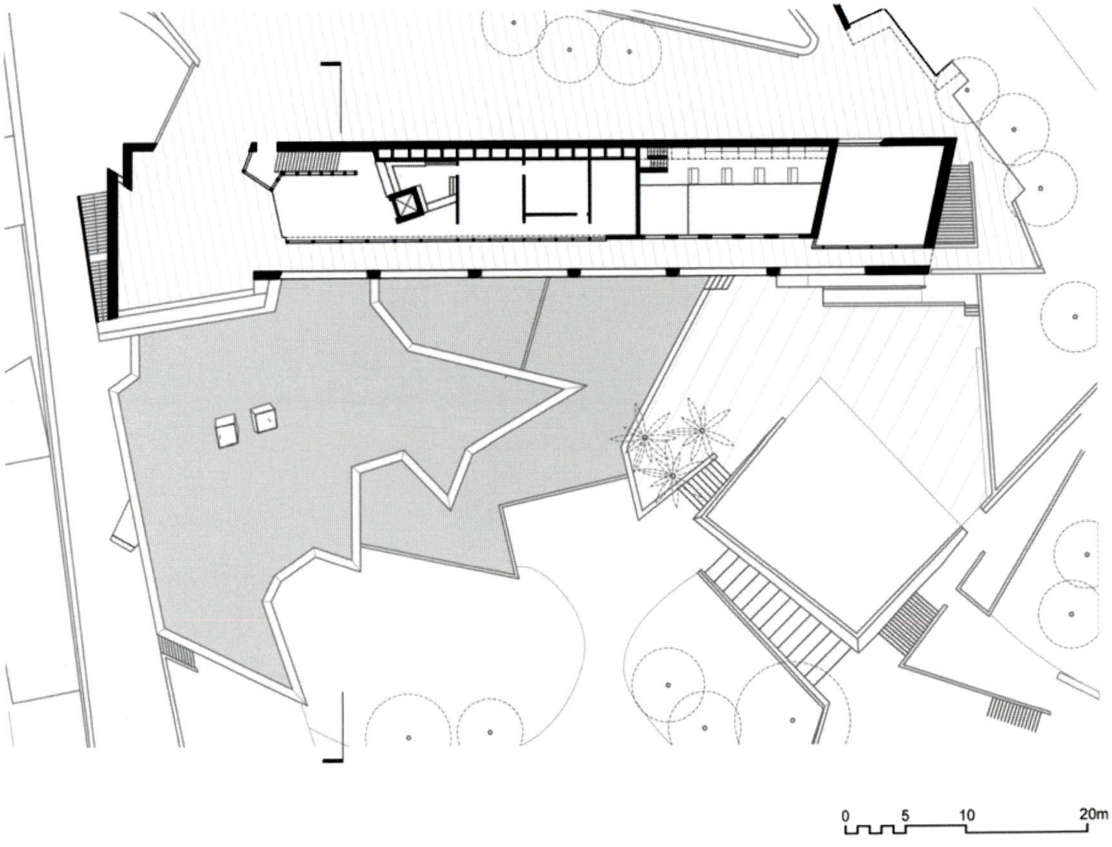

The Pilar and Joan Miró Foundation at Palma, Mallorca, was established in 1981 when Miró and his wife donated his studios and the works that they contained to the City of Palma. In 1989 the Foundation commissioned Rafael Moneo to build a further building on the site at Son Abrines. This accommodates a library and auditorium, along with ancillary functions, such as administration offices, a shop and a cafeteria. There is a temporary exhibition gallery and a major place for the display of Miró's works (Figures 8.1–8.3).

The site is a south-facing slope lying below Son Abrines, Miró's original house and studio, and the studio that was built for him between 1954 and 1956 by Josep Lluis Sert. This situation allows the building to sit unobtrusively in its context and to exploit the special qualities of the bright southerly light. The entrance to the building is through open logia formed in a two-storey, east–west oriented, linear pavilion. This frames a dramatic view of the sea seen across the water-covered rooftop of the principal gallery space – the so-called 'star space' – that lies below, extending into and defining the sculpture-filled garden.

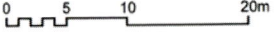

0   5   10   20m

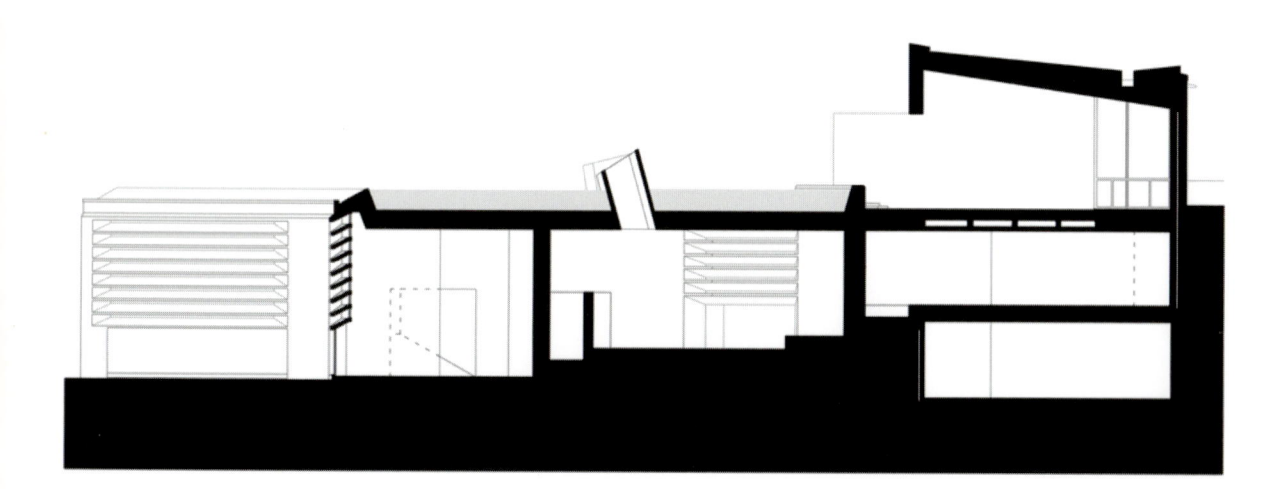

8.2
Cross-section looking west

8.3
Exterior looking west

The relation of interior and exterior is complex and precisely controlled, conditioned significantly by the intrusions into the surroundings of the site that have occurred since Miró moved there in 1956, as suburban development has progressively encroached. Moneo has written:

> the ... building reacts with energy to the hostility of the environment. The countenance of the star-shaped volume is like a fort, ready to defend itself against supposed enemies on the horizon. Its sharp edges cut critically into the cityscape – as if one were seeing an abandoned bulwark – the gallery's volume ignores its surroundings, or better, responds to the neglect and disregard implicit in the constructions on the once attractive hillside ... The Foundation resists, confronts or ignores its environment. For this reason the windows jut out, framed in concrete diaphragms, in order to free us from the lamentable urban story outside. Only one single window is low enough to allows us to have any contact with the garden, upon which our eyes inevitably settle their gaze.[5]

From the entrance loggia a staircase descends to a lower foyer from which all of the principal spaces of the building open up. In the present discussion it is the exhibition space that most concerns us. We already understand something of Moneo's intense and highly specific reaction to the surrounding *environment*. In this case the term refers ironically to the brutal human interventions into the landscape, rather than the climatic context that is our principal concern here. The effect is to render this an intensely internalised building whose external form – 'like a fort' – takes its cues from the topography, both natural and man-made, rather than from any abstract and idealised notions about the display of works of art. But the nature of Miró's work is such that it provokes an original and striking interpretation of both the topography and the environment of the art museum:

> The gallery's interior, we might say, endeavours to draw close to its content, the work of Miró – a work that has always celebrated liberty and life – and presents itself as a fragmented and inapprehensible space, able to create a spatial atmosphere true to the spirit of Miró's painting ... [T]he design has deliberately fled from any repetition, from any series or parallelism ... Our desire is that the paintings within will feel at home, and will float ungraspably in the atmosphere of the hall, itself so difficult to apprehend.[6]

Here is a 'programme', if that is an appropriate term for such a statement, which manifestly rejects the generalisations of the conventional art museum, in either

its technical brief or its conventional architectural interpretation. Generalities are replaced by a specific response to the nature of the art. Consequently, the questions of form, of material, of illumination, are fundamentally reconsidered, 'the design has … fled from any repetition, from any series or parallelism.' – precisely the characteristics of the conventional gallery. The aim is 'atmosphere', a term that we have met earlier in exploring the terminology of the architectural environment,[7] and which is a more appropriate expression of Moneo's intentions.

At first encounter, the 'hall' is, in Moneo's term 'ungraspable' (Figure 8.4). It offers none of the familiar clues of repetitive, visible structure or of the obvious devices of environmental management. In their place we encounter a layered and descending territory within which art works, paintings and sculpture, are disposed in relation to each other, grouped by virtue of medium, material and size. Gradually, however, another kind of order becomes apparent as the eye and mind adapt. Illumination is both natural and artificial. Daylight enters through tilted shafts, cut through the rooftop pond, a strongly directional opening in the west wall, devised to admit light but not view, and a screen of alabaster that occupies almost the whole of the faceted southern wall, behind a system of fixed concrete louvres that soften the harshest midday sun (Figure 8.5). Beneath this, clear glazed openings bring views of the garden, but precisely edit the visibility of the wider surroundings of the building (Figures 8.6 and 8.7). Quite straightforward, adjustable spotlights fixed directly to the concrete ceiling provide artificial light. These allow adjustments to be made, as the exhibition is rearranged from time to time. Against this setting the works of art are grouped and then regrouped as the visitor moves around the space, following the alternative routes that are offered.

As Carlo Scarpa's Gipsoteca Canoviana shows,[8] the design of a museum devoted to the work of a single artist is clearly a different problem than one for the display of a generalised collection. Knowledge of the works to be displayed allows a specific response to their character. This permits, perhaps demands, a break from the dominant typological tradition of art museum building.

In writing about his design for the Sainsbury Wing of the National Gallery in London, Robert Venturi drew a distinction between *invention* and *convention*, coming down in favour of the latter as the basis of his scenographic, Soane-influenced design.[9] Moneo, on the other hand, seizes the opportunity to break with convention and to bring his powers of invention to bear on the reinterpretation of the nature of the art museum as he responds to the site and context at Son Abrines and to the nature of Miró's art. His description of the building concerns itself with his responses to the negative qualities of the surroundings and the positive attributes of Miró's paintings and sculptures. The building works with topography and orientation, form and material, opacity, translucency and transparency, natural and artificial light, fabric and plant – all the elements of environmental management – to create a new and individual setting for art and, hence, to further the evolution of the architecture of the art museum.

8.6
Alabaster screen and glazed opening

8.7
External detail of south façade

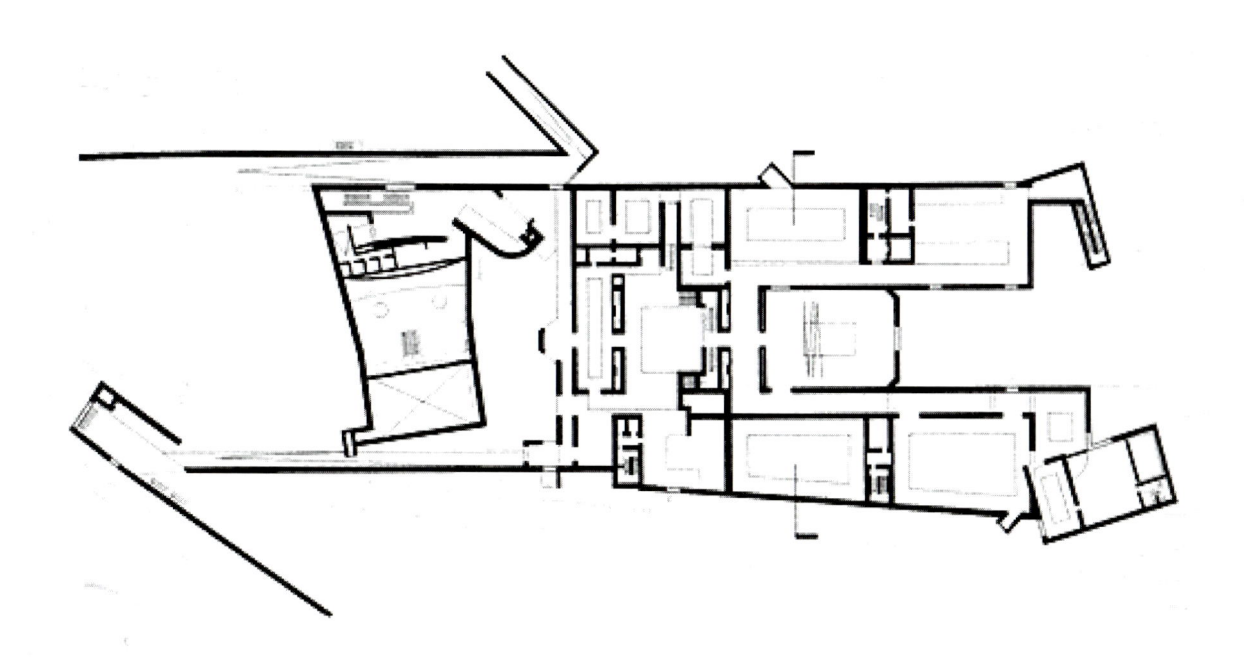

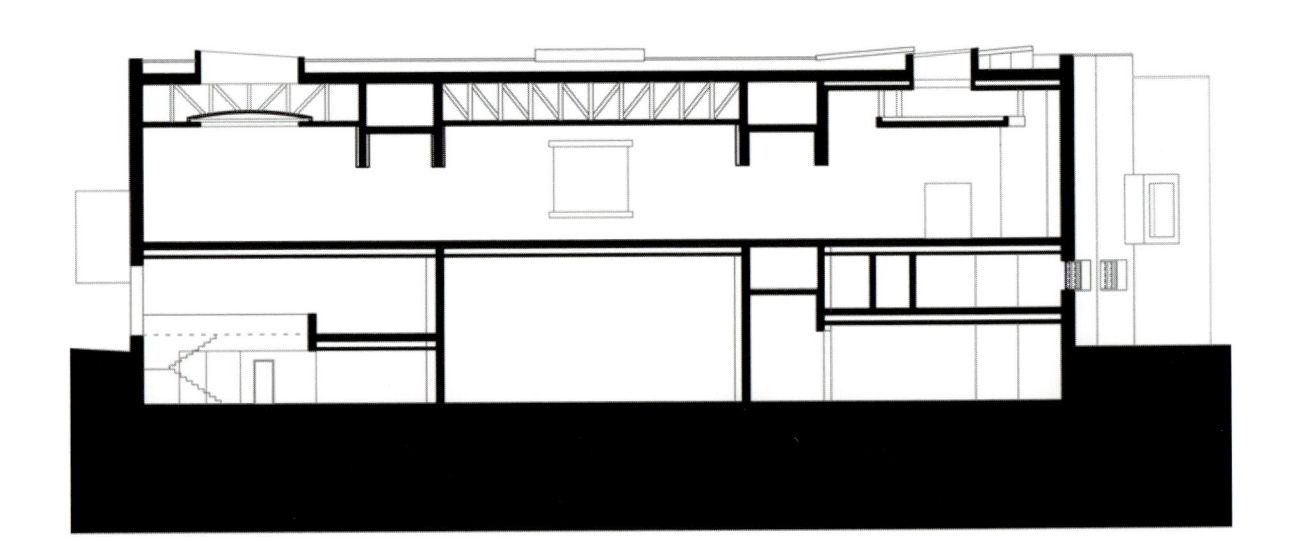

The Serralves Foundation, Oporto, Portugal (1991–1999)

Alvar Siza's building for the Serralves Foundation at Oporto is also in a suburban location.[10] Here, however, the conditions of the well-established park in which the building stands provoke nothing like Moneo's critical reaction to the sprawling commercial development that surrounds the Miró Foundation. The important collection of the Serralves Foundation contains works that represent most strands of contemporary art: painting, print, sculpture, mixed media, video art and digital techniques. The building also plays host to temporary exhibitions. It would be difficult to imagine the adoption of the conventional model of the art museum in the face of this programmatic complexity and uncertainty. A more likely strategy might be to turn to the mechanical 'perfection' of a sealed enclosure served by mechanical systems, in the manner of the Centre Pompidou, providing infinite flexibility in response to the indeterminate programme.

Siza's design could not differ more from the idea of a museum as a 'machine for art'. The new building lies close to the north-western boundary of the park and develops a complex relationship with the topography. A narrow, canopied passageway leads to a courtyard from which the building is entered. The plan of the building is primarily an orthogonal pavilion that responds by subtle inflection to the informal topography of the site as it extends southwards from the entrance sequence (Figure 8.8). It terminates in a three-sided courtyard open to the park beyond and across which the building makes a series of self-references. Upon this lucid spatial structure the cross-section steps down following the southerly slope and the building's envelope, in its detail, is punctured by a rich variety of openings: windows and rooflights, that have both practical and symbolic purpose in establishing the nature of the exhibition galleries (Figure 8.9).

In his earlier design for the Galician Centre for Contemporary Art at Santiago de Compostela (1988–1993), Siza explicitly engaged with the historical tradition of the top-lit gallery.[11] Here a wide patent-glazed rooflight sits above a relatively narrow opening in the roof slab. Beneath this a light-deflecting, inverted 'table' serves to reflect light onto the white painted ceiling and then back towards the walls (Figure 8.10). This can be interpreted as a transformation of the Soanian model in response to the demands of art conservation and to the brighter light of northern Spain. A similar element is found at Serralves where it operates more as a symbol of the gallery tradition than as a practical device.

At Serralves Siza utilises a variety of rooflights, some with inverted 'tables', others with translucent lay lights, and diverse window configurations, used in various combinations with artificial light sources, to illuminate, both literally and metaphorically, a sequence of galleries that allow diverse arrangements of equally diverse works of art (Figures 8.11–8.13). The intention seems to be to bring light to the architecture and to maintain connections with the external world, rather than to mechanically illuminate the art. This is a poetic, undogmatic environment that unassumingly informs the experience of the museum environment. Kenneth Frampton has described the Galician Centre for Contemporary Art in the following terms:

> Siza's architecture depends as much upon the materials and the general tone of the ambient light as it does upon the specific nature of the space. White marble revetment and light timber floors and furnishings, plus walls and ceilings finished in plaster and painted white above the dado level, jointly ensure that the museum is filled with scintillating light that, in places, becomes muted as the day unfolds. [12]

The same may be said of Serralves, and these buildings propose an architecture of the museum that acknowledges the practical and poetic legitimacy of the historical type, but adapts this, as a technical device and as a determinant of architectural space, to meet the conditions in which contemporary art is exhibited.

The Walsall Art Gallery, Walsall, UK (1995–2000)

Moneo's and Siza's respective architectures are technologically undemonstrative. These art museum buildings, of necessity, incorporate extensive mechanical systems of environmental control, but these are given their place unobtrusively in relation to structural configurations and spatial topographies that are themselves subtle and undogmatic in form and expression. They are a far cry from literal interpretation of Kahn's distinction between 'served' and 'servant'.

A long way from the sunshine of Mallorca and Portugal, the Walsall Art Gallery, by Caruso St John, in an industrial town in the English Midlands, also addresses questions of the environment for art and of the relation of services to structure and space (Figure 8.14).[13] The building is designed to provide space for temporary exhibitions that embrace the wide diversity of contemporary art practice. It also houses a unique, permanent collection of works, the Garman Ryan collection. This is a group of works in all traditional media – oils, watercolours, drawings, sculpture in stone and bronze – that has its origins in the private collection of the sculptor Jacob Epstein. In addition, the Gallery has a more general permanent collection that it has assembled since its foundation in 1892. There are also an archive, education rooms – the Children's House, administration, a café and a restaurant. While space for visiting exhibitions can be, probably should be, generic and neutral, the presentation of permanent collections and, in particular, of a unique, if idiosyncratic, collection raises questions of interpretation and specific context.

The art museum: art, environment, imagination – Moneo, Siza, Caruso St John, Zumthor **169**

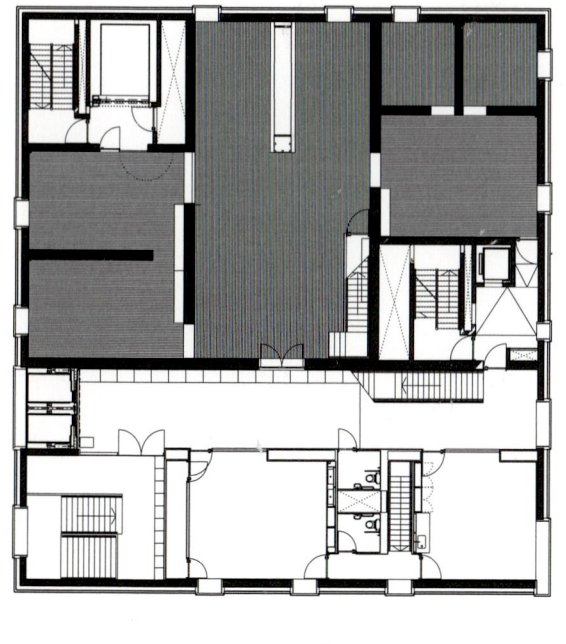

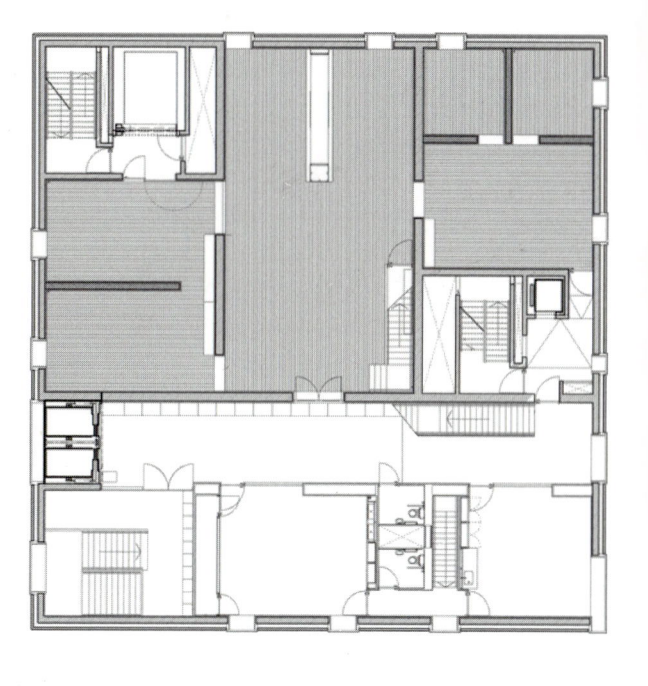

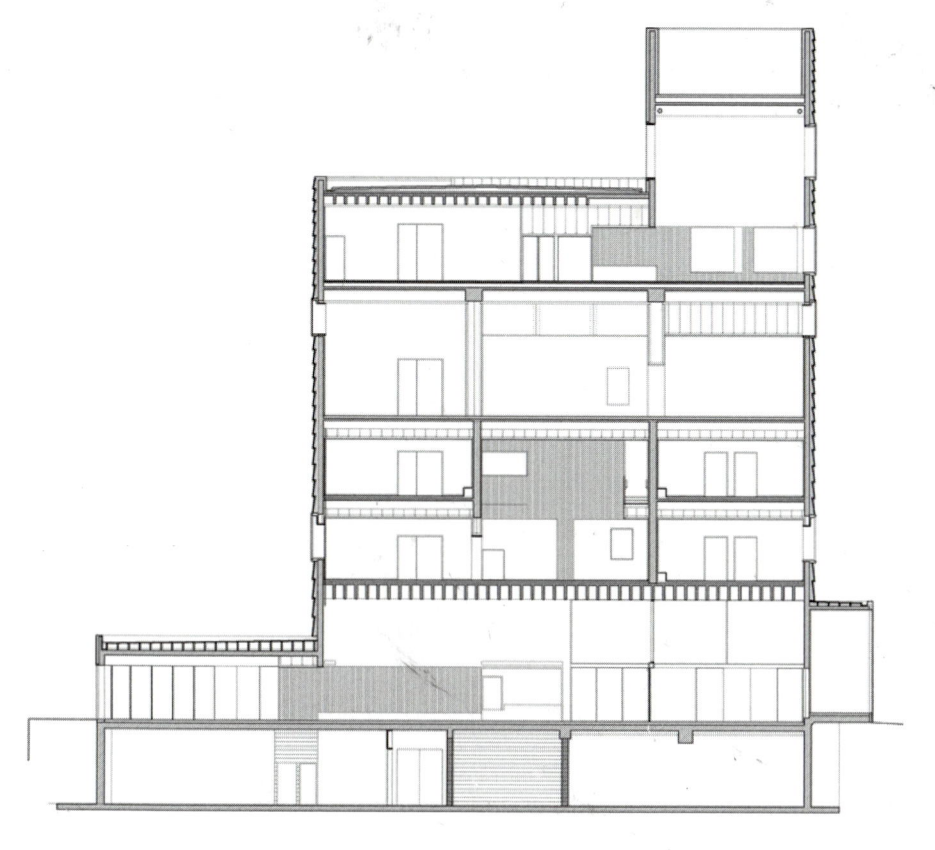

8.15
Plans, Garman Ryan Collection (left),
temporary exhibition galleries (right)

8.16
Cross-section

The building takes the form of a square tower that rises above a wider base (Figures 8.15 and 8.16). A staircase rises and criss-crosses its way past the galleries, finally arriving at the restaurant on the top floor, with panoramic views across the town. This arrangement prohibits the use of conventional top-lit galleries. The temporary exhibition galleries occupy the floor below the restaurant and their presence is expressed on the façades of the building by bands of horizontal glazing. Within the galleries these appear as clerestories above the hanging walls (Figure 8.17).

8.17
Temporary exhibition gallery

In detail, the clerestories are a sophisticated combination of window and artificial light source. Two skins of translucent glass define a wide cavity, which contains artificial light fittings and motorised blinds; the void also acts as an extract plenum for the air conditioning system. In the traditional top-lit art gallery the golden rule is to place the rooflight outside the cone of vision of the viewer. This is to avoid visual glare when regarding the work of art. This is why the design manuals almost always prohibit the use of clerestorey windows. At Walsall, the layers of diffusing glazing and the intervention of the white adjustable blinds are designed to keep the relative brightnesses of the picture wall and the light source within comfortable limits. The ambient light is supplemented by spot sources that illuminate individual works of art. After dark, light flows into the galleries from the clerestories – now luminaries – and outwards, like a beacon, across the town. At one point this engineered functionality becomes illusion where a 'clerestorey' is continued across an internal partition, masquerading as a window, but is in fact purely an artificial light source.

The Garman Ryan Collection is arranged on two levels around a double height volume at the centre of the building (Figure 8.18). In scale and materiality this is more domestic than institutional and calls to mind installations such as that at Kettle's Yard in Cambridge, where a similarly individual collection is housed in a group of medieval cottages later extended at a domestic scale by Leslie Martin (Figure 8.19).[14] At Walsall, the 'house' is fictive not actual, but is an absolutely appropriate response to the collection and to the donor's requirement that the works should be exhibited in defined thematic groupings. The cellular layout with small windows alludes to domestic building, but is manifestly an element of a modern building. Although they have windows, these rooms are predominantly artificially lit and are fully air-conditioned. The windows provide relatively little practical illumination for the art works. Cross-shaped light fittings, fixed directly on the timber ceilings, are the principal light sources.

The building has a specific tectonic in which construction and material are predominant over structure and in which an extensive and complex mechanical services installation is concealed. Unlike Kahn at Kimbell, this is achieved without overt articulation of the 'servant' spaces in the topography of the building. Two principal vertical service ducts, each within a circulation core, travel the full height of the building from the basement plant room. Horizontal services are located above the suspended ceilings of the Garman Ryan Gallery and also serve the temporary galleries above. At this level the services are accommodated within a concrete frame structure at the centre of the plan around which steel stud frames support plaster skins, in effect forming large service voids (Figure 8.20). Air is supplied to the galleries through continuous slots at the head of the walls and extracted through the clerestorey windows.

In this building we are far removed from the practices of environmental determinism. Its necessarily extensive services installations find their place within a hierarchy of interest that is primarily poetic and tectonic. The space for art is reinterpreted by, on the one hand in the Garman Ryan Gallery, reference to the informal setting of private, domestic display, and, on the other in the temporary exhibition galleries, to a reconfiguration of the conventional, functional relationship between the art work, light source and viewer. To achieve this, 'servant' spaces are woven into the tissue of the building rather than inscribed onto it.

8.18
Interior, Garman Ryan Collection

8.19
Leslie Martin, Kettle's Yard Gallery, Cambridge. Art in a domestic setting.

8.20
Walsall Art Gallery, the temporary exhibition galleries under construction. The framed structure allows flexibility for the installation of the mechanical services.

Kunsthaus Bregenz, Austria (1990–1997)

The art museum stands in the light of Lake Constance. It is made of glass and steel and a cast concrete stone mass which endows the interior of the building with texture and spatial composition. From the outside the building looks like a lamp. It absorbs the changing light of the sky, the haze of the lake, it reflects light and colour and gives an intimation of its inner life according to the angle of vision, the daylight and the weather … The multi-layered façade is an autonomous wall construction that harmonizes with the interior and acts as a weather skin, daylight modulator, sun shade and thermal insulator. Relieved of these functions, the space-defining anatomy of the building is able to develop freely in the interior. [15]

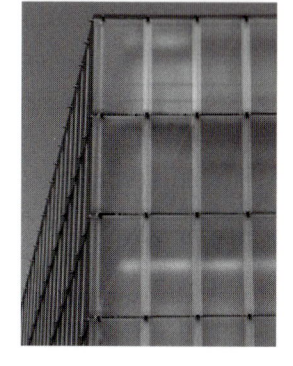

8.21
Peter Zumthor, Kunsthaus Bregenz, lake front

8.22
Façade detail

8.23
Ground and upper floor plans

In 1997, Peter Zumthor completed the Kunsthaus Bregenz (Figure 8.21). It is clear from the emphasis of the architect's description of the building that it is intellectually and actually concerned with the relation of light and art – a building that 'looks like a lamp'. Clad in shimmering glass shingles that reflect and refract the ever-changing light of the lakeside, its appearance immediately conjures associations between transparency and illumination (Figure 8.22). But the building is not merely a symbol of light, beyond first appearances it offers a fundamental re-evaluation of the nature of the art museum both in its relation to the nature of contemporary art and to the capability of contemporary technology to support the reinvention of the art space (Figure 8.23).

The analysis began with a simple diagram illustrating the horizontal flow of light as it might pass through the glazed envelope and the voids between the structural walls (Figure 8.24). In the tradition of the art museum, the section is almost always more significant than the plan, and it is the section of the Kunsthaus that reveals the clarity and originality of the building (Figure 8.25). Within the open-jointed external glass skin there is a completely sealed enclosure of concrete walls and glass. At ground level, light flows horizontally into the entrance hall through both layers of glazing, exactly as shown in Zumthor's sketch, and the polished concrete soffit of the first floor slab is exposed to view. Thereby, the structural logic of the building is demonstrated. But the three upper floor galleries are, in effect, separate enclosures. Each floor is wrapped by a continuous, unpunctured, perimeter concrete wall, whose function is to enclose, not to support, and each space is capped by a taut glass ceiling, suspended 'man high'[16] below the concrete slab.

On its journey into the galleries, daylight passes through the two vertical planes of glass and is then refracted through the horizontal plane of the ceiling. Geometrically the configuration of solid and void is, as the section demonstrates, akin to a clerestorey, with strips of glazing above the gallery walls. But the interposition of the horizontal glass of the ceiling diffuses and redistributes light into the galleries,

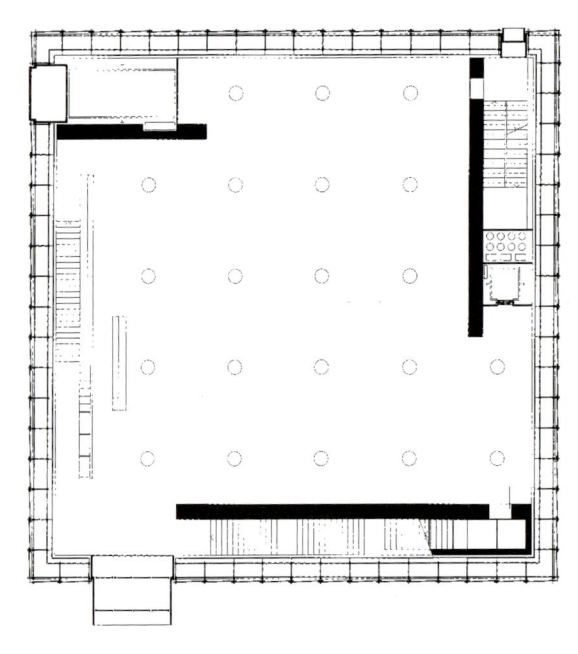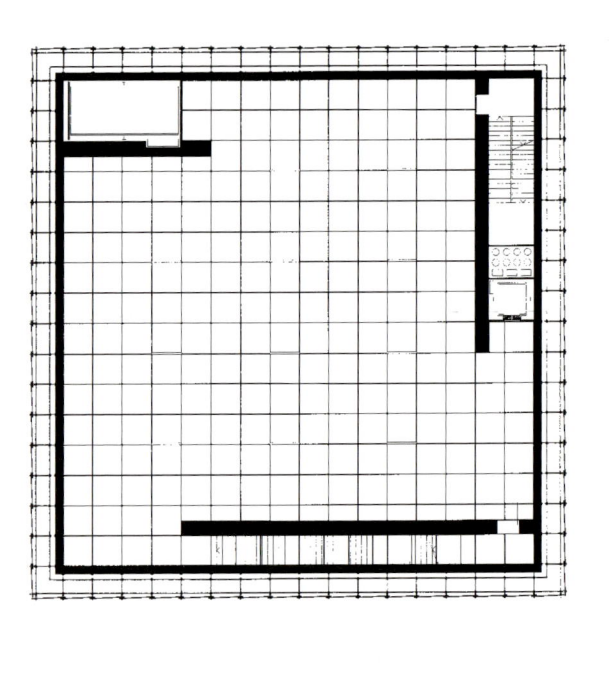

brighter at the perimeter than the centre (Figures 8.26 and 8.27). The effect is quite unlike a clerestorey-lit space. Inevitably, because of the progressive obstruction of layers of diffusing glazing, the light levels are low, but they vary subtly as the sky changes from season to season and as the sun tracks from east to west. Peter Buchanan has vividly described this process:

> In winter the whole volume above the glass ceiling can become filled with horizontal sunlight which is diffused downwards with no detrimental effect on the artworks. At the height of summer, the geometry generally prevents serious penetration of the sun's rays, though blinds are automatically lowered over the glass walls if solar intensity becomes too great. [17]

Zumthor himself has observed:

> We feel how the building absorbs the daylight, the position of the sun and the points of the compass, and we are aware of the modulations of light caused by the invisible and yet perceptible outside environment. And in the heart of the building the light is modulated by the three wall slabs which bear the rooms. [18]

The void above the glass ceiling contains an array of purpose-made light fittings that are controlled by a sensor mounted on the roof of the building. These can be controlled, individually or in groups, in response to the ambient light or to meet the needs of specific exhibitions. The apparent simplicity of the layered façade conceals, in fact, an extremely sophisticated environmental machine. A thick layer of thermal insulation is attached to the outer face of the *in situ* concrete walls. Coils of water pipes are located within the sealed enclosure and the adjustable blinds that Buchanan writes about are suspended in the void between the outer and inner layers of glazing (Figure 8.28).

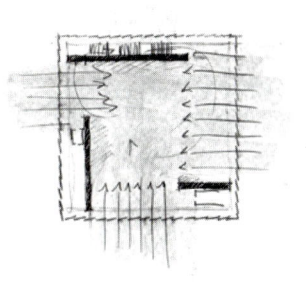

In the design of most modern art museums, the conventional response is to install a full air-conditioning system to safeguard temperature, humidity and air quality. At Bregenz a totally different strategy is used. Temperature control in the building utilises the thermal mass of the concrete structure. Coils of water pipes are encased in the *in situ* concrete of the floor slabs and enclosing walls and these circulate water drawn from deep in the ground beneath the building – from a depth of 27 metres (Figure 8.29). This provides cooling in the summer and a gas boiler is used to raise the water temperature to provide heat to the building in winter. The ventilation system introduces air through a gap at the junction of the floor and the enclosing concrete walls and this is extracted through the ceiling void into the slab of the floor above. Under normal conditions this is purely a ventilating system, there is no need to provide cooling or heating (Figure 8.30).[19]

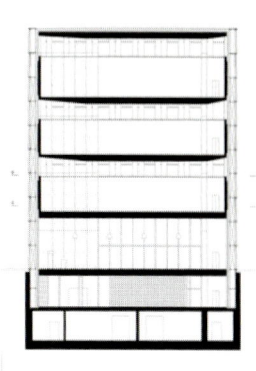

8.24
Plan sketch, south to the top

8.25
Cross-section

By adopting this unconventional approach to the museum environment, Zumthor has achieved an original synthesis of means and ends. The power of the building derives from the clarity and economy with which space, material, structure, enclosure and environment are brought together. Friedrich Achleitner eloquently summarises its qualities:

> Since the supporting concrete walls function as both heater and cooler by means of an integrated system of pipes and a constant water temperature, an additional moment of physical and psychological stability joins the visual. One cannot maintain that this predilection of Zumthor's to reach toward the essential – the laws of nature – in all that he does intends to suppress the technoid, the machine-like, the mechanistic. However, in the reduction, in restraining this 'world' in the visible, there lies a powerful psychological moment – as it were, a liberation of the view toward essential things.[20]

The art museum: art, environment, imagination – Moneo, Siza, Caruso St John, Zumthor **177**

8.27
Upper-floor gallery

Type and counter-type

Throughout its modern history the architecture of the art museum has been influenced by environmental concerns. The need to organise natural light to illuminate works of art fundamentally shaped the first specialised gallery designs and established the principal features of the typology. This influence has persisted for two centuries, even as the technology of artificial illumination has developed. In the last decades of the twentieth century, prompted by the demands of fine art conservation, the potential of the artificial environment – illumination, temperature control, ventilation – has played an ever-greater role. The four buildings discussed in this essay may all be considered in relation to this history.

At the Miró Foundation, Rafael Moneo responded defensively to the uninspiring suburban context, but found inspiration in Miró's works and in the brilliant light of Mallorca. The 'star' space is without precedent in the history of the art museum, where galleries are almost always orthogonal. The illumination is complex, issuing from small, punched rooflights, shaded cowled openings in the walls – these cannot really be described as windows – and the diffused sunlight that passes through the louvre-protected alabaster screen to the south, all supplemented in some measure by artificial light. This is, in Venturi's useful distinction, between *invention* rather than *convention*, but remote as it may seem from Soane's Dulwich Gallery, it is just as clearly concerned with the issues of the relation of art to light to the viewer. It is informed by principle applied to the problem and is not the product of arbitrary form making.

At the Serralves Foundation, Alvaro Siza perhaps stays closer to the tradition, and offers a particularly lyrical interpretation of it. His inverted 'light tables' refer to the convention of the top-lit art gallery, but their juxtaposition with large, often screened windows, and discreet artificial lighting creates spaces that reject the formality of most galleries. Works are seen in constantly changing relationships to their setting; sometimes against plain white walls, sometimes in silhouette against a window. The configuration of the building, particularly at the point where the re-entrant courtyard opens to the south, provides numerous connections between inside and out, drawing the landscape and glimpses of the building itself into the field of view, quite different from the extreme interiority of the conventional top-lit box.

Caruso St John's tower of a gallery at Walsall presents another view of the contemporary art museum. The specific conditions for display and the actual nature of the Garman Ryan Collection have led to another kind of interpretation of the domestic as the setting for art. These spaces are intimate in dimension and materiality, and with views out onto the town, but simultaneously satisfy all the technical environmental requirements of the modern gallery. In contrast, the temporary exhibition galleries are neutral and generalised. The seemingly contradictory device of clerestorey lighting is made, by careful engineering, appropriate to the needs of these spaces and the diverse forms of art that they exhibit.

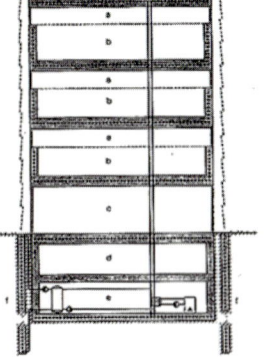

8.28
Façade detail

8.29
Cross-section showing the
fundamentals of the embedded
heating and cooling system

8.30
Sketch showing air supply and
extract arrangement at edge of floor
slab

The Kunsthaus Bregenz, also in some respects a tower, attempts no such differentiation. Its glass skin encloses three virtually identical deep galleries, stacked one above the other over the free space of the entrance hall. These are used exclusively for temporary exhibitions of contemporary art – in all its diversity of media.[21] All that is seen is glass or concrete. Inside, the vertical glass shingles of the exterior are transformed into a luminous horizontal ceiling that hovers above the polished concrete floor, and just touches the tops of the enclosing concrete walls. In *The Architecture of the Well-tempered Environment*,[22] Rayner Banham wrote about 'exposed power', citing the foul air stack at the Marseilles Unité, the external ducts of Albini's La Rinascente Store in Rome and the service towers of Louis Kahn's Richards Memorial Laboratories as examples of the increasing significance of environmental devices as 'decoration'. In most recent work, however, it has become the practice to discreetly conceal environmental services in ducts and voids within the building fabric. This is the case at Miró, Serralves and Walsall. At Bregenz, the services are also invisible, but because they are embedded, or embodied, in the structural mass of the floors and walls, these become, in fact, a new kind of exposed power, the ultimate integration of structure and services.

In these four buildings the architecture of the art museum has escaped from conformity to type. They present wholly different notions of the kind of space in which art, and particularly the art of the twentieth and twenty-first centuries, should be exhibited. These innovations derive from many sources, but in every case the act of environmental imagination, in conception and realisation, plays a powerful role.

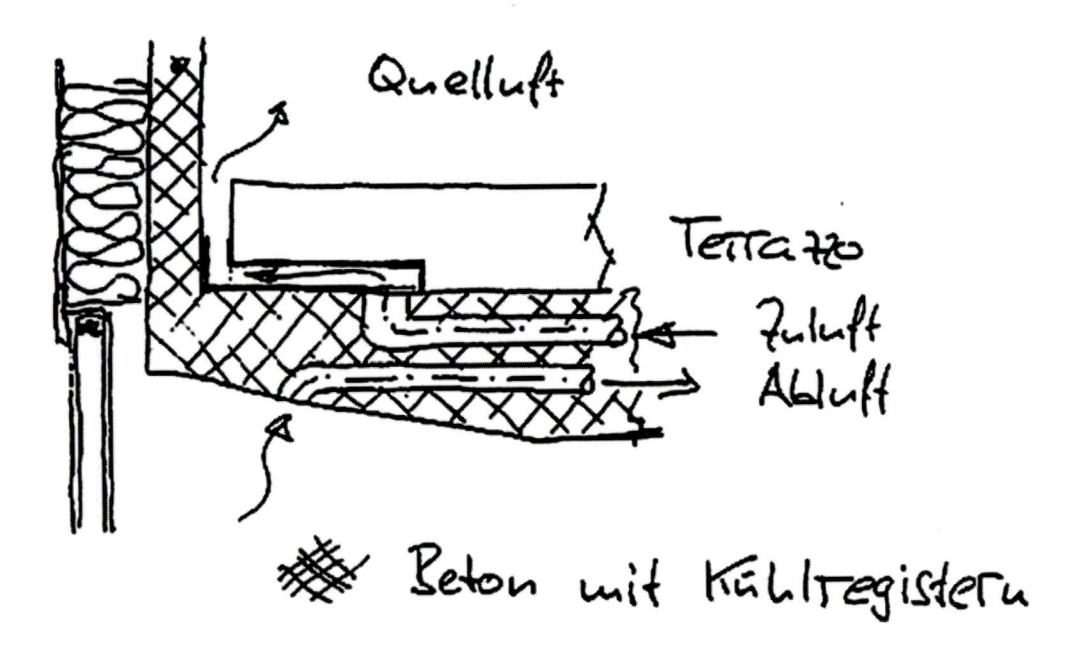

Notes

1   Nikolaus Pevsner, *A History of Building Types*, Thames and Hudson, London, 1976.

2   See Essay 2 for discussions of these two buildings.

3   Essay 4 explores Kahn's theme of 'served and servant' in detail.

4   This project is described in detail in Dean Hawkes, 'The Sainsbury Wing', in Dean Hawkes, *The Environmental Tradition: Studies in the Architecture of Environment*, E & FN Spon, London, 1996.

5   Rafael Moneo, 'Project Description', in *Fundació Pilar I Joan Miró a Mallorca: Guide*, Electa Espāna, S. A., Madrid, 1993.

6   Ibid.

7   The *Oxford English Dictionary* defines 'ambiance/ambience' as 'the character and atmosphere of a place.' See Introduction.

8   See Essay 5, 'Carlo Scarpa: "I wish I could frame the blue of the sky"'.

9   Robert Venturi, 'From Invention to Convention in Architecture', The Thomas Cubitt Lecture, Royal Society for Arts, London, 8th April 1987, first published in *RSA Journal*, January 1988, reprinted in Robert Venturi, *Iconography and Electronics upon a Generic Architecture: A View from the Drafting Room*, MIT Press, Cambridge, MA, 1996.

10 The standard reference for Siza's works is Kenneth Frampton's, *Alvaro Siza: Complete Works*, first published in Italian, Electa, Milan, 1999, first English edition, Phaidon, London, 2000. This is usefully supplemented by Philip Jodidio, *Alvaro Siza*, Taschen, Cologne, 1999.

11 This is illustrated in detail in Pedro de Llano and Carlos Castanheira, *Alvaro Siza: Obras e Projectos*, catalogue of an exhibition at the Galician Centre for Contemporary Art, 1995.

12 Kenneth Frampton, 'Architecture as Critical Transformation: The Work of Alvaro Siza', in Frampton, *Alvaro Siza*, op. cit.

13 The technologies of the building are described in detail in, Katherine Holden, *et al.*, 'Walsall Art Gallery', *The Arup Journal*, no. 2, 2000. The functional and physical integration of its architecture and engineering is discussed in Dean Hawkes and Wayne Forster, *Architecture, Engineering and Environment*, Laurence King, London, 2002.

14 Kettle's Yard is illustrated in Leslie Martin, *Buildings and Ideas: 1933–1983*, Cambridge University Press, Cambridge.

15 Peter Zumthor, Introduction to, *Kunsthaus Bregenz*, Archiv Kunst Architektur: Werkdocumente, Verlag Gerd Hatje, Ostfildern-Ruit, 1999, also in *Peter Zumthor, Architecture and Urbanism*, Extra Edition, February 1998, A+U Publishing Company, Tokyo.

16 Ibid.

17 Peter Buchanan, 'Mystical Presence: Art Museum, Bregenz, Austria', *Architectural Review*, December 1997.

18 Peter Zumthor, op. cit.

19 Technical information is based on 'Kunsthaus – Technology', from its website, http://www.kunsthaus-bregenz.at.

20 Friedrich Achleitner, 'The Conditioning of Perception or The Kunsthaus Bregenz as an Architecture of Art', in *Kunsthaus Bregenz*, op. cit.

21 Since its opening in 1999, the Kunsthaus has hosted shows by Louise Bourgeois, Jenny Holzer, Donald Judd, Jeff Koons, Roy Lichtenstein, Gerhard Merz and Rachel Whiteread, among others.

22 Rayner Banham, *The Architecture of the Well-tempered Environment*, The Architectural Press, London, 1969. The logical conclusion of this line of thought might be found in Piano and Roger's Centre Pompidou, Paris, 1971–1978, and Roger's Lloyd's Building in London, completed in 1984.

Essay 9
Sacred Places
Zumthor, Siza, Holl

Essay 6 examined the interpretation of the Christian church that was the product of the last years of Sigurd Lewerentz's life.[1] In the churches of St Mark at Björkhagen and St Peter at Klippan, Lewerentz realised a remarkable synthesis of the elements of architecture (*form, material* and *environment*) that was without precedent and, even though these buildings are widely admired, without direct progeny. They stand as the products of an original imagination, enigmatic and provocative. But, most significantly, they declare the potentiality of the methods of modern architecture to give expression to the sacred.

The present essay returns to the subject of the sacred environment, as it has been further explored in the work of, respectively, Peter Zumthor, at the Chapel of St Benedict at Sumvigt in Switzerland (1985–1988), Alvaro Siza, in his design of the church of Santa Maria at Marco de Canavezes in Portugal (1990–1996) and Steven Holl, with his St Ignatius Chapel on the campus of Seattle University in the United States (1994–1997).

St Benedict's Chapel, Sumvigt, Switzerland (1985–1988)

The buildings of Peter Zumthor have attracted wide attention in recent years. Through the realisation of a relatively modest number of quite small buildings he has issued a challenge to many of the assumptions and procedures that have held sway in the theory and practice of architecture. At the heart of his work there lies a deep engagement with architecture's capability to engage the senses and emotions:

> the quest for the new object that I shall design and build consists largely of reflection upon the way we really experience the many places of our so different dwellings throughout the world – in a forest, on a bridge, on a town square, in a house, in a room, in my room, in your room, in summer, in the morning, at twilight, in the rain. I heat the sounds of cars moving outside, the voices of the birds, and the steps of the passers-by. I see the rusty metal of the door, the blue of the hills in the background, the shimmer of the air over the asphalt. I feel the warmth reflected by the wall behind me. The curtains in the slender window recesses move gently in the breeze, and the air smells damp from yesterday's rain, preserved by the soil in the plant troughs.[2]

With these perceptions in mind, the tiny chapel of St. Benedict offers a wonderful opportunity to explore the environmental imagination (Figure 9.1). Its very situation, high on the northern slopes of the upper Rhine Valley, is the starting point. Its scale and materiality take their cues from the scattered houses of this mountain community, but its form and detail declare its special purpose. It seems to be inevitably of the place:

> Every new work of architecture intervenes in a specific historical situation. It is essential to the quality of the intervention that the new building should embrace qualities which can enter into a meaningful dialogue with the existing situation. For if the intervention is to find its place, it must make us see what already exists in a new light. We throw a stone into the water. Sand swirls up and settles again. The stir was necessary. The stone has found its place. But the pond is no longer the same. [3]

9.1
Peter Zumthor, St Benedict Chapel from south

9.2
Plan

9.3
Section looking north

On first encounter, the building might be considered to be more about the tectonic than the environmental, but Zumthor has insisted that such conventional categories and distinctions have little relevance for him:

> The sense that I try to instil into materials is beyond all rules of composition, and their tangibility, smell and acoustic qualities are merely elements of the language that we are compelled to use. Sense emerges when I succeed in bringing out the specific meanings of certain materials in my buildings, meanings which can only be perceived in just this way in this one building. [4]

The first impression within the chapel is of utter simplicity (Figures 9.2 and 9.3). This is conveyed by the combination of clear form, repetitive and comprehensible structure illuminated by the continuous band of the clerestory window. The conventional east–west orientation of the Christian church renders this configuration asymmetrical through the play of light, more intense from the south than the north. Although the interior is brightly lit and all is literally visible, the richness and complexity of the building progressively come 'into view' in a way that is analogous to the process of visual adaptation, in which we are able gradually to adjust to lower light levels as we go from brightness to darkness (Figure 9.4).

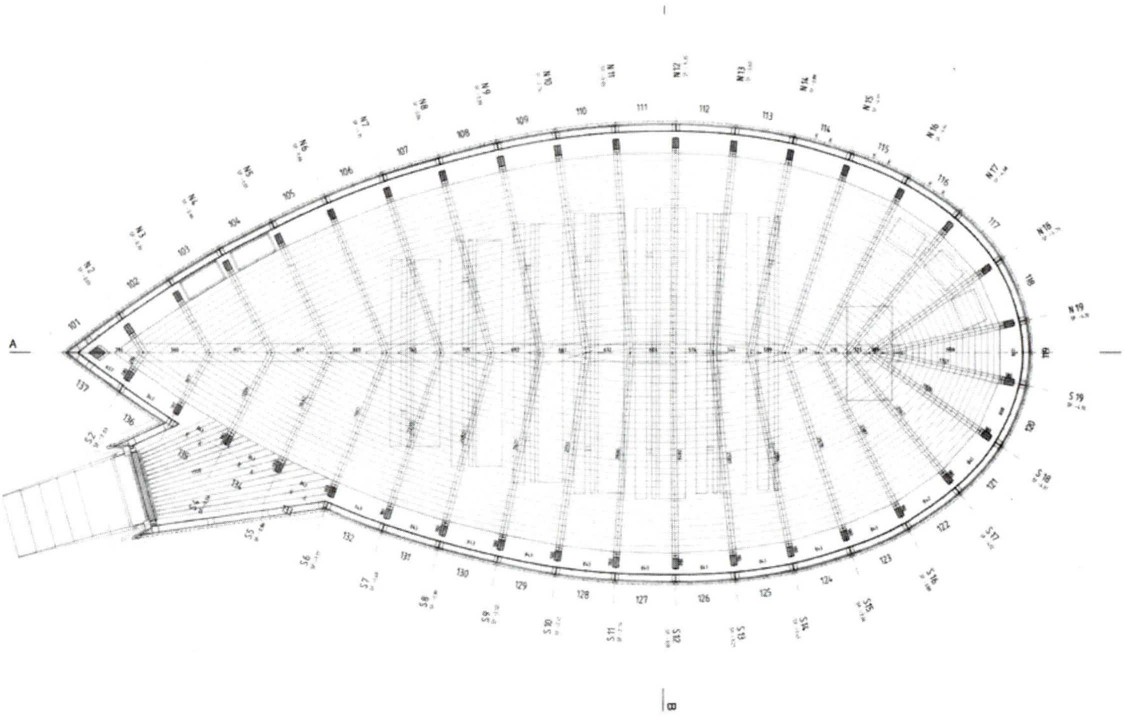

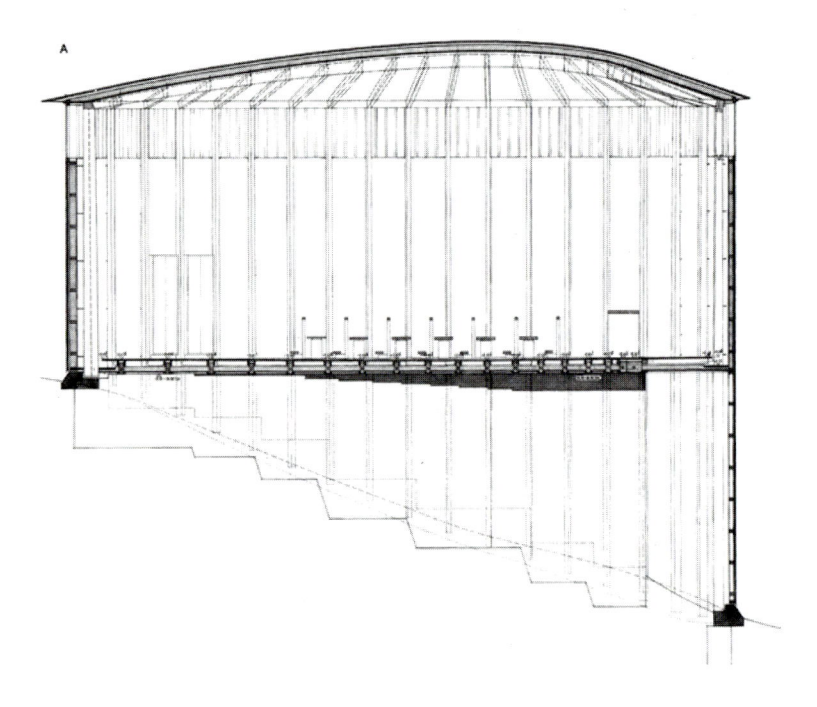

9.4
Interior looking east

9.5
Interior detail

The dully-silvered finish of the plywood lining of the walls attracts the light from the clerestory and, by inter-reflection, animates the space. A specific artefact of this process is the intensification of brightness that occurs by inter-reflection between the natural timber of the structural columns and the silver wall (Figure 9.5). Another detail that comes to the attention is the fine tapering of the mullions of the clerestory. This, in the manner of the moulded glazing bars of old window frames, softens the contrast between mullion and sky and thereby avoids glare (Figure 9.6). As the sun follows its daily course across the heavens, the space is animated by the ever-changing play of sunlight on the interior. Once again, the simplicity of the continuous clerestory, in its relationship to the non-orthogonal plan, produces effects of surprising richness.

Zumthor has proposed:

9.6
Clerestory detail

> In architecture, there are two basic possibilities of spatial composition: the closed architectural body which isolates space within itself, and the open body which embraces an area of space that is connected with the endless continuum … Buildings which have a strong impact always convey an intense feeling of their spatial quality. They embrace the mysterious void which we call space and make it vibrate.[5]

St Benedict belongs to the first of these categories. There is an intense focus upon the 'space within itself' that is the almost inevitable effect of the absence of windows at eye-level. This effect is rendered particularly powerful by the minute scale of the chapel. But there is simultaneously a sense of the vast scale of the terrain, the 'endless continuum', outside, promoted by the view of the sky seen through the clerestory.

Acoustically the building has the particular qualities that follow from the use of light timber construction. It is responsive to human presence, sounding every footfall, and there is an audible awareness of the almost imperceptible movement of the structure with gentle creaks. One is aware of bird song and the sound of the wind in the trees of the mountainside – all of which is expressive of the nature of the building itself and of its relationship with its site.

High in the mountains the building is exposed to extreme winter weather. The response to this couldn't be simpler. The timber construction permits a high standard of thermal insulation to be achieved within the structure and electrical heating elements concealed beneath the pews produce warmth exactly where it is needed. The only other 'service' is the array of electric lamps that hang from the roof, following the plan form, to provide night-time illumination. In their simplicity these are absolutely in accord with the whole conception of the building.

9.7
Alvaro Siza, Santa Maria de
Canavezes, exterior from north-west

9.8
Plan

9.9
Long section looking south

9.10
Cross-section looking east

Santa Maria, Marco de Canavezes, Portugal (1990–1996)

I wanted to make a church that felt like a church and not a building with a cross in it. I wasn't interested in this primitive notion of how a symbol could determine the character of a building. So I tried to achieve something I would call the character of the church …

If you try to think of a good cross in modern architecture, I can only think of the ones designed by Le Corbusier in Ronchamp or La Tourette, or the one of Barragan and not much more. There are very few contemporary churches that have this atmosphere that is difficult to describe, that make you feel that you are in a sacred building. I think that the purpose of this project should be to insert this fraternal relationship between men and this atmosphere.[6]

The church is located just outside the centre of the town of Marco de Canaveses, in an area of undistinguished modern development. It sits on a podium above a dual carriageway road (Figure 9.7). This elevation above its surroundings enables it to establish a strong presence in this nondescript context. The podium is constructed from the local granite. The white, orthogonal volume of the church rises from the podium and a granite dado of variable height negotiates the transition of material.

The plinth is occupied by the mortuary chapel that is approached from the lower level through a small, enclosed garden and cloister. The curved forms of the chapel reflect those of the church above. The church is a simple rectangle, 30m x 16m in plan. To the west two projections either side of the grand entrance doors (10m high x 3m wide) contain, to the north the baptistry and the belfry to the south. Within this simple formal scheme spatial complexity is achieved through manipulation of the details of plan and section (Figures 9.8–9.10).

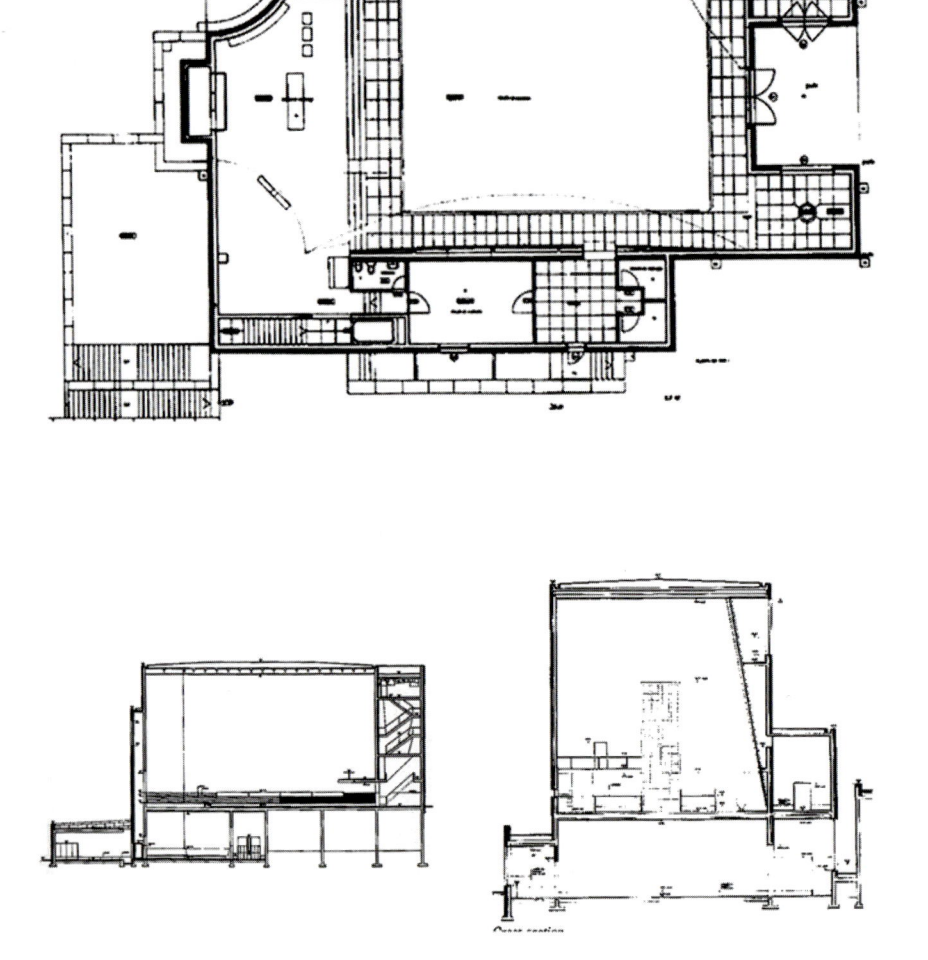

The essence of the enclosure lies in the asymmetry between the north and south faces. To the south, the tall vertical wall rises uninterrupted from floor to ceiling. It is penetrated only by a long, horizontal window. The north wall is a leaning, convex surface that terminates in three large clerestory windows (Figure 9.11). At the east, it intersects the convex form of the nave at the point where it hovers above the side chapel. The interior is predominantly white with all the walls and the ceiling finished with matt paint. The west, south and east walls have a dado of white tiles, whereas the north wall is painted over its full height. The main area of the floor and that of the sanctuary are of wide-boarded hardwood, whereas the rear of the nave, the baptistry and the bell tower are floored with white marble. The principal light of the space is from the north-facing clerestory (Figure 9.12). The lower, horizontal window in the south wall illuminates only the sliver of floor close to it, and will admit direct sunlight only at limited times of day. The north wall itself is primarily illuminated by light reflected back from the clear, blank surface of the south wall.

For Siza, the clerestory in the north wall carries significant associations:

You have this angle that gives some depth to the windows. You can see the light comes in but you don't see the actual windows in perspective. This was obtained in old churches naturally with the thickness of the construction, but today we do make walls about 40cm so I tried to reintroduce this quality of thickness and density. This space resulting from the curve is also accessible upstairs to clean the glass. A lot of old churches have this kind of veranda. I would look, up at it, and there would never be anyone there, and I would wonder how it was accessed and who goes there. I projected this sense of wonder here. [7]

9.11
Interior looking east

9.12
Clerestory detail

9.13
Detail of west end of nave with organ
gallery

9.14
Baptistry

Looking west, the tile-lined baptistry and, to a lesser extent, the belfry are the most brightly illuminated parts of the entire composition (Figures 9.13 and 9.14). The overall effect is calm, but full of subtle differentiations as the forms and materials respond to the predominantly shadowless illuminance. This also contributes to a sense of thermal comfort that is the outcome of the volume, its heavyweight construction and the absence of direct sunlight. On a hot summer's day, the interior was very cool at midday. A further, subtle contribution to the sense of calm and cool is provided by the sound of running water that is instantly apparent on entering the building. This comes from the baptistery, where water constantly issues from the font into the recessed stone basin in which it sits. The acoustic effect of this is probably accentuated by the materiality and sheer height of the baptistry tower.

This is a building that gives precedence to 'atmosphere' over the tectonic. The materiality of the building is primarily of surface – white-painted plaster, white tile, white marble, timber, granite – than it is of expressed construction. In a Kahnian sense, light is perceived as a building material. The subtle differentiations of brightness that play within the volume of the church invest it with a rich calm (if that is not a contradiction in terms) – serenity. The three physical parameters of environment – heat, light and sound – all have a role in establishing the atmosphere – low, calm light, cool, still air and the quietly audible sound of running water.

All of this works to dissociate the interior from the untidy bustle of the town outside. This effect is reinforced by the visual control that is achieved by the horizontal window in the south façade. This directs the attention towards the hilltops of the distant horizon rather than to the road and nondescript modern urban buildings in the foreground.

St Ignatius Chapel, Seattle University, USA (1994–1997)

Steven Holl began his engagement with the St Ignatius Chapel when he gave a lecture, 'Questions of Perception', at Seattle University in the winter of 1991. In this, he described, 'a phenomenology of architecture'. The lecture argued for a heightened development of spatial and experiential dimensions through individual reflection on the senses and perception'.[8]

As the project developed, Holl discovered connections between these ideas and the teachings of St Ignatius of Loyola, the founder of the Society of Jesus, which place emphasis on the role of the five senses in the act of contemplation. These led him towards a particular metaphor of light – light from above – and the relation of darkness and light – of consolation and desolation. It was out of these discoveries that the concept of the chapel as 'a gathering of different lights' emerged. This was expressed in the sketch, 'Seven Bottles of Light on a Stone Box', which became the central idea of the building. The completed building is very clearly a translation of the 'Seven Bottles' drawing into physical, tectonic, environmental form, perhaps one of the clearest expressions of the relation of technics and poetics (Figure 9.15).

But the translation of metaphor into concrete reality is a complex matter in which many decisions and judgements are made. The churches of Zumthor and Siza demonstrate totally contrasted approaches to the relation of the tectonic and the environmental and St Ignatius differs from both. The exterior construction of the building translates the 'Stone Box' of the conceptual sketch into a composition of twenty-one, 'tilt-up' precast concrete panels (Figure 9.16). These support a tubular steel roof structure, zinc clad externally, that shapes the bottles of light. The internal wall surfaces, partitions and the complex rooflights are formed in metal lath finished in textured, hand-trowelled plaster. The floor has a polished concrete finish. Tectonics and environment are brought together ingeniously by the manner in which, with just one exception, all the window openings in the walls occur at junctions between the concrete panels. The consequence of the tectonic system is that the form and materiality of the interior are independent of the exterior construction. This allows the manipulation of light, its intensity, distribution and tonality, rather than the expression of any structural logic, to be the basis of the architecture.

The question of orientation lies at the heart of the play of light in Christian architecture. In conventional church forms the dominant east–west axis projects asymmetrical light upon symmetrical space and captures the distinction between morning and evening. The orthogonal grid of the Seattle University campus lies almost exactly upon the cardinal points. The chapel thereby effortlessly observes the convention. But Holl's response, perhaps conditioned by the context and dimensions of the site, is unconventional. The long axis of the enclosure runs north–south and the building is entered from the south (Figure 9.17). From the enclosed and brightly lit narthex a processional route moves northwards to enter the nave at its south-west corner. From here the space unfolds as the asymmetrical vault, with its supporting arches, establishes the dominant east–west axis. Within this prospect complex and

diverse patterns of illumination play across the textured plaster and are reflected, inverted and transformed in the polished concrete of the floor. The chapel of the Blessed Sacrament is north-lit, facing out towards the city beyond the campus. Almost all the light enters indirectly from concealed or screened openings. Colour is introduced, in an almost baroque manner, either through coloured glass or by reflection from concealed, painted surfaces. The white plaster is animated by a rich disposition of many hues (Figures 9.18–9.20). Holl precisely reports the process by which these effects were conceived and executed:

> The procession is lit by diffused natural sunlight. In the nave a yellow field is combined with a blue lens to the east, and a blue field with a yellow lens to the west. In the chapel of the Blessed Sacrament, an orange field is coloured by a purple lens. The choir has a green field with a red lens. The reconciliation chapel combines a purple field with an orange lens. The bell tower and pond both have projected light and reflected natural light. [9]

As time passes, from morning to evening and from winter to summer, these elements project an ever-changing light over the chapel. This is particularly evident on bright days and, perhaps most of all, on the days of rapid change from bright to cloudy that are characteristic of the western seaboard climate of Seattle. But even under dully-overcast conditions the light has an incandescent quality, seemingly brighter than intuition would allow.

Artificial light is not regarded as a merely functional night-time substitute for daylight and sunlight. From all viewpoints the interior is punctuated by hand-made, clear glass lamps, suspended from the vaults or spaced upon the walls. These are lit at most times, regardless of the quantity of natural light, and with their pin-point brightness, add a further dimension to the nature and meaning of the interior. After dark the artificial light is projected outwards through the rooflights, the building becomes an emitter rather than receiver of light, at some times throughout the night.

Hearing is given high priority in Ignatian philosophy and has been given careful attention in the development of the design. In a small space acoustics should not be a particular problem, direct sound being predominant over reflected. The combination of the small volume of the chapel and the acoustic absorption of the textured plaster surface produces a comfortable reverberation. Nonetheless, the formation of the curved, plaster surfaces is precisely regulated to make sure that their foci lie either outside the space or above the height of human audibility (Figure 9.21). This calculation is graphically represented in the long section of the building.

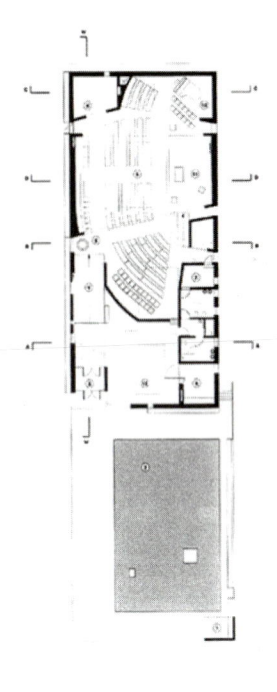

9.17
St Ignatius, plan

9.18
Nave, looking east

9.19
Chapel of the Blessed Sacrament

9.20
Reconciliation Chapel, detail

Lying unobtrusively behind the powerful visual presence and calm acoustic of the building is a wholly modern heating and ventilating plant. Seattle has a temperate climate without extremes, cool winters and warm summers. Heating is necessary in winter and the apparatus of modern environmental engineering ensures that the building satisfies late twentieth-century expectations of thermal comfort. Summer comfort is maintained by mechanical ventilation without cooling. This is practical and straightforward, but the physical incorporation of the system in architecture of this originality is not self-evidently simple. The clear topographical differentiation of Kahn's 'served' and 'servant'[10] would be at odds with the whole conception of this building and this demands that service should be provided by other configurations.

A mechanical room is located beneath the eastern edge of the nave and choir from which air is distributed beneath the floor to enter the building discreetly through a variety of locations. Fixed seating in the narthex and at the rear of the nave conceal air grilles and the *poché* formed by the metal lath inner structure contains supply ducts in the chapel of the Blessed Sacrament and the choir. The void between these two spaces is, in effect, a return air duct, as is disclosed by the presence of high-level grilles. Supply grilles are also found in the risers of the sanctuary steps and in the partly concealed flanks of the gilded reredos (Figure 9.22).

The environmental imagination

In the European tradition, the alternative schools of gothic and classic dominate Christian architecture. Zumthor's and Siza's buildings might be said to represent a contemporary continuation of that distinction. The Chapel of St Benedict is a refined essay in expressive construction and, at Santa Maria, materiality is concealed behind an almost uniform, applied surface of 'white' – inside and out. Each position has a fundamental and profound effect on the respective building's environmental qualities. Holl's St Ignatius' Chapel may, perhaps, be placed in the classic model, but perhaps baroque would be more appropriate, although the expressed, expressive, tectonics of the exterior might be distantly interpreted as gothic.

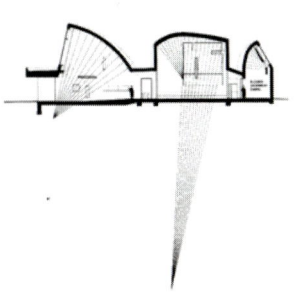

St Benedict manifestly offers shelter from the elements of the often-harsh climate in which it is set. Its copper roof and sheathing of shingles speak of enclosure and protection. Inside, Zumthor arranges structure, material and light so that their interaction creates a rich and complex setting for worship. The apparatus of modern environmental systems is reduced to the expression of the simplest of light fittings and the heating system is simply and artfully concealed from view.

The cubic, white volume of Siza's Santa Maria, with its roof concealed by a parapet, is less evidently concerned with the question of shelter. The uniform whiteness of the interior allows subtle gradations of light to be visible and serves to invest the space with an appropriate calm. Once again, the devices of service systems are absent from view to sustain the purity of the white space.

9.21
St Ignatius, section showing acoustic radii of roof vaults

9.22
Sanctuary, detail of reredos

Its immediately apparent complexities make Holl's St Ignatius Chapel different from either of these. In comparison with Zumthor's or Siza's restraint of both means and ends, Holl is elaborate and exploratory in adapting the technologies of modern construction and environmental management to give form and expression to his 'phenomenology of architecture' and its particular interpretation of Jesuit belief.

What is common to these buildings is environmental *imagination*. This is the ability to envision the outcome of the conjunction of form and material, set within the physical facts of the climate and locale, in ways that inform and enhance the purpose and meaning of a building. This lies at the very heart of the architectural project.

Notes

1   Essay 6, 'Sigurd Lewerentz: Architecture of Adaptive Light'

2   Peter Zumthor, *Peter Zumthor Works: Buildings and Projects 1979–1997*, Lars Müller Publishers, Baden, Switzerland, 1998.

3   Peter Zumthor, 'A Way of Looking at Things', in *Thinking Architecture*, Birkhäuser, Basel, Boston, Berlin, 1999.

4   Ibid.

5   Ibid.

6   Alvaro Siza, interview with Yoshio Futagawa in *Alvaro Siza, GA Document Extra*, no. 11, 1998.

7   Ibid.

8   Steven Holl, *The Chapel of St Ignatius*, Princeton Architectural Press, New York, 1999.

9   Ibid.

10 Essay 4, 'Louis I. Kahn: The Poetics of "Served" and "Servant"'.

Essay 10
Airs, waters, places
Therme Vals

Body and environment

In Victor Olgyay's, *Design with Climate*[1] there is one of the most wonderful images of modern architectural science (Figure 10.1). A man (looking, from the rear, uncannily like Ronald Reagan) stands exposed to all the conceivable means by which he might exchange heat with his surroundings. His body produces heat by the metabolic processes of human physiology (1 a–d). He absorbs radiation from the sun, from glowing radiators and from non-glowing objects and surfaces (2 a–c). Heat is conducted to his body from the surrounding air, if warm, and by contact with surfaces (3 a, b). He is affected by the condensation of atmospheric moisture (4). The man then may lose heat by radiation to the sky – if it is cool – and to cold surfaces in his surroundings (5 a, b). Heat may be conducted away to surrounding cool air and to any cool surfaces with which he is in contact (6 a, b). Finally, heat may be lost by evaporation through the respiratory tract or from the skin (7 a, b). In the image, all these processes are depicted operating simultaneously. Thankfully this circumstance would be inconceivable in any practical environment except, perhaps and unspeakably, in a torture chamber.

I use this image, and its accompanying commentary, to demonstrate that thermal environments, even those that we define as 'comfortable' are complex in combining in some measure processes of conduction, convection, evaporation and radiation. When we extend our terms of reference to include the luminous and acoustic aspects of building environments, in all of their potential diversity, we can see that, even as we go about our most ordinary daily business, we are surrounded by an elaborate environmental cocktail. In order to meet conventional codified notions of 'comfort', we find that practical environments tend towards the middle ranges, neither too hot nor too cool, neither too bright, too dull, too loud, nor too quiet. On the other hand, as is shown in many of the significant works of architecture discussed in the preceding essays, the most memorable and remarkable architectural environments often break the bounds of convention. They discover combinations of the environmental elements that, by some particular emphasis or relationship, enrich the experience of inhabitation, whether this is of a house, a museum, a church or a laboratory.

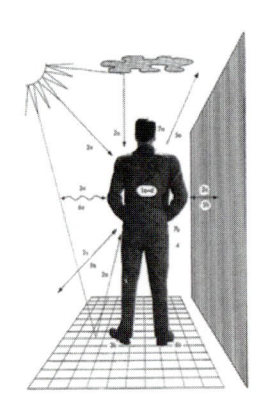

10.1
Heat exchange between man and surroundings

Therme Vals

To conclude these essays on the environmental imagination in architecture I have chosen to examine Peter Zumthor's Therme Vals. This building, completed in 1996, embraces all the elements of heat, light and sound in distributions and combinations that extend beyond most conventional circumstances. Above all, this is an environment of the senses. Unlike the conventions represented by Victor Olgyay's besuited man, where contact with the environment is limited and decorous, at Vals we enter an altogether different and infinitely more sensuous condition.

The valley of Vals rises southwards from the town of Ilanz on the Vorderrhein. High in the valley, 1,200 metres above sea level, a spring rises from the mountainside. Since the nineteenth century the spring has served a spa and it is here, close by an existing hotel, that that Peter Zumthor placed his building (Figure 10.2). In describing its essential nature he has written:

> The building takes the form of a large, grass-covered stone object set deep into the mountain and dovetailed into its flank. It is a solitary building, which resists formal integration with the existing structure in order to evoke more clearly – and achieve more fully – what seemed to us a more important role: the establishing of a special relationship with the mountain landscape. [2]

It is this acute awareness of the mountain that defines and characterises the environmental experience of the building. Examination of the plan (Figure 10.3) and the cross-sections (Figure 10.4) immediately conveys an understanding of the intimacy and richness of the relationship of the construction to the topography and geology of the valley. From the plan we may note how the density of the building, its 'geological' formation, changes as it unfolds from its innermost depths, by the indoor central pool with its surrounding monoliths of the load-bearing 'stones' and towards the alternation of solid and void that constitutes the eastern edge. We can also note how the topography of the building opens towards the south, terminating in the open-air pool and its terraces. The cross-section reveals the 'cut-and-fill' of the building into the mountain slope. These properties directly influence the environmental experience of the building. As a bather you arrive at the north-western corner of the plan deep in the mountain and progress through ever-changing environments towards the more open eastern and southern extremities. You first pass through exquisite, boudoir-like, polished hardwood changing rooms and emerge on a gallery above a stepped ramp that leads towards the internal pool (Figure 10.5). On the journey downwards you have, first, a view across the central pool then, at the foot of the ramp, as you turn eastwards, you are presented with a framed view of the opposite hillside (Figure 10.6). From here you explore at will the variety of sensory experiences that the building offers. [3]

10.2
Therme Vals, rooftop

10.3
Plan at pool level

10.4
Cross-sections looking south

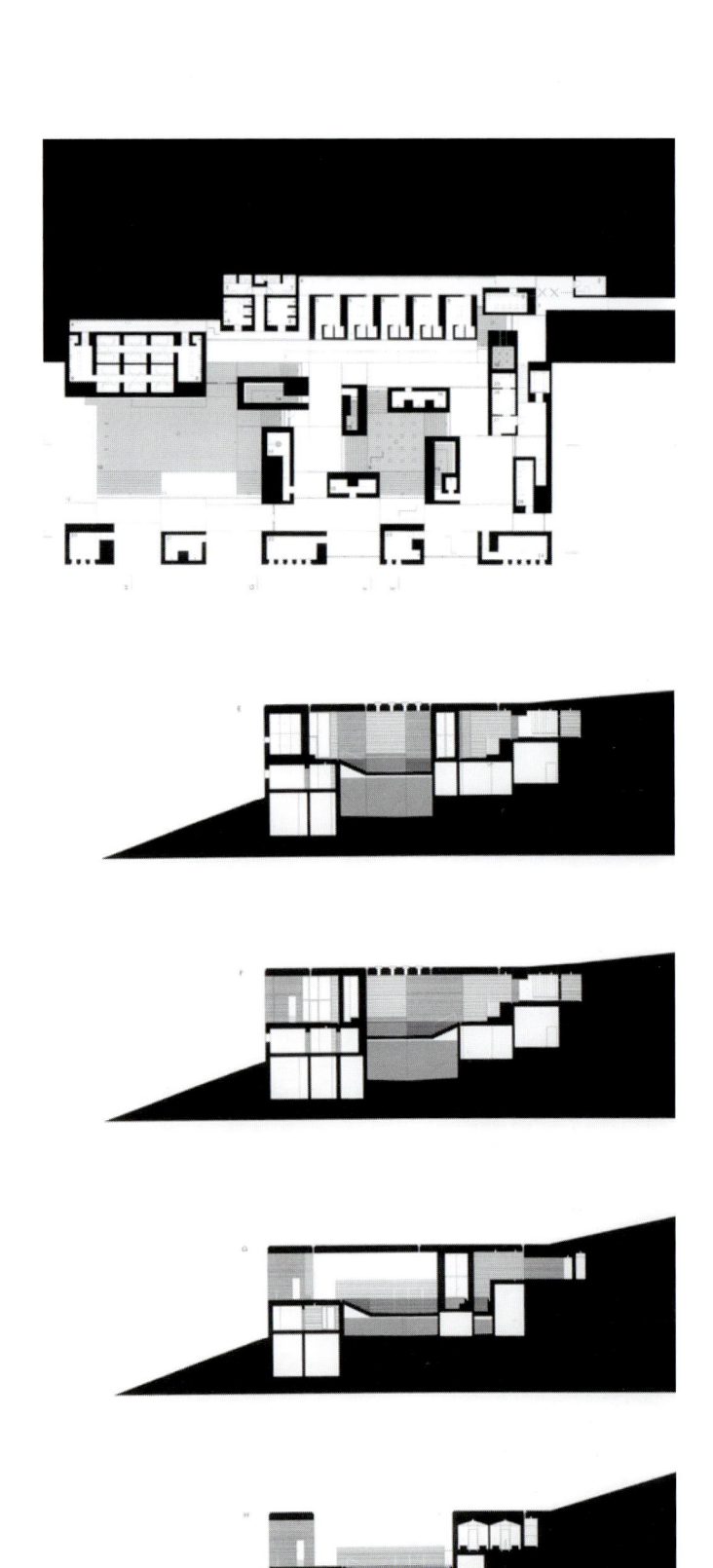

10.5
The stepped ramp looking south

10.6
Looking east from the foot of
the stepped ramp

Experience and environment

The primary experience of the spa is of bodily immersion in the waters, with their diverse temperatures, but over and above this the building offers a complex synthesis of sensory stimuli. The bather encounters, in endless combinations, the atmosphere, or *aura* as Friedrich Achleitner has insisted, [4] its temperature, humidity, luminosity, scent and the sound that it carries.

Visually the environment ranges from the wholly artificial light of the spaces within the 'stones'; the glittering dark of the interior zones, with orchestrated brightnesses of the narrow shafts of light that enter with surprising brightness between the roof slabs and small hanging lamps, whose light is more absorbed than reflected by the striated surfaces of gneiss stone (Figures 10.7–10.9); the iridescent blue of the array of rooflights above the central pool the bright daylight of the eastern gallery and, finally, the full brightness of the sky bounded by the horizons of the mountains rising above the outdoor pool.

The water that flows from the mountain spring at Vals is at a temperature of 30°C and it is water and its temperature that define the thermal environment of the building. Within the spa the central pool is at 32°C, a fact declared by a brass sign, set in a shaft of daylight cutting down the gneiss stone wall. The outdoor pool is at 36°C, to compensate for exposure to the ambient temperature. Elsewhere, as voids within the stone masses are discovered, the bather may choose from a variety of water temperatures, contrasting the heat of the fire bath at 42°C with the 14°C chill of the nearby cold bath. The 'flower' bath is at a gentle 30°C and offers olfactory pleasure as gentle scents rise from the jasmine petals that float on the surface of the water. The successive chambers of the Turkish bath offer a yet more extreme thermal experience that is emphasised further by the dim illumination, the swirling, steam-filled, heavily scented atmosphere.

Throughout the spa the acoustic is as diverse and as subtle as the waters. In a conversation with Steven Spier, Zumthor has stated that, 'I believe that buildings should sound the way they look.' [5] This seemingly simple statement conceals a subtle and original grasp of environmental relationships. In purely physical terms the acoustic of a space is the product of its geometry and its materiality. It is, in the reductive terms of building science, a function of volume and sound absorption. [6] The four principal materials that define the internal spaces of the spa (stone, concrete, glass and water) have almost identical acoustical properties, all offering very little absorption of sound. Nonetheless, Zumthor's manipulation of orthogonal geometry establishes many different relationships of volume and material that influence the perceived sounds of the building. By some almost magical process, the building seems to quieten its users. Conversation is hushed as bathers move about the building and discover and respond to its acoustics, so that the impression is quite unlike the reverberant clatter of a conventional indoor swimming pool. To rephrase Zumthor's statement about the sound of buildings, the look of the building tells you what sound to make, or indeed in some instances to be silent. Perhaps the most striking instance is

10.7
Central pool, 32°C

10.8
Natural and artificial light sources

10.9
The outdoor pool

set deeply into the north-west corner, below the point of entrance, where an almost concealed passage leads to the 'spring grotto' (Figure 10.11). In this tall volume of rough-faced stone a unique acoustic effect is created. The echoing reverberation of the space somehow provokes bathers to hum or sing as they sense the acoustic. In the outdoor pool, where the roofless acoustic is that of the valley rather than of the building, the force of three water jets creates a continuous percussive rhythm as it strikes either the surface of the pool or the backs of bathers (Figure 10.10). All these effects are the product of 'natural' acoustics, the bather 'plays' upon the building almost as a musician plays an instrument. In one unique place, the 'sounding stone', you encounter the 'artificial' sounds of a recorded composition specifically written for the building by the composer/percussionist Fritz Hauser. Here you are the receiver rather than the producer of sound, passive rather than active.

Zumthor often speaks of his interest in music:

> the slow movements of the Mozart piano concertos, John Coltrane's ballads, or the sound of the human voice in certain songs all move me.
> The human ability to invent melodies, harmonies and rhythms amazes me.
> But the world of sound also embraces the opposite of melody, harmony and rhythm. There is disharmony and broken rhythm, fragments and clusters of sound, and there is also the purely functional sound we call noise. Contemporary music works with these elements. [7]

He has also noted the relevance for architectural thought of John Cage's compositional process where

> he is not a composer who hears music in his mind and then attempts to write it down. He has another way of operating. He works out concepts and structures and then has them performed to find out how they sound. [8]

The analogy of architecture and music can be dangerously misleading, often banal, but it seems to be useful in attempting to describe something of the sonic essence of Therme Vals. In his conversation with Steven Spier,[9] Zumthor tacitly acknowledged that his approach to the acoustics of the building – and to its lighting – rejected conventional normative prescriptions in favour of reference to 'a personal body of experience'. In the light of this it is possible to represent the *sound* of Vals by analogy with Zumthor's characterisation of the nature of contemporary music and his reference to Cage's compositional method. The acoustic experience is of 'fragments

and clusters of sound' as speech, footfall and the sound of rippling water are inter-reflected about and within the complex spatial organisation of the building.

By its nature, architecture, particularly architecture as concrete as that at Vals, can only partially subscribe to the indeterminacy of Cage's music. Working with the facts of material and volume, the acoustic outcome is inevitable, could be a matter of calculation and, when constructed, be almost certainly beyond modification. It is here that Zumthor's resort to 'a personal body of experience' comes into play. As he told Spier:

> I have to get into all the possible qualities which could be brought, which arise within me, out of my memory, experiences, fantasies and images, to generate this building. And I do this without any programmatic ideas in my head ... The way I have been brought up helps me to start really independently from rules, books, and things, so that I can try to be true to what I feel. [10]

Just as Cage's music is free, but not arbitrary, Zumthor's architectural method is supported by the security of memory and experience, one might call this 'informed intuition', in the search for the solution. The unique and complex sounds of Therme Vals are not the result of calculation and analysis. How could such aims have been codified? But they are the result of a process in which elements of memory and experience – of environmental imagination – are brought to bear on the qualities of the evolving design.

Selected bibliography

This presents the principal books that are referred to in the text. Citations of essays, articles and other sources are given in full in the Notes to each essay.

Ahlin, Janne, *Sigurd Lewerentz: Architect*, Byggförlaget, Stockholm, 1985, English edition.

Architectural Monographs, *Sir John Soane*, Academy Editions, London, 1983.

Assunto, Rosario *et al.*, *La Rotunda, Novum Corpus Palladianum*, Centro Internazionale di Studi, di Architettura "Andrea Palladio" di Vicenza, Electa, Milan, 1988.

Baker, Geoffrey H., *Le Corbusier: The Creative Search*, Van Nostrand Reinhold, New York, E & FN Spon, London, 1996.

Baldwin, James, *Collected Essays*, The Library of America, New York, 1998.

Banham, Reyner, *The Architecture of the Well-tempered Environment*, The Architectural Press, London, 1969.

Benton, Tim, *The Villas of Le Corbusier: 1920–1930*, Yale University Press, New Haven, CT, 1987.

Bernan, W., *On the History and Art of Warming and Ventilating, Rooms and Buildings, etc.*, G. Bell, London, 1845.

Blundell-Jones, Peter, *Modern Architecture Through Case Studies*, Architectural Press, Oxford, 2002.

Blundell-Jones, Peter, *Gunnar Asplund*, Phaidon, London and New York, 2005.

Boesiger, W. and Girsberger, H. (eds), *Le Corbusier 1910–1957*, Les Editions d'Architecture (Artemis), Zurich, 1967.

Brawne, Michael, *Louis I. Kahn and the Kimbell Art Museum, Fort Worth, Texas, 1972*, Phaidon, London, 1992.

Brooks, H. Allen, *Le Corbusier's Formative Years: Charles-Edouard Jeanneret at La Chaux-de-Fonds*, The University of Chicago Press, Chicago, 1997.

Brownlee, David B. and De Long, David G., *Louis I. Kahn: In the Realm of Architecture*, Rizzoli, New York, 1991.

Caldenby, Claes and Hultin, Olof, *Asplund*, Rizzoli, New York, 1986.

Carmel-Arthur, Judith and Buzas, Stefan, *Carlo Scarpa: Museo Canoviana, Possagno*, Edition Axel Menges, and Stuttgart/London, 2002.

Chabannes, Marquis J. B. M. F., *On Conducting Air by Forced Ventilation, and Regulating Temperature in Dwellings*, Patent Calorfiere Fumivore Manufactory and Foundry, London, 1818.

Collins, Peter, *Changing Ideals in Modern Architecture: 1750–1950*, Faber & Faber, London, 1965.

Cook, John W. and Klotz, Heinrich, *Conversations with Architects*, Lund Humphries, London, 1973.

Cooper, Jackie (ed.), *Mackintosh Architecture: The Complete Buildings and Selected Projects*, Academy Editions, London, 1978.

Cruickshank, Dan (ed.), *Timeless Architecture*, The Architectural Press, London, 1985.